To Evange

always remember:
You've got to accentuate
the Positive & eliminate
the negative.
God bless you,
Jack Segal

Psl 31
("Be strong & have courage")
(Joshua 1:6, 7, 9, 18)

Focus on the Bagel, Not on the Hole

Rabbi Jack Segal

SUNBELT EAKIN Austin, Texas

All names marked with an asterisk (*) are Pseudonyms

FIRST EDITION

Published in the United States of America
By Sunbelt Eakin Press
A Division of Sunbelt Media, Inc.
P.O. Drawer 90159 Austin, Texas 78709-0159
email: sales@eakinpress.com
website: www.eakinpress.com

1 2 3 4 5 6 7 8 9
1-57168-602-9

CONTENTS

PART TWO:

The Thing That Costs The Least
But Does The Most Is A Pleasant Smile

ACKNOWLEDGMENTS

My Book, *Focus On The Bagel, Not On The Hole,* was not really a unilateral act. My secretary, Sue Werner, labored regularly at the computer to bring forth the final text from my handwritten manuscript. And even though my handwriting was not of the caliber of many physicians, who require code breakers to decipher their script, still, it took time, great patience and steady diligence to type what I had written.

But when Sue had to leave me, I was again fortunate that Renee Mueller, one of the synagogue secretaries, was able to "pick up the baton" and finally conclude my book, and she did a yeoman's job at that task.

In addition to Sue & Renee I was blessed that Lisa Unsell and Vickie Cornejo also volunteered to help me in my other synagogue activities. There were occasions when Lisa had to save me by finding lost chapters in my computer.

Plaudits galore, however, are also due to Linda Brandt, Bernadine Rosenblatt, and Rae Uzick, who acted as my "eagle eyes" to proofread the book and also offer suggestions as to the composition of the text. Their advice, recommendations, and opinions were always considered and most of them were incorporated in the book.

Deep appreciation is also extended to Jan Zollars who gave birth to the cover diagram. It is simple but profound, plain but elaborate, unassuming but meaningful. It indicates the true meaning of my book—concentrate on the main substance and ignore the unreal; be optimistic and not pessimistic; never give in, never give up.

The book, therefore, is the product of teamwork. I simply acted as the "quarterback" and my team helped me get to the "goal line".

Virginia at Eakin Press once again helped bring my latest book to fruition. She helped me with my first book of the trilogy, *When Man Closes Doors, God Opens Windows,* and I am quite positive that she will be helping me again with the third book of the trilogy, *Remember What You Still Have Left, Not What You Have Lost,* that I am presently writing.

But my greatest inspirations were the members of my family: Toby, my wife, who always encouraged me to write these stories of my life; my children (Jeffrey, Michael, Lisa and Scott) and their spouses (Shelley, Sharon, Matt and Dena) who were often major characters in my stories; and my grandchildren (Jordan and Josh; Shawn; and Ali, Nicole and Zach) who always inspired me to continue writing because they, too, were sources of ideas that eventually found their way into my stories. Every Friday night, and every holiday, those in Houston would grace our *Shabbat* table and add life, vitality, and spice to the spirit of the day. They added to the verve and drive to motivate me to continue my writing.

Yes, I retired from the pulpit rabbinate in 1996 but I have still been active in performing life cycle events, speaking throughout Texas and the United States, working in my office every day, delivering the benediction at the conclusion of services every *Shabbat* morning, and being available for Counseling for the many members and friends of Beth Yeshurun Congregation. I was the rabbi of Beth Yeshurun for more than thirty-one years and during that time the more than 2,300 families at the congregation became part of my "extended family". I owe a great debt of thanks to all members of the synagogue who have always encouraged me "to be myself" and to do the things that I thought were important. May God's blessings always be upon them.

INTRODUCTION

It was November 18, 1995. Itzhak Perlman was the star of the evening. Lincoln Center in New York was a sell-out. Everyone had come to hear the master violinist whose sounds seemed to be born in heaven and delivered through the virtuosity and wizardry of his fingers and violin.

However, his "presentation" always began before he put his bow to his violin because as a child he had been stricken with polio and simply getting to his place on the stage was a major effort. He had two metal braces on his legs and he would walk with the aid of crutches. It was obvious to one and to all as he walked across the stage that he was in pain even though his face radiated a broad smile. But when he reached his chair he sat down, put his crutches on the floor, removed the brace on one foot and then did likewise to the brace on the second foot. Then he bent down, picked up his violin, and motioned to the conductor to begin the musical concert.

However, very early in the concert something went wrong. It was obvious to everyone in the concert hall. After the first few bars one of the strings on his violin broke. Everyone could hear the sound of that string as it snapped because it sounded like a gunshot in the muted hall.

People who came for the concert said to themselves, "Darn it, the concert will probably have to be postponed for at least fifteen minutes until he can put on his braces again and go to his room to choose another violin or until someone can bring him several violins so that he might choose one for the concert."

But the audience was stunned and overcome when Mr. Perlman resorted to neither option. He merely hesitated for a moment, closed his eyes, and motioned to the conductor to begin again. The orchestra began and he joined them as if nothing had transpired. He played with a zeal, fire, and power that truly transfixed those in the audience. They could not believe what their ears were hearing. Everyone knows that it is impossible to play a symphonic work with only three strings. You know that; I know that; and every musician and audience knows that. However, on November 18, 1995 Itzhak Perlman refused to know that. He refused to allow the word "impossible" to remain in *his* dictionary or *his* mental frame of mind. The audience could actually see him recomposing the work in his mind. In fact, it seemed as if he was attempting to create new sounds from the surviving three strings that had previously never come forth from them.

And when he concluded the concert there was an initial total silence in the hall, a heavy silence; however, then everyone rose simultaneously and the applause was tumultuous and pandemonic. People were applauding with their hands, stomping with their feet, whistling through their lips, and loudly calling forth words of praise and acclaim. The audience refused to be silenced or hushed. Then, Mr. Perlman smiled at the audience and raised his bow to quiet the audience. In a respectful tone he stated: "You know, sometimes it is the artist's task to find out how much music you can still make with what you have left."

His words were not merely for music-lovers. They were for all of us. Too many people live in the past, bemoaning their losses and wailing about their misfortunes and injuries. Others remain in a state of denial and cannot move forward. They are frozen in the past and cannot make any headway. They concentrate on "what should have been" and ignore "what still can be." Those people focus on the hole rather than on the bagel and lose the potential of the future. Yes, many have been hurt, others have been maimed, still others have lost much, and still many more have been "dealt a poor and unfair hand," but for life to STILL be meaningful we must FOCUS ON THE BAGEL AND NOT ON THE HOLE.

Yitzhak Perlman refused to moan to his audience, "Sorry, the show's over. The maker of the violin did not string it properly." He refused to give excuses. He concentrated on his abilities, on his intellect, and on his skills, and he produced a masterful presentation.

During World War II, a Boston-raised paratroop sergeant, Harold Russell, lost both of his hands in a demolition accident. He thought his future was now non-existent. He believed that he would never be able to share his life and express his love to the girl he wanted to marry. He saw only a past—only that which was behind him, nothing that was before him.

But his girlfriend convinced him that the future was still his for the making. True, it would be different from that which he had dreamed of before the war but it could still be a productive one and a romantic one. She taught him to look forward and not to concentrate on the past. The past can never be brought back but the future can be a fertile and creative era.

Russell eventually was convinced of her philosophy of life and he said, "IT IS NOT WHAT YOU HAVE LOST, BUT WHAT YOU HAVE LEFT THAT COUNTS." Too many of us squander precious energy, time, and courage dreaming of things that were and never can be again, instead of dedicating ourselves to realities and the heavy tasks of today.

Harold Russell focused his mind on the future—on the bagel, on the possible, on the thinkable, on the conceivable, on the likely—and not on the hole, the impossible, the unthinkable, the inconceivable, and the unlikely. He went on to become an actor and win two Academy Awards in 1947 for his performance in "The Best Years of Our Lives." Later, he wrote an autobiography that was published in 1949, *Victory In My Hands,* while spending a good deal of time working for various handicapped and veterans' causes. Still later, he made several appearances on TV's "China Beach." In the 1980's, Russell returned to the big screen where he made "Inside Moves," a film about handicapped people who formed a support group, and he also acted in "Dogtown" in 1997 when he played a small town cigar store owner. He died on January 29, 2002 at the age of 88. He never looked backward to weep about his past. He merely looked forward to see what he could achieve and accomplish in the future.

This book consists of 25 stories of events that I personally experienced. Some show frustration while others indicate exhilaration. Some betoken disappointment while others denote satisfaction. However, never is there a finale of crying out, "I give in; I give up." Never do we hear the words of Job's wife (Job 2:9), *"Baraych Elohim vamet,"* "Renounce God, and die." On the contrary, "Praise God, and live."

This sentiment was preached and lived by the French artist Renoir who for two decades, during the latter part of the nineteenth and the early part of the twentieth centuries, lived a life of pain and misery. Rheumatism racked his body and distorted his fingers. Often, great beads of perspiration would appear on his forehead when he would grasp his paintbrush in his hand and painfully attempt to apply the paint to his canvas. It was obvious to all that he was in deep pain.

After a while, he no longer could stand while painting and had to be placed in a chair. In fact, at times a physician had to be called to administer sedatives, but his suffering and misery never disappeared.

But Renoir always went on. Even though he was in pain he continued painting.

One day, his disciple Matisse could not bear to see him in such misery and agony and therefore asked him, "Master, why do you continue to go on every day? Why do you torture yourself?"

But Renoir did not respond by cursing his fate. He merely stared at one of his favorite canvases and softly responded, "The pain passes, but the beauty remains."

Yes, he could have concentrated on his pain, anguish, and

affliction. But he refused. He chose to focus his mind and his thoughts on his favorite canvases—on the bagel and not on the hole.

It is my hope that people will concentrate on the tune "You've Got to Accentuate the Positive, Eliminate the Negative" and not focus on the melody "Blues in The Night."

May God bless you!

Part One

Hope Sees The Invisible, Feels The Intangible, And Achieves The Impossible

Chapter 1

"O God, What Are You Doing to Me?"

The year 1981 was *not* a good one for my family.

Early that year, my second son, Michael, was intentionally shot *in the head* during a robbery in Austin, Texas, when he was a student at the University of Texas. The three who shot him intended to kill him for the $2 that he had in his pocket, and it was truly a miracle that he survived and was able to progress to graduate from college, Graduate School, become a Social Worker, marry, and have a daughter.

It was very difficult for me to accept the fact that Michael was now handicapped. He had *not* been in an accident caused by thoughtless speeding. He had *not* been drinking and fallen down the steps. He had *not* been involved with drugs and shot by those who claimed he had not paid them. Michael had been studying in the library of the University of Texas in Austin for an Organic Chemistry exam when the chimes of the clock struck midnight and he decided to take his girlfriend, Sharon, home. But he had no gasoline in his car and he stopped at a convenience store to purchase $2 worth—because that was all the money he had at that time.

He entered the convenience store during a robbery, and the mastermind of the burglary merely cried out to his cohorts, "Waste the dude," and they shot him in the head, in cold blood, execution style, and they laughed at their violent and savage act as they exited from the store. They had killed a college kid, they thought, and that made them happy and satisfied.

It took me weeks and weeks before I felt comfortable again to stand on the pulpit before my congregation. Yes, I was an adult. I was a rabbi. I supposedly "conversed" with God every day but I felt that God had let me down. What had Michael ever done to be afflicted so viciously? I had always preached to my congregants that God was a compassionate God. I told them that the Bible stated (Exodus 34:6), "The Lord is . . . merciful and gracious . . . keeping mercy unto the thousandth [generation], forgiving iniquity and transgression and sin. . . ." But where was the compassion in allowing a young boy to be shot in the head—a young boy who wanted to become a physician and help the suffering?

I had always emphasized from my pulpit that God was a loving God. The prophet Malachi had quoted God as saying (Malachi 1:2), "I have always loved you."

But where was that love in simply standing by and doing nothing while allowing three thugs to injure and wound, bloody and almost kill a youngster who always stretched forth his hand to help others?

As the months rolled by, the overabundance of activities of every day made that perplexing and painful question partially evaporate and dissipate as a cloud attacked by a gust of wind. It was like a constant headache for which the sufferer takes aspirins. The headaches do not totally disappear. They are merely concealed and camouflaged by the analgesic effect of the aspirins. The pain does not completely vanish. It is merely superficially cloaked. So, too, my theological problems never really dissolved. They merely hibernated.

A month after Michael was hurt I visited a 12-year-old boy at M.D. Anderson Cancer Hospital. He had been studying for his Bar Mitzvah when he was diagnosed with cancer. The doctors told his mother that the boy's future was very grim. He had not reacted positively to his medication, radiation, or chemotherapy. The doctors even told her that they did not think he would reach his Bar Mitzvah date, his thirteenth birthday, a little less then a year away.

When I entered his room, I could see the severity of his condition. Every time he moved, I could see the pain on his face and I could hear a groan come forth from his throat.

As I held his mother's hands, she said to me, "It hurts me to say this, Rabbi, but why is God punishing me, my husband, and especially my son so severely? What did my young son ever do to God? Why is God torturing him so severely?"

She dabbed several tears away from her eyes and continued. "He is an Honor Student in his class. He even attends a Religious Day School in New York where we live. His entire class is reciting *Tehilim* [chapters from the book of Psalms, as is traditional in Orthodox Judaism when someone is ill] for him as his *Rebbe* [religious subjects teacher] has instructed them. He observes all the *mitzvot* [biblical and rabbinic commandments] meticulously. He *davens* [prays] every morning, afternoon, and evening—and he is only twelve." More tears gushed forth from her eyes as she mentioned his young age. "He observes *kashrut* [the Dietary Laws as specified in the Torah]. What more does God want of him?" And she pursed her lips in anger and confusion as she mentioned the word "God."

The young woman who could not have been more than 35 began weeping uncontrollably. She did not know what to say or do and I did not know what to say or do, so I merely held her hands and then hugged her as her sobs went unabated.

The pretty, young woman then ceased crying for a moment, looked up at me with tension written all over her face, glared at me, and continued, "My husband and I have been married for 14 years. We have three sons, and Jeremy*, here in bed, is my eldest. Jason*, my husband, has given me everything that a woman could desire: money, a big house, jewelry, overseas vacations, cruises—everything. But my greatest delight and my most precious gems have been my children."

Once again the young woman began to weep bitterly, and she emphatically added as a postscript, "Why is God punishing us? What did *we* ever do to *Him?* Does He enjoy seeing us writhe in pain? Is He a cruel God, Rabbi? I always thought He was an understanding and compassionate God." And once again, tears began cascading down from her eyes.

I sat with her for over an hour, merely holding her hands, but never attempting to answer her questions—because I myself really did not have an answer for her piercing inquiries. Those same religious problems were also presently festering in *my* mind—since Michael had been so wantonly and maliciously attacked. "What was the purpose of evil in this world and why were the innocent and the good the casualties of these attacks?" Those questions continued to haunt me each time I saw a young person suffering—and I saw that situation so often.

Yes, the passage of time had somewhat shrouded these stinging questions for me but time was never able to totally eliminate them. I continued to perform my daily duties—but with less verve, less enthusiasm, and less energy. These damaging doubts constantly caused me to become emotionally upset each time a similar situation presented itself.

A week after visiting the young woman from New York and her ailing son at M.D. Anderson Hospital I was informed that one of the non-Jewish workers at my congregation, Don*, had lost a young grandson. The boy was only five years old but had been killed in an auto accident when a drunk driver had broadsided the car in which the young child had been riding. The youngster had been sitting next to the door where the collision had occurred, and the police stated that he had been killed instantly.

Both Toby and I attended the funeral to pay our respects and express our condolences to the entire family—and the family was truly appreciative.

At the service, the minister spoke about Jesus being in heaven and waiting to personally greet Lester* at "the Pearly Gates." Then the minister hesitated for a moment and posed to those present at the funeral the same question as the one presented to me by the young mother at M.D. Anderson Hospital: "Ernestine* and Jim* loved Lester more than a groom loves his bride. They treasured him more than we treasure the air we breathe or the water we drink. That child gave them more warmth and pleasure than we derive from the sun that shines upon us each day. Lester's parents' eyes twinkled with pride each day more than the stars twinkle each night after the sun sets simply because they had a five-year-old son whom they loved so much."

The minister hesitated momentarily, sighed heavily, looked straight into Lester's mother's eyes, and then proceeded. "If that is all true, WHY did God take him from Ernestine and Jim?" His voice reverberated with strength and volume as he cried out the word "WHY?", and he continued shouting that word louder and louder five times: "WHY—WHY—WHY—WHY—WHY?"

Again he hesitated for a moment as all eyes were now focused on him. There was not a dry eye in the church. Everyone present wanted to hear the answer to that "Million Dollar Question."

The minister then raised his head upwards and simultaneously raised his arms toward the ceiling as if directing them toward the heavens. "The answer to that question is,"—and the minister presented his answer one word at a time, "God—needed—Lester—even—more—than—his—parents—needed—him."

Within a flashing moment, fifteen to twenty people cried out, "Yes, God needed Lester more than Ernestine and Jim needed him," and I looked toward Lester's parents who were holding hands to comfort each other—and they were both shaking their heads as if acquiescing with the minister, even though tears were rolling down their cheeks like a waterfall in the Guadalupe Mountains of Texas.

The minister continued, "Even though Lester was only five, he was a soloist with our choir last Christmas and everyone *raved* at his singing, and *shouted* at his dancing, and *applauded* his antics. He was the star of the show."

As the minister enumerated Lester's attributes, people sporadically called out, "Yes sir" or "You are right" or "How true; how true."

Smiles quickly appeared on almost all faces as if they were in agreement—even on the faces of Ernestine and Jim. The minister then loudly cleared his throat: "God needed a young soloist for His heavenly choir—and he chose Lester." The minister's eyes were now piercing those of Ernestine and Jim as the parents weakly replied, "You are right; you are right; God needed a young soloist for his heavenly choir—and Lester was the best. He was God's personal choice. How fortunate we are. God pointed directly at *our* family and chose *our* Lester."

I slid down in my seat as if I wanted to disappear as the minister spoke, and Toby glanced at me as if she could not believe her ears.

When the hour-long service was concluded, Toby and I approached the grandfather who worked at my synagogue to once again express our condolences. "Did you hear my preacher?" Don smiled at us as if a heavy burden had been removed from his shoulders. "Lester's now the lead soloist in God's heavenly choir. How blessed we are."

I shook his hand and Toby kissed him and we left.

On the way home, Toby and I spoke about the peace of mind seemingly achieved by Don, Ernestine, Jim, and so many others present who were told that Jesus himself had chosen Lester for the lead singer in God's choir.

As we drove home, I was like a steaming radiator on a 1929 Ford, but I did not want to discuss with Toby *my* theological problems with God. It was not that I doubted the existence of God but I found it difficult at that time to fulfill the biblical Commandment (Deuteronomy 6:5), "And thou shalt *love* the Lord thy God with all thy heart, and with all thy soul, and with all they might." At that time, *I* could not even love God with my little pinky. In fact, *I* could not even put the word "love" in the same sentence with the word "God." I merely listened as Toby shook her head and told me how sorry she felt for the parents to be obliged to listen to the minister's comments, but she added, "However, they seemed to derive some spiritual comfort from his words." And then she added, "It's almost impossible for me to believe."

By coincidence, one week later, I read in the *Jewish Herald Voice* (the Jewish weekly newspaper of Houston) that an Orthodox congregation in Houston was hosting a speaker who would be lecturing on, "Why Does God Permit Evil And Pain in Our World?" and I purchased a ticket to hear him.

About three hundred and fifty people were present to hear the speaker discuss this complex and formidable question.

He was obviously an Orthodox rabbi. He wore a long black jacket; a black beard shrouded a good portion of his face; upon his head precariously rested a thick *yarmulke* (skull cap); at his ears were *pay-yot* (side curls) that he placed over and around his ears; and *Tzee-Tzeet* (fringes as described in Numbers 15:37-41) flopped and fluttered freely over and under his jacket as he opened it because of the warmth of the auditorium.

The rabbi posed all the traditional and rational questions that evening but in a slightly different manner:

"Could a *loving* God inflict pain upon His children?

"Could a *compassionate* God be happy when an innocent little child contracts cancer?

"Could a *tender* God ever deliberately take a mother away from her family because of leukemia when this would cause so much pain and anguish to the husband and children?

"Could a *charitable* God allow a faithful father and husband to be killed in an auto accident when this would cause his beloved widow and orphans to consequently be placed in a financial and emotional limbo?

"Could a *benevolent* God knowingly and willingly permit wars that devastated nations and countless respectable and honorable human beings?"

The speaker continued, pointing his index finger at the audience as he rattled off piercing and searching questions one after the other, and each time he asked another question his voice rose until he almost shouted the last of his five questions.

He hesitated momentarily, breathed heavily, and then pounded his right fist in the palm of his left hand and strongly called out, "God knows everything that *is* happening in this world, that *has* happened in this world, and that *will* happen in this world. In fact," he added with greater strength and greater volume, "God is involved in everything that happens in this world. Nothing happens without God's OK and God's knowledge."

And to indicate that that was not merely a personal, subjective interpretation of Judaism but rather a foundation stone of Jewish belief, he added, "*I* didn't make that up. That's what the *Talmud* tells us." He hesitated momentarily, stared into a sea of doubting faces, and added, "The Talmud says in Chullin 7b, '*En adam nokeph etzba-o mil-ma-ta, ella im ken mach-ree-zin alav mil-ma-la.* No one stubs his finger in this world unless it is first decreed [by God] in the heavens.' Whatever happens in this world—even cancers, illnesses, auto wrecks, wars, and pain—everything is done with God's knowledge—everything is done with God's planning."

People were shifting in their seats. It was obvious that they were upset by his comments. However, a big broad smile appeared on his face in spite of the doubting reaction of the audience.

"But there is an answer to all those questions," he continued with authority in his voice and complete belief on his face. "Did you ever read the book of Job?" he cried forth with assuredness. "That book gives us the answer.

"When Job was perplexed by those same questions—Why did his children die? Why did he lose all his wealth? Why did he become so afflicted with such terrible diseases?—God answered his questions by asking *him* [Job 38:1ff.], 'Where were *you* when *I* laid the foundation of the earth? Tell it, if you have any understanding [of it]. Who fixed her measurements, if you know it? . . . Who laid her cornerstone?' "

The rabbi hesitated for a moment, smiled broadly, and continued on like the Mississippi River. "God was telling Job that

Job simply did not understand God's actions. They were too complex and too complicated for his *human* understanding. One must be *superhuman* to fathom God's actions—and we are *not* superhuman."

The rabbi then pointed his right index finger again at the audience, shaking it as if admonishing those present, "Don't you remember the words of the prophet Isaiah? He said in the name of God [Isaiah 55:8], *'Lo moch-sh'vo-tai moch-sh'vo-taychem.* My thoughts are not comparable to your thoughts.' We operate on different wavelengths and different frequencies."

As the rabbi looked about the auditorium it quickly became obvious to him that he had made a dent into the skepticism of his audience, and he continued his thrust. "Have you ever gone to Italy and observed Michelangelo's statue of David? Stare at his fingers," and the rabbi raised his hands and focused on *his* fingers. "*Mine* are normal, but *David's* are much larger than normal. They look as if he's suffering from some congenital ailment. As you stare at them you say to yourself, 'How can this be the famous statue? Michelangelo goofed. Michelangelo has made a mistake.'

"But if you stop staring at the one *small* and *tiny* part of his body and look at the total statue and listen to the guide explain *why* Michelangelo purposely and intentionally gave David oversized fingers, you will understand the beauty of the *entire* work. Staring at a *small* part of it leaves you confused and baffled, but examining the *entire* piece shows you beauty and elegance."

It was obvious that the rabbi was gaining the confidence and approval of the majority of his audience who were primarily Orthodox. Then, the rabbi went on to add the *coup de grace.*

"If a person had a telescope that would focus *only* on Arnold Schwarzenegger's big right toe that had a pimple on it, not knowing whose toe it was, that person would probably say, 'This is gross; this is ugly; this is repulsive.' And he would be correct because all he could see would be a pus-like and infected toe.

"However, if the telescope would focus on Arnold's *entire* body," and the rabbi now raised his voice, "the viewer would see an Atlas, a Hercules, a man with an iron shape, a world champion body builder—a unique treasure in this world."

The rabbi banged his hand on the lectern and cried out, "You cannot concentrate on a *small* portion of the whole." His voice now thundered. "You don't understand how it all fits together if you only concentrate on a small piece of the whole.

"Have you ever worked on a five hundred piece puzzle?" The rabbi smiled as his voice became more placid and tranquil. "When you look at one piece, you don't know if it goes to the right or the left, the top or the bottom. However, two weeks later, when you've completed the jigsaw puzzle, you understand the importance of that one piece. *With* it, the puzzle is complete. *Without* it, the puzzle is incomplete.

"So, too," the rabbi added as his voice now thundered and boomed, again, "it is with God. Only *He* sees the entire jigsaw puzzle. *We* only see the individual pieces—and we do not understand of what importance they are—but *God* does understand why we have *each and every* piece in the puzzle."

The speaker continued for about ten more minutes and concluded his talk to a robust and vigorous round of applause.

Afterwards, he was surrounded by well-wishers who told him:

> "You answered the question that has been bothering me since I was a youngster."
>
> "You solved the problem that caused me to leave Orthodox Judaism ten years ago. I can now return with a clear and understanding mind."
>
> "Your lecture was the best I have heard in many years."
>
> "I have not entered a synagogue since my daughter was killed by a driver who had overdosed on drugs. You have given me the key to unlock the door to reenter my *shul* [synagogue]."

People were pumping his hand and congratulating him. It seemed to me as if they thought that he was Dr. Sabin or Dr. Salk announcing the discovery of a new vaccine to eliminate a dreaded disease.

However, as I drove home that evening I was snorting and fuming, raging and ranting. The rabbi's solution to the age-old question of evil in the world had not only not satisfied me, it had actually exacerbated and aggravated *my* problem. It was like rubbing salt on an open wound. What did he mean when he quoted the Talmud that stated that no one ever stubs a toe without God being involved in that act, that everything that occurs in this world is with God's permission and tolerance, even evil. At least that is the way *I* heard his words.

Did that mean that God was involved in my Michael being shot? Did that mean that God was involved in six million Jews being murdered by Hitler? Did that mean that God was involved in twelve year old Jason being afflicted with cancer and five year old Lester being killed by a drunk driver? That was too outlandish and too incredible to believe or even comprehend.

To whom could *I* talk to discuss this subject? To whom could *I* open *my* wound and *my* hurt and *my* stress in order to receive a comprehensive and acceptable reply? I therefore decided to make an attempt to be my own "doctor" and my own "psychologist."

I remembered how my *zayde* (grandfather) had answered me when I was ten and World War II had begun. I had asked him, "*Zayde,* why is it that Hitler is such a bad man? Why is it that he hates the Jews? What did we ever do to him? We Jews served in the German army during World War I. Some of the best scientists in Germany were Jewish. The Jews were loyal to their country. Why does Hitler hate us?"

Then I hesitated for a moment as he stroked his white beard, twirled his *pay-ot* (side curls), and took a deep breath. But before he could reply to my questions I added a more penetrating query. "Why doesn't God stop him? God took the Jews out of Egypt—that was a miracle. God gave Moses the Ten Commandments—that was a miracle. God sent an angel to stop Abraham from sacrificing Isaac—that was a miracle. God even destroyed the cities of Sodom and Gomorrah because they were bad and evil—that too was a miracle."

I then looked my *zayde* directly in the eyes, penetrating straight through his head, and in my youthful naivete asked, "Why doesn't God perform another miracle *now* and stop Hitler—or even kill him? God did it in the past. Why can't he do it now?"

I waited with mouth agape for my *zayde's* reply. He always had an understandable answer for all of my religious questions, but this time he seemed to lack his normal zeal and enthusiasm. He hesitated longer than usual and therefore I once again asked him, "*Zayde,* what is God waiting for? If in the past he helped Abraham, Isaac, Jacob, Joseph, Moses, David, Solomon, and so many more Jews, why can't He now help the Jews in Berlin and the other cities of Germany? The Nazis have already burned every synagogue in Germany. Some people are even saying that the next thing Hitler will burn will be the Jews themselves."

My *zayde* continued stroking his beard and with a deep and heavy sigh he replied in Yiddish, "*Men fraygt nisht kein kashess fun Gott.* [We do not ask questions of God. He knows what He's doing. *We* just don't understand His actions.]"

Zayde then arose from his chair, walked into his bedroom, closed the door—and that was that. I thought I heard him weeping, but I could not be sure.

That reply did not satisfy me one iota when I was ten years of age and it surely did not satisfy me when I was the father of three sons and one daughter.

I then recalled the mental torment of the prophet Habakkuk who lived about twenty-six hundred years ago and personally experienced the tyranny of the Babylonians and the destruction of the City of Jerusalem.

Habakkuk raised his eyes toward the heavens and shouted at God (Habakkuk 1:2-3), "O God, how long shall I cry and You will not hear; how long will I scream about violence and You will not save?"

Yes, the prophet refused to echo my grandfather's reply, "One does not ask questions of God and about God." Yes, *he* shouted at God. Yes, *he* was angry at God. But no answer came forth for Habakkuk concerning his profound question. He, too, was like me. We were both tormented by a logical and legitimate question: Why does not God come forth to help and save his loyal and faithful people? Does He enjoy seeing them being tormented? This is not the first time that God's innocents have been unfairly and inhumanely treated.

Habakkuk's question to God did not help me understand why my Michael had been so violently attacked without God sticking out His hand and shouting, "You can't do this to him."

I then remembered the great Hassidic defender of the Jews, Rabbi Levi Yitzchok of Berditchov (in the Ukraine), a noble and famous Hassid (pious Jew), of the late 18th century.

The Hassidic literature tells us that on one occasion, Rabbi Levi Yitzchok stood in the center of a very large circle that he had drawn in a field, raised his eyes and arms toward the heavens, and cried out to God, "Master of the universe, when a simple Jew drops his *tephillin* [prayer boxes worn daily by traditional Jews in conformity with Deuteronomy 6:8], he picks them up and kisses them. O God, the Children of Israel are *Your tephillin.* They are now lying in the dirt and mud being bloodied and butchered by their neighbors, and I ask, 'Why don't You do what the simplest Jew knows that he should do—pick them up—kiss them—and redeem them?'"

But as I thought of Rabbi Levi Yitzchok's complaint and protest to God, I realized that he, too, received no reply. His non-Jewish neighbors in the Ukraine continued to bloody and butcher his congregants. No miracles came forth from the heavens to save them or even aid them.

And, again, I continued to be plagued by *my* question of God, "What did Michael ever do to be treated so harshly and violently? He wanted to be a physician, to help mankind, not harm mankind. He wanted to bring light where there was darkness, warmth where there was frost, smiles where there were tears. Why was he so violently hurt—and *You* did not protect him?"

I then remembered another story about Rabbi Levi Yitzchok of Berdichov.

It was the evening just after *Yom Kippur* (the day when Jews do not eat or drink for 25 hours and pray to God for an entire day for forgiveness for their sins), and the Rabbi heard a faint knock on his door. He opened it and noticed that it was the town tailor who was shaking as if he had seen the dead reappear in life.

"What happened? Why are you here?" the rabbi asked with a puzzled expression on his face.

"I have committed a terrible sin," the tailor replied while trembling uncontrollably.

"How could you sin?" Rabbi Levi Yitzchok asked as he raised his shoulders in disbelief. "I personally saw you sitting in the synagogue for the entire day and your prayers could be heard by me all day long as you sat only two rows away from me."

"I came to *shul* last night to ask God for forgiveness," the tailor meekly replied, "but when I opened my *Machzor* [holiday prayer book] the words often refused to come forth. So, intermittently during the service I wrapped myself in my *Tallit* [prayer shawl] and constructed my own prayers.

"I said, 'O God, I know I have committed many sins during the past year. Several times I did not *daven* [pray] at the scheduled time. I was late. I even remember one day when I was in a hurry I ate a *knobble* [garlic] sandwich and did not recite the *Hamotzee* [prayer over the bread]. I even recall once last year passing a beggar and not placing a *kopec* [a coin] into his metal cup. I am truly sorry for these transgressions and I promise, O God, I will improve during the coming year.'"

The tailor hesitated for a moment, his face became pale, and he looked down on the ground; however, he continued. "But You, O God, *You* have also committed many grievous crimes during the past year. *You* permitted my sister-in-law Zlotte's baby to die in child birth; *You* also allowed my so called non-Jewish neighbors to burn down my tailor shop; and *You* did not even help my son Motke when he was attacked by two thugs, robbed, and so badly beaten that the doctor had to amputate his right leg."

The tailor then stood up straight, braced his shoulders, pursed his lips, and raised his voice. "So, God, I have a suggestion. Let's make a deal—if You forgive *me,* I'll forgive *You.*"

The rabbi saw that tears were welling up in the tailor's eyes. But upon hearing this, Rabbi Levi Yitzchok grabbed the tailor's hands, placed his face next to his congregant's face, and slowly and softly spoke to him. "You made a mistake. How could you let God off so easily? You had Him in the palms of your hands but you only asked for forgiveness for *yourself.* You could have *forced* Him to redeem *the entire world.*"

However, I remembered that that was the end of the story. The rabbi had not stated how the tailor could have *forced* or *coerced* God to do anything. And no miracles were forthcoming; and little babies continued to die in childbirth; and Jewish stores continued to be burned by so called neighbors; and thugs continued to bloody innocent Jews on the road, in their homes, in their shops, and in their schools. God obviously saw what was happening but no comment was coming forth from Him.

And again I silently asked, "God, how could You allow my fine boy to be hurt so badly and so maliciously?"

I guess if I were a simple layperson, this problem would not have bothered me so intensely. But every week I visited the hospitals, sometimes three or four times a week. Beth Yeshurun averaged about sixty-five funerals every year, and I officiated at more than fifty of them. Every week and almost every day since I arrived at Beth Yeshurun I was encircled and enveloped by someone who was asking me, "*Why* doesn't God answer my prayers?" or "*Why* does God permit pain and evil in this world?" or "*Why* is God punishing my little child? What did he ever do to God?" or "If God is supposed to be so good, why does He permit so much pain and suffering in this world?"

Until Michael was hurt, this was merely a theoretical, philosophical problem to me, but since Michael was hurt, it refused to leave my mind and evaporate.

And then, about eight months after Michael was shot and almost killed, I received a phone call at about 11 P.M. from the

Emergency Room at St. Luke's Hospital in Houston. The receptionist, in a somber voice, said, "I'd like to speak to Rabbi Segal."

"Yes, I'm Rabbi Segal," I replied nonchalantly.

The receptionist apologetically responded, "Rabbi Segal, we'd like you to come down to the Emergency Room of St. Luke's Hospital immediately. A young man, Jeffrey Segal, your son, was brought into the E.R. an hour ago. He was the victim of an act of violence and I was asked to contact you, your wife, or both of you."

For a moment I could not reply. How could this be happening again—twice in a little more than half a year—first Michael and now Jeffrey? Had someone put out a "contract" on my family? Had God put out a "contract" on my family?

"How is he," I rapidly asked as I quickly regained my composure and my breath.

The receptionist continued in her solemn voice, "I really don't know. I was merely asked to contact you and see whether you could come down tonight?"

"I'll be there in ten minutes," I blurted forth without hesitation.

My heart was beating like the tail of a frightened rabbit who had just encountered a fox.

Telling Toby was another traumatic ordeal. She knew that something tragic had occurred as I held her tightly to relate my brief conversation with the receptionist.

Tears once again gushed down her face. "How could this be happening to us again?" she sobbed as her hands shook. "I'm still suffering from Michael's accident. Are we a cursed family?"

Toby continued to weep but we quickly got into the car and sped to the Emergency Room, arriving there in only eight minutes.

We walked quickly into the E.R. and were immediately greeted by Dr. Greenfield*, an eminent neurologist, who was also a member of my congregation.

"Rabbi, Toby," he greeted us with a wan smile on his face. "The first thing I want to tell you is that Jeffrey *will be* okay. True, he suffered some severe blows but he will be O.K."

Dr. Greenfield then motioned to a small room, directed us toward it, and continued, "Let's sit down and I'll tell you what we were able to piece together. Then you'll go to see Jeffrey. We're just finishing tests on him."

We sat down but I was "sitting on *shpilkess*" (extremely tense). "Jeffrey told me what had happened," Dr. Greenfield continued. "He was returning from your home at 6:30 this evening where, he told me, he had had a spaghetti dinner. He was riding his bicycle to his home because he loves to exercise. But it was pretty dark and when he got to about 100 yards past the United Orthodox Synagogue on Greenwillow, he noticed that a car was going to pass him on his left, and the fellow was blasting away on his horn. Jeffrey said that he moved to the right toward the sidewalk, but he noticed a young fellow sticking his head out of the passenger's side of the car swinging a baseball bat.

"Jeffrey said that it all happened within five seconds, if that long. The young fellow swung the bat as he passed Jeffrey and hit him flush across his shoulders. Jeffrey said that he remembers nothing after that blow."

Dr. Greenfield removed his handkerchief from his pocket to wipe his glasses.

The tension was too great for me. "But what happened to Jeffrey?" I quickly interjected as I breathed heavily.

"Well," Dr. Greenfield continued, "Jeffrey was knocked unconscious. He suffered a broken clavicle [collarbone], a broken scapula [shoulder blade], a broken rib, and he also suffered a slight concussion. However," the doctor quickly added, "he *will* quickly recover. He's young; he's healthy; he's athletic; and he's a student at our Baylor College of Medicine, and I'm positive that after a few days he'll be able to return to class."

Dr. Greenfield now had a broad smile on his face. "It will take more than a blow from a baseball bat to really hurt Jeffrey. Luckily that fellow was not Babe Ruth and did not hit Jeffrey on the head. He's sore in body now but he is alive and all the physical problems will soon go away. I can't emphasize how lucky he is that the blow was not three inches higher on the head. I hate to tell you—but it could have been fatal."

Dr. Greenfield grimaced as he stated what could have been. He hesitated for a moment and then went on. "Jeffrey is also sore in mind. He wants to get out of the hospital *now* and start searching for the fellows who attacked him. He keeps telling me that it was a black Plymouth that held his attackers and he wants to go out NOW to find them. But I told him to lie down and be still." The doctor smiled warmly and continued, "I told Jeffrey that if he didn't do what I told him I'd have his professors give him flunking grades." Dr. Greenfield smiled heartily again but Toby and I remained stone-faced. We were not in the mood for humor.

The doctor then reached out for Toby's hands and sympathetically went on. "Toby, this is *not* like Michael's case. Jeffrey will recuperate completely in just a few days."

Once again tears came forth from Toby's eyes and she sobbed, "Thank you, doctor; thank you, doctor."

Toby and I were then escorted by Dr. Greenfield to one of the examining rooms where Jeffrey was lying. He was very angry and inflamed.

"Those rotten, stupid fools," Jeffrey fumed as he added several expletives. "For no reason at all they beat me over the back and tried to kill me. I'll get them and show them what a *nunchuk* [an Okinawan weapon made of two pieces of wood connected by a chain] is. I wonder how *they'll* feel getting hit with a *nunchuk* over the head."

Both Toby and I knew that it was not good for him to get excited at that time so we tranquilized him with some small talk and asked him to tell us what had transpired and how he felt.

"How I feel?" he fumed. "I hurt all over—but I'll get better. But those [expletive] goons will feel my *nunchuk*."

Jeffrey hesitated for a moment, shook his head, and went on. "The entire incident is really quite hazy." He repeated to us exactly what Dr. Greenfield had told us and then added, "Beyond that, I don't remember anything. I only remember seeing a bat coming toward me—and that's all. The next thing I remember is waking up in the hospital. But my friend Albert* filled me in on what happened afterwards.

"I was knocked unconscious right in the middle of the

street. But I was lucky. Just by coincidence, my friend Albert, who lives with me, was driving home past United Orthodox Synagogue and he saw someone lying in the street. He did not recognize who it was, but as a medical student he quickly pulled over to the curb and jumped out to give first aid. He was startled to see that it was me, Jeff, on the ground.

"So, after making sure that I was still alive, he ran to the nearest home and pounded on the door in order to call 911. But the old lady inside refused to open the door. She must have thought that he was a thief or a gangster or a criminal and shouted at him that if he did not go away she was going to call the police.

"Finally, after knocking on three doors, someone allowed him to enter and call 911. Luckily, he was able to flag down another car beforehand and get the young fellow to signal oncoming cars to avoid me." Jeffrey shook his head in amazement, gritted his teeth, and snorted. "I could have been killed by someone running over me."

Jeffrey was obviously tired and exhausted, and after talking to him for about an hour he fell asleep. The nurse told us that they wanted to keep him for observation for another day but all the beds in the hospital were taken and he would have to remain in the E.R. until the morning when a room would become available.

Toby not only looked exhausted and depleted but she was truly emotionally consumed and prostrate. Her eyes were red from tears and I told her to go home. I said that I would remain with Jeffrey all night until he was moved to a room in the morning. She did not want to leave but I strongly insisted on it—and she left.

Jeffrey slept all night and did not awaken until the nurse came to check his vital signs at 7 A.M. His first words were, "I'm starved." They took him in a wheel chair to a private room as I said "Good-bye," gave him a kiss and a warm hug, and told him that I was merely going home to shower, change clothes, and shave. I told him that both Toby and I would soon return.

While going through the lobby as I was leaving the hospital I met a fellow rabbi who told me that he regularly visited patients early in the morning. He looked at me, shook his head, clenched his teeth, and pontifically commented, "Jack, what's the matter with you? You look terrible. You don't have a tie; your pants are wrinkled and baggy; your jacket is rumpled; you look as if you haven't shaved in two days; and it seems as if you don't own a comb. What's the matter with you?" And he added as a postscript, "Go home and look presentable. You're the representative of the Jewish people at this hospital. What will the gentiles say when they see you in such a disheveled manner?"

However, I quickly told him what had happened to Jeffrey and that I had spent the entire evening in the Emergency Room sitting in a chair.

The rabbi listened attentively and then philosophically commented in his Charles Laughton manner of speaking. "I feel sorry for you, Jack. God is obviously testing you," and he expanded the words "testing you." "First it was your son Michael who was shot and almost killed. What a tragedy that was," and his eyes focused upwards. "Now it is your son, Jeffrey, who was bludgeoned and also almost killed. God, I believe, is testing you Jack as He tested Abraham almost four thousand years ago when his son, Isaac, was almost sacrificed on a mountaintop. But God is testing *you* more than He tested Abraham, Jack. With you, Jack, it has involved *two* of your children, Michael and Jeffrey. With Abraham, it involved only *one* of his sons." The rabbi shook his head from right to left and then from left to right as if the entire experience was incomprehensible to him.

I was truly getting upset and unsettled by his statement because he was an *extremely* liberal rabbi. It was my feeling that he did not believe a word he was saying because he had once told me that he did not literally accept that biblical story but rather symbolically interpreted that incident of God telling Abraham to sacrifice his son Isaac. He had told me that to him it indicated the Jewish principle that the Jews were opposed to human sacrifices. It was an allegory. It was a myth. It was a fable. God was attempting to teach the Jews a major principle of Judaism: "Do not be like the people amongst whom you live. They believe that it is a religious act, a noble deed, to give up and sacrifice your most precious object to God to show your attachment to Him, even if that object is your son. Judaism, on the other hand, says, absolutely not! No *human* sacrifices. That is improper. That is unethical. That is immoral. That is inhuman. Sacrifice a ram if you must sacrifice something—but *never* a human being. In fact, God does not even want your animal sacrifices, as the Bible states [I Samuel 15:22], 'Does God want your burnt offerings and your sacrifices? Behold, listening to God is far better than bringing Him a sacrifice; to be attentive to His Commandments is far more important than bringing Him the fats of rams.'"

However, the rabbi spoke so often to Christian groups, and he knew that the vast majority of his audiences literally accepted the Abraham-Isaac story, that he automatically, as if he was on auto-pilot, told me: "Jack, God is testing you." He then pointed his finger at me and pontificated, "Jack, remember the German proverb, 'He who has never tasted what is bitter does not know what is sweet.'"

With that comment, the rabbi looked at his watch and surprisingly stated, "I didn't realize how late it was. I must go. See you soon." And he was off. I did not even get a chance to say "Good-bye" to him. I only saw the exhaust of his quick departure. However, his last comment irritated me profusely.

The next weeks were not easy ones for me. Yes, Jeffrey left the hospital after only two days but he was still sore and aching. However, it was obvious to me that had he been hit on the head instead of the back—he could have been killed; had a car not seen him unconscious on the road—he could have been killed. It was only a miracle that saved him.

Every time I entered the synagogue, every time I ascended the pulpit to preach a sermon, every time I entered a classroom to discuss Jewish philosophy, every time I counseled a disturbed and distressed congregant in my office, my mind was saturated with the question, "O God, why are you doing this to us?"

I was becoming obsessed and overcome by that question.

Then, suddenly, one day as I was driving along West Bellfort Avenue that question refused to leave my mind. I turned on the radio and listened to a talk show. It didn't help. I put on music. It didn't help. I tried listening to a cassette recording. It still did not help. That question refused to leave me. It was now haunting me and intimidating me.

There was an apartment complex and some stores with a sizable parking area adjacent to the corner of West Bellfort and Chimney Rock, so I quickly pulled into the parking area, turned off the ignition, closed my eyes, gritted my teeth, began breathing heavily and quickly, and embarked on a silent conversation with God.

"God, I still don't know how you could do this to us. I remember listening to that Orthodox rabbi quoting the words of Rabbi Hanina [Hullin 7b] that no one ever stubs his toe unless it is ordained, ordered, and decreed by God." I breathed in heavily and continued with my silent conversation with God. "That, to me, is ridiculous. It's even worse than that. It's absurd and preposterous."

For a moment I hesitated as a few beads of perspiration appeared on my forehead. "That would mean that everyone who entered M.D. Anderson, Methodist, St. Luke's, and Hermann Hospitals with major ailments were sent there by *You*." I squinted more tensely. "That would declare that You, God, had a daily quota. Today You need ten cancers, eighteen heart attacks, four car crashes, six leukemias, seven strokes, and many more terrible and terrifying sicknesses."

Once again I hesitated for a few moments and then brashly silently snorted as I bit down on my lower lip. "If I believed that, I would quickly apply for the position of Vice President of Madalyn Murray O'Hair's atheist organization. It is impossible and inconceivable for me to believe that You knowingly and willingly inflict pain and ailments, sickness and suffering on countless innocent individuals—including little babies. That's not *my* God. Someone who needs such a daily quota to be filled is cruel and ruthless, inhumane and savage, barbarous and sadistic."

It was obvious to me that one should not speak to God in such a rough and arrogant manner but I was angry and resentful, internally fuming and towering with rage.

"I have spent my life preaching the principles of Judaism, speaking about a *loving* God and a *compassionate* God. My God is obviously not the same God as that of Rabbi Hanina. How could anyone believe in such a God? How could anyone worship a God who *intentionally* wrecks families, hurts babies, and inflicts pain on countless good-hearted and warm-hearted men and women?"

I sat in the car for about five minutes. No answers entered my mind. Then, all of a sudden, it was as if a computer had begun operating. I remembered what I had once read in the Commentary of the *Hertz Bible*. Thoughts galore began running through my mind as I sat supposedly quietly but actually internally uneasy and disturbed. In fact, I was more than that. I was mentally volcanic and eruptive.

I was a rabbi, the spiritual leader of a very large congregation, and I did not really have an answer to a basic question that bothered everyone some time during his or her lifetime: Why is there so much pain in the world? Why does God allow it?

Rabbi Hertz spoke of King David. David's life consisted of one problem after another: one son attempted to slay him; another son raped one of his daughters; another son could not wait until his father died so that he could become king; David fell in love with two married women and impregnated one of them while her husband was fighting for Israel in the front lines; nations galore wanted to see David dead. David, too, was confronted by my problem: "O God, how can *You* do this to me?"

But David refused to accept that so-called Jewish philosophy that God was involved in every act that transpired on this earth. On the contrary, David said (Psalm 91:15), "*Imo anochi b'tzarah,* [I am with you in your distress]." David, it appeared to me, believed that God was saying to all of us, "I am holding your hand; I feel your pain; I am suffering with you; I am weeping with you." God was *not* inflicting the pain on us. He was suffering *with us*. He was *not* imposing these afflictions upon us. He was attempting to comfort us in our own hours of suffering. Rabbi Hanina's words that God was involved in everything that happened on this earth, including our suffering, was foreign to David.

I could also see before me Rabbi Hertz's comments about the Israelites during the time of the Judges when the armies of Ammon invaded the Holy Land and smote the Jews mercilessly and unrelentlessly. But the Jews repented, wept before God, and showed Him their pain. The Bible states (Judges 10:16), "*Vatiktzor nofsho ba'amal Yisra'el,* [And God's soul was aggrieved for the trouble being experienced by Israel]." God was weeping because Israel was weeping. God was suffering because Israel was suffering. God was in pain because Israel was in pain. God was *not* inflicting the aches and agony and anguish upon Israel. On the contrary, God was experiencing them together with Israel.

My face was flushed but my mind was running in high gear. I could still see the Hertz Commentary floating before me and I could see my favorite prophet, Isaiah, standing before the Jews and proclaiming (Isaiah 63:9), "*Bechol tzaratam lo tzar,* [In their affliction, He was afflicted.]" God was telling the Jews that God suffers together with them. He has no quotas of heart attacks, cancers, strokes, and other debilitating diseases that must be fulfilled every week. He does not get a commission for inflicting pain on innocent men, women, and children. No! God writhes in pain with us; God suffers with us; God is afflicted with us; God agonizes with us; God convulses with us. He merely holds our hands and sympathetically cries out, "Hold on. We *will* make it. We *will* overcome this tragedy. I will *always* be with you."

As I sat in my car, breathing heavily, biting down harshly and rigidly on my lower teeth, squinting through the small apertures of my eyes, it seemed to me that I was having a dialogue with God and I was angry with Him. He was apologizing to me and saying, "Jack, when I created this world I had to make a decision: should *man* enjoy total freedom of choice, the freedom to do as he pleased, or should *I* be totally omnipotent and powerful and be able to always interject My actions and change man's actions when I felt that his actions would lead to problems and painful results? Jack, My decision was to give man *bechirah,* freedom of choice.

"In my Bible, I stated [Deuteronomy 30:19], *'U-vacharta bachayim,'* 'You should choose life.' *You* are the master of your soul. *You* are the controller of your own actions. *You* are the director of your own conduct. *I* cannot mix into your behavior. Otherwise you will simply be a mannequin, a puppet, but not a human being.

"*I* do *not* inflict pain on innocent people. *I* want my children—the human beings of the world—to be upstanding individuals and enjoy life. But, like every parent, we are sometimes disappointed by some of our offspring. Occasionally, they disillusion us and cause us dismay, shame, and humiliation by going off on an improper and immoral path—and all *I* can do is weep."

My breathing was still fast and irregular. Tears welled up in my eyes—but my mind continued this theoretical dialogue.

"Jack, I could not have my children enjoy *both* freedom of action and the protection of my actions if they slipped and were going to be hurt. One can only be fish *or* fowl—but not both.

"I can only 'hug and hold' my children when they are hurt and try to encourage them to continue to go forward. Jack, I cannot completely take away your pain. I can only mollify it and soften it. I cannot remove all your tears. I can only help you dry them. I cannot prevent you from being knocked down. I can only help you get up again."

For a moment, I felt some relief, but as I drove away, gunning my car as I drove it off the parking lot space, my anger toward God was once again rekindled. In previous years, before I began to ask penetrating questions because of my own personal hurts, my God was omnipotent and completely powerful. Now, my "dialogue with God" had painted a God limited in ability. God did not stop the three thugs from shooting Michael or almost killing Jeffrey because He wanted human beings to be free and unhampered in regard to their actions—even if they were harmful and damaging to God's other children. I could not totally comprehend this—but what other option did I have?

However, this attitude created an equally brazen question: Why would a person pray to God? Why would I recite a personal prayer to God, a *Mi Sheberach* (prayer for the health of a specific human being) if God could not, or would not, intervene on a hurt person's behalf?

My mind was swimming. My reasoning abilities floundered from right to left and left to right. I was more confused now than before. The traditional rabbinic apologists did not offer me solutions that were acceptable, and contemporary philosophies left me cold.

The next morning, before I went to help Michael with his therapy I once again recited the traditional prayer that I had been reciting three times every day: *"Refa'einu,"* "Heal us, O Lord and we *shall* be healed; save us and we *shall* be saved; for You are our hope. Grant a perfect healing to *all* our wounds. May it be thy will, O Lord our God, and God of our fathers and mothers, to speedily send a perfect healing from heaven, a healing of soul and body to Michael Segal and Jeffrey Segal, sons of Toby and Jack Segal, for You are a faithful and merciful physician. Blessed are You, O God, who heals the sick of the entire world."

I felt uncomfortable reciting that prayer. However, even though my *intellect* rebelled against it, my *emotions* embraced it. Yes, my *logical* thinking pushed me *away* from it, but my *sentiment* drew me *toward* it. What else did I have to hold onto? That prayer of my youth had always brought me hope, and even though my rational thinking now brought forth many questions about it, I could not jettison it or abandon it. My instincts refused to allow me to forsake it and desert it.

I kept remembering a brief poem that I had learned in Religious School when I was a youngster.

God respects:
Not the *arithmetic* of our prayers—
how *many* they are;
Not the *rhetoric* of our prayers—
how *elegant* they are;
Not the *music* of our prayers—
how *melodious* they are;
Not the *logic* of our prayers—
how *methodical* they are;
But the *sincerity* of our prayers—
how *heartfelt* they are.

• • • • •

An eight-year-old boy sat on top of a load of wood in a wagon. The wagon was drawn by two horses which ran swiftly down a steep hill. After the frightening ordeal, the child's mother asked him, "Well, my boy, what did you do?" And the boy replied, "I prayed to God—and hung on like a beaver!"

—Author Unknown

CHAPTER 2

A Woman With Courage

There are very few things that I can recall from the age of six, but this I will never forget.

My father had relatives living in Richmond, Virginia, and my mother thought that it would be good if she, my older brother Marty (who was then nine), and I would go to Richmond to strengthen family ties. So, my mother packed two suitcases and we were off to the South.

It was 1935 and I was a first grader. It was the first time that I visited the South, having been born and raised in Brooklyn, New York.

We were welcomed very warmly and hospitably by my father's cousin and I was introduced to another six-year-old boy who lived next door to our relatives. I was told that the boy would play with me during the day when my mother and brother were elsewhere.

It was good playing with him. He had loads of toys, more than I had ever seen in any six-year-old's home in Brooklyn.

However, on the third day that we were in Richmond, and when I was playing in my new friend's home, a Black woman entered his family's home—and I noticed that she entered through the rear door, not like everyone else who entered through the front door. My new friend, Jimmy* told me that she was Beulah*, their maid. She was short, slim, always had a big smile on her face, and was about sixty years of age.

Several hours later, while Jimmy and I were playing in his back yard, and Beulah was hanging clothes to dry on the line, she said to Jimmy in a motherly manner, "Jimmy, can ya please get me some watah to drink? It's hot today."

Jimmy did not reply. He simply scampered off toward the kitchen and quickly returned with a glass quart bottle that normally contained milk. However, this time it was half filled with water—and he gave it to Beulah.

She drank heartily in one protracted swig the entire half-filled bottle of water, exhaled heavily, placed her hands on Jimmy's shoulders and softly pronounced, "You ah a very good boy, Jimmy. You ah a very good boy." Beulah tapped Jimmy on the head, went over to the trash can, broke the glass milk bottle, threw the glass shards into the can, covered the can, and returned to hanging out the clothes to dry.

"That Beulah is a real nice lady," I commented to Jimmy as we were playing with his tricycles.

"She's O.K.," he quickly replied without picking up his head to look at me.

However, something bothered me, and as a six-year-old I merely asked him directly. "Why does Beulah walk in and out of your house through the back door? Doesn't she know where the front door is? Everyone else knows where it is. She's the only one who uses the back door."

And before he could reply I added another question. "Why did you give her a milk bottle for her water? You've got loads of glasses in your kitchen. They're all over the sink. And why did she break the bottle after she finished having her drink? My mother always throws out the empty milk bottles when we're finished. Everybody else in your house drinks from a glass or a cup. I've seen it. Why does Beulah drink from the milk bottle?"

Jimmy looked at me as if I was from another planet. "Are you a Yankee?" he quickly retorted as he squinted his eyes and pursed his lips. She's Black and we're all White," he shouted at me. "Only Whites enter the front door and only Whites drink from glasses. In our home Blacks come in from the back and they drink from milk bottles." And before I could make a comment, Jimmy stood up tall on his tricycle and emphatically stated, "We don't keep Black drinking bottles. Tomorrow, my dad will have another one for her. My dad checks with my mother every night to make sure that all drinking bottles used by Blacks in our home are broken every day."

Before I could utter a word, even in confusion, Jimmy reflexly commented, "Let's get back to playing."

I was only six, but even at that young age I knew that this action was different, strange, and—unfair. My mother also had a woman come in once a week to wash clothes. She, too, was Black, but my mother never had her drink from a glass milk bottle and then break it at the end of the day. Our Black woman used the same dishes and utensils that we did.

And she did not enter our house through the rear door. True, our house did not have a rear door. We lived in a three-family house, but that was not the reason that she entered through the front door. My parents treated her just like anyone else in the family.

I was really confused—but I was only six years of age, so I went back to the tricycles and continued playing with Jimmy.

The next day, my mother decided to take my brother and me downtown to see the sights of Richmond. We rode a bus for about twenty minutes and alighted in the center of the city. We spent about two hours there seeing statues of Civil War Generals, eating sandwiches, and licking our ice creams.

Then my mother said that it was time to return home. We caught a bus returning to my father's cousin's neighborhood; however, the bus was packed—like sardines in a can. So, the three of us stood in almost the center of the bus.

I looked about in an inquisitive manner and I noticed something strange. Almost all the Black people on the bus were seated in the last two rows. Several other Black men and women were standing; however, they too, were concentrated in the rear of the bus. "What a coincidence," I thought.

However, I did notice that one Black man was seated in the middle of the bus, adjacent to my mother, my brother, and me. He was the only Black person not focused at the rear of the bus. I thought, with my six-year-old logic, that all the Black people had been the first ones on the bus and, therefore, had automatically migrated toward the rear. However, I rationalized, the one man close to us had gotten on the bus later.

We must have been driving for about two minutes when the bus shuddered. All the people who were standing let forth, "I'm falling," or "Watch out," or "What happened?" or some other confused comment as they fell forward banging into each other. My mother was lucky that she was able to grab onto a strap hanging from a horizontal pole near the ceiling, and my brother and I grabbed onto her. But several people who were standing fell and had to be helped to their feet—but no one was hurt, only angry.

No one knew what had occurred, what had precipitated that abrupt stop. Several people called out, "Did we hit a car?" or "Did we hit a person?" Others cried out, "What happened? What happened?"

But the answer quickly became obvious to those aboard the bus when the driver rapidly squirmed through the crowd toward the area where we were standing. "What the heck are you doing here?" he shouted at the Black man seated not more than a foot from where my mother was standing. The driver removed his sunglasses and continued his vitriolic diatribe against the Black man. "Get your fat [expletive] off the seat. You belong in the back with your own people, not here with the White folk."

The driver continued to shout insults and affronts, indignities and slurs at the Black man, and several white people chimed in, "That's right;" "You belong in the back;" "You should know your place on the bus."

I was confused and I could see fear written all over my mother's face. And as the man rose from his seat to escape toward the rear, with shame and also fear pasted all over his face, the driver continued to shout obscenities at him. "You Black [expletive], didn't you see the lady with the two kids standing next to you?" and he pointed at my mother, my brother, and me.

My mother's eyes opened wide and her mouth became unbolted as if she was about to gasp for breath. The driver was making her the center of the controversy, but it was obvious to me that my mother wanted to crawl into a small hole and be as inconspicuous as possible, but no small hole was available.

"That White woman is just as tired as you are," the driver continued to shout at the man as he wormed his way toward the rear, with many White men and women casting insulting gazes at him. "You should know where you belong, you Black [expletive]. This is not the first time you've been on a bus."

When the man arrived in the cramped area occupied by the Blacks, the driver turned his attention to my mother, as he was now standing right next to her. "Ma'am," he pleasantly pronounced as a smile progressed along his face, "the seat is now yours. You can sit down on it." And he took his handkerchief out of his back pocket and wiped the seat off for my mother.

My mother's heart was beating out of control. "Oh, thank you; however, I'd rather stand," she quickly countered with a contorted smile on her face.

"Oh no, this is your seat," the driver quickly insisted. "I purposely stomped on the brakes when I saw that Black [expletive] sitting in the White section." He hesitated for a moment, breathed in heavily, and shook his head. "Please excuse my strong language. I didn't mean to use that vile word. But he should have known that that was not his seat. That seat was for you," and he pointed his hand at the seat. "Please be seated, ma'am."

My mother's lips seemed to quiver. Eyes galore were directed toward her. But she breathed in heavily and parried, "Thank you very much for your thoughtfulness. But I cannot sit. I have back problems and sitting down would cause me great pain."

"Don't worry," the driver replied as his smile continued to broaden. "Just hold onto me. I'll help you into the seat."

I thought my mother was going to collapse out of shame and fear but she had a reply for each of his comments. "Even if I can be seated, it will be torture getting up when we leave."

However, the driver was persistent. His smile did not leave his face. “I told you not to worry. I’ll personally help you even when you get up.”

My mother was desperate. She did not know what to say, but automatically and instinctively out of her mouth came four Yiddish words, “*Gay brech ah foos.* [Go break your leg.]” And my mother smiled brightly at the driver. She was surprised at the audacity of her comment and she did not know what his response would be.

“What did you say?” the driver queried as his smile quickly left his face.

My mother continued to smile at the driver as if the smile was painted on her face, and she slowly responded, “*Gay brech ah foos.* [Go break your leg.]” But this time she said it very slowly.

Immediately, the driver’s smile returned to his face. “Thank you for your blessing,” he exultingly stated as he articulated each word individually. “I guess you’re Catholic but I don’t speak Latin. Thanks again for your blessing—even though it was in Latin.”

My mother heaved a heavy sigh of relief, but immediately another woman slid into the seat and strongly called out, “It’s getting late, driver. Let’s start moving.” Echoes of her sentiments quickly came forth from at least a half dozen other passengers.

The driver squirmed back to his seat, put the bus into gear, and off we went.

My mother squinted a quick look toward the Black man. He was grimacing as if he was totally appalled by his action of acquiescence and submission but resigned to the realization that any acts of mutiny on his behalf would have quickly resulted in his arrest. My mother shook her head to herself as if expressing an inner feeling of, “How pitiful it is that seventy years after the Civil War, Black people in the United States are still being treated in the South like second class and third class citizens. In fact, they are not even being treated as citizens at all.”

But, then, the totally unexpected occurred. We had been driving no more than thirty seconds when we heard what sounded like the blast of a rifle shot. It was definitely an explosion. Many women, both White and Black, shouted in fear and instinctively lowered their heads. "[Expletive]," the bus driver cried out, "it's a blowout," and he began slowing down the bus as it began rocking from side to side. But no more than an additional ten seconds transpired before we heard another explosion, this one much louder than the first. Again there were shouts of fear and heads were lowered. "Someone's shooting at us," several people were shouting and screaming. My mother automatically held my brother and me close to her to protect us from any eventuality.

"[Expletive]," the driver bellowed once again, "it's another blowout. Nobody's shooting at us." He was fuming and smoldering and he quickly brought the bus to a quick stop.

"Everybody off," he roared in obvious anger as he opened the door. "There's a pharmacy down the block. I'll call for another bus to pick us up. I'm sure he'll be here pretty soon."

The driver opened the front and center doors and was the first to alight from the bus. Immediately, he began helping the White people as they descended from the bus. The Black people were totally ignored by him as they left through the center door.

As my mother descended from the bus, the driver stretched forth his hand to help her down the three steps. "The seat was rightfully yours," he commented to my mother as his grimace evaporated from his face and he flashed a smile of contentment toward her. "Today was a really tough day; however, your Latin blessing defused me." The driver hesitated for a moment and then added, "You seem to be a holy woman. I wonder if I could impose upon you a request for another blessing. I'm a religious man and I go to church every Sunday even though it's a Baptist Church. Prayers are very important to me, and, as I said, today was a tough day for me."

However, before my mother could respond, a Black woman approached the driver and softly inquired, "How long do you think it will take before the other bus will come? I don't want to be late for work."

But the driver abruptly turned toward her and began shouting again, "I'm busy right now, you Black [expletive]. When he comes, he comes."

My mother felt she was going to collapse. Not only did she feel fear from this driver, but she also felt embarrassment and shame for the Black woman who had merely asked a simple and logical question but had received a vituperative and abusive reply—and for no reason at all.

"Of course I'll give you another blessing," my mother replied with a "Mona Lisa smile" on her face, and seven Yiddish words came forth from her lips. *"Brech bay-der fees oon bay-der hent, tzu-za-men.* [Break both feet and both arms, together.]"

An explosive smile burst forth on the driver's face. It was as if he had been personally blessed by the Pope himself. "Thank you; thank you; thank you," he enthusiastically and ebulliently responded as he grabbed my mother's two hands.

"I'm late. I've got to go," my mother quickly stated as she released her hands from his, grabbed my brother's hand and my hand, and walked off toward a taxi stand on the corner.

However, she stopped abruptly, turned around toward the driver, smiled warmly again, and called out toward him, *"Du bist ah shvuntz oon a drek.* [You are a low-life, good-for-nothing, and a scalawag.]" Once again she grabbed our hands and directed us toward the cab but we could hear the driver crying out, "Thanks again. God bless you for those heartfelt prayers."

• • • • •

1) "I'm no martyr. I just had a hard day at work. My feet were hurting, and I was too tired to give up my seat."

—Rosa Parks, Mother of the Civil Rights Movement

2) "When it comes to success, the choice is simple. You can either stand up and be counted, or lie down and be counted out."

—Maggie L. Walker, America's First Black Female Bank President

Chapter 3

Never Give In! Never Give Up!

Normally, when a Jewish boy is thirteen years of age he celebrates his Bar Mitzvah (participates in the ritual indicating that he has religiously "come of age"). However, Howie* did not become a Bar Mitzvah until he was fourteen years old because he had been lax in his attendance at Religious School, had missed many of his Bar Mitzvah classes, and had not enthusiastically studied his lessons—but eventually he achieved his goal. He celebrated his Bar Mitzvah in the Chapel of our synagogue on a Saturday afternoon, rather than in our Sanctuary on a Saturday morning.

Ice skating was the epicenter of Howie's life. After school and on weekends he was always at the ice skating rink. In fact, Howie played on an amateur hockey team. The hockey players were all fifteen, sixteen, and seventeen years of age, but Howie was tall—almost six feel tall—and he could hold his own against all the big boys.

One day, Howie and several of his friends gathered together on the street outside his mother's office. They were waiting for his mother, Shirley*, to take them to the skating rink. She usually left work at 4 P.M. and it was now 3:15 P.M. They all had their ice skates with them and they were boasting about what they were going to do on the ice.

However, Howie shouted at all of them and eventually attracted their attention. "I saw something on TV last night that I'm going to do for you when I get my skates on," Howie boasted to his friends. "It's cool as ice and only the best can do it." His friends began snickering because Howie always bragged how superior he was on the ice.

"I'm gonna do it," Howie boasted, "and I'll bet that none of you will have the courage or the guts to do it with me."

All of Howie's friends stared at him and one finally shouted, "Tell us about it. Show us what it's all about."

Howie stood up tall. His chest expanded as if he was going to demonstrate some twists and turns that only he could do but the others could merely wish that they could execute. Then, in a flourish, with his eyes gleaming with pride, he related to them what he had seen on TV the previous night.

"That skater was stupendous," Howie trumpeted. "His skates were on his feet and he took some lighter fluid and put it all over the blades on his two shoes. He then took a match and lit the blades. For a moment it seemed that he was going to cremate himself. Fire was all around him. But he quickly began to skate—and the fire no longer enveloped him. He was merely like a 747 jet with the exhaust flames coming out of the jet engines."

Howie stared at his friends whose eyes were agape. They were mesmerized by his story. "I wondered how he was going to stop," Howie continued. "His speed was causing the flames to shoot out behind him, but as soon as he would stop, the fire was once again going to be all around him."

Once again he gazed at his friends. They were still totally quiet. It was as if everyone was wondering to himself, "Do I have the courage to do that?"

But Howie continued. "When the skater came to the end of the rink he jumped. It was unbelievable."

The four boys were now gawking at Howie. "He jumped into a ten-foot by ten-foot pool of water," Howie laughed, "and the fire was quickly extinguished. Not even a hair on him was singed. And when he was later interviewed he merely smiled and said, 'The heat of the fire merely kept me warm as I skated around the rink.'"

The four boys quickly broke their silence by shouting, "Cool," "That's terrific," "I'm sorry I missed it," and "I'm going to do that some day."

Howie took his ice skates and shouted back at them, "I'm going to do it today when I get to the rink."

The boys thought that that was merely braggadocio, grandiloquence, and the pompous words of a fourteen-year-old younster, but Howie grinned at them and took out a can of lighter fluid from his jacket. "You guys don't believe me," he snickered. "Well, just watch me," and he removed the cap on top of the can, squeezed a jetstream of lighter fluid over the blades of his shoes, and then repeated it a second time. "This is for good luck," he shouted at them. "I want my shoes to look like a B-1 bomber, powerful and mighty."

But the second squirt of lighter fluid partially missed its mark and hit Howie's pants and shoes. "This stinks," he quipped to his friends as he attempted to wipe the fluid off his pants with the padded arm of his jacket. "Gads, now my arm also stinks," he joked with his friends as they growled in glee. "I better wait five minutes until it all dries up."

Howie waited about three minutes and then removed a pack of matches from his pocket. He did not have any patience. He wanted to get to the rink as soon as possible. "I got these last night at the Razorback Restaurant* where my parents took me for dinner. The food was stupendous there," he added, "but my parents didn't see me take the matches when we left." They all laughed as Howie tore a match from the book of matches.

The first attempt to ignite the match was unsuccessful. He struck it several more times but no flame came forth. Howie threw away that spent match and tore out another one. This time he held the match close to its head and struck it with force. Immediately, it brought forth a fire and Howie's finger was charred. Instinctively, he cried out, "Damn it," as he dropped the match upon his pants.

Then, everything happened so very quickly. Initially, the four friends burst forth with shouts of glee—Howie had burned his fingers while striking a simple match. But within two seconds the so-called spent match had ignited Howie's pants—and that quickly spread to the arms of his jacket and to his shoes. The lighter fluid may now have been dry but its existence was still present in his clothing.

Howie was shouting and screaming. He was obviously in great pain. His friends were attempting to throw dirt and sand and earth on him but they were not having any effect on extinguishing the flames. On the contrary, Howie was now almost totally engulfed in fire. It was now quickly spreading upwards on his chest. Howie was pounding on the flames with the palms of his hands—but he was losing the battle. Everyone was shouting and screaming. Then, one boy took off his jacket and threw it over Howie, but he could not get close to him because of the fire, and the jacket was not effective in snuffing out the fire.

Because of the loud noise from the screaming, Shirley, Howie's mother, went to the window of the office with the intention of telling the boys to be quiet and wait for her to finish her work. But she saw the flames and she quickly recognized that it was her son, Howie, who was totally immersed in the flames. She shouted, "Oh my God."

However, she had the presence of mind to grab her long coat that was hanging in the closet and she ran out toward her son. It only took about a minute before she reached him but he was no longer running about. He was now lying on the ground crying out and howling. The boys were continuing to throw earth and sand on him but to no avail. The lighter fluid was still feeding the flames. They could not get close to him without getting singed, and his friends' jackets were too small to be effective.

But Shirley, with the courage of a mother, held her full length coat out in front of her and pounced upon her son, quickly enwrapping him in the coat. The flames were gone as quickly as they had appeared.

Shirley had been singed but she did not indicate any pain. "Call 911," she shouted at Howie's friends. However, they seemed paralyzed with disbelief as to what had happened. They seemed incapacitated. They were merely staring at Howie on the ground. "Immediately," Shirley again roared at them as if she was a Marine Drill Instructor, and the three boys quickly ran off toward her office.

Howie was moaning and groaning. He was in shock and Shirley removed the coat from him to ascertain the severity of the wounds; however, as soon as the coat was on the ground the fire that had previously enveloped Howie once again erupted. The oxygen and the intense heat and the residue of the lighter fluid quickly initiated another flame and conflagration.

Once again, Howie was shouting and screaming, wailing and screeching. Once again, Shirley could see the intense pain in Howie's eyes. Once again, Shirley feared that she was losing her son.

Quickly, she again enveloped Howie with her long coat, and once again the flames slackened and were finally extinguished and snuffed out as she patted every part of his body to attempt to put out every last spark and flicker of flame. This time she did not attempt to view the damage by removing her coat. But once again she shouted at the boys, "Call 911 immediately."

The boys ran out of her office. "The ambulance is already on its way," the shortest boy whimpered as he ran toward Shirley. "What can we do? What can we do?" they all chimed in.

"Pray for him," Shirley quickly retorted, "and start doing it right now." The realization was quickly enveloping Shirley that Howie was very badly hurt, severely hurt, and it would take a miracle to help him. His hands were lying limp before her and she could see that they looked roasted and toasted. There was no more flesh upon them; however, she did not want to touch them or him because she felt that she might impose on him some additional hurt and damage.

Within four minutes, two ambulances arrived with six paramedics and technicians. They were quickly briefed by Shirley and the boys as to what had transpired, and after placing Howie on a gurney, carrying him into the ambulance, and inserting an I.V. in his arm, he was whisked off to Hermann Hospital where burn victims had their best chance for survival.

Shirley accompanied Howie in the ambulance to the hospital and immediately called Raymond*, Howie's father, from the hospital Emergency Room. Doctors galore worked for hours on

Howie while Shirley and Raymond waited nervously in the Waiting Room amidst many friends and family members who had gathered there after hearing the traumatic news. Sporadically, a nurse would exit from the Emergency Room to compassionately inform Shirley and Raymond of the severity of Howie's case—but that he "was still hanging on" and that "the doctors were doing their best for him."

At 2 A.M. the Senior Surgeon in charge of Howie's case came out of the Emergency Room, sat down with Shirley and Raymond, grasped Shirley's hands, and softly spoke to both of them as the friends and family encircled them. "Your son has been very badly burned," and the surgeon emphasized the word "very"; however, when he saw Shirley grimace and tense and stiffen, he added, "but he is young and strong, and there is a chance that he will be able to overcome the burns and shock to his body."

The doctor went on: "The first thing we had to do was stabilize him, which we've achieved—at least for the present time. We also had to remove skin and flesh that were burned beyond saving. The next twenty-four hours are critical. They will give us a hint as to whether he will be able to survive this trauma."

Shirley held tightly onto Raymond's hand as she listened to the doctor intimate that Howie might not even survive. Tears appeared in the corners of her eyes as she fought valiantly to restrain an uncontrolled flow. Raymond merely sat there as if he was a stone statue. He did not move or stir or budge. It was as if he was mesmerized with fear.

Once again, the surgeon continued as he held onto Shirley's hand. "If everything goes well during the next few days, we are going to move Howie to the Burn Center in Galveston. They specialize in treating children. That will be the best place for him. We'll have him flown there by medical helicopter."

Shirley could no long restrain the flow of tears and Raymond embraced her. "Meanwhile," the surgeon suggested, "all we can do is wait. Time is the best helper and ally for Howie. The longer he hangs on, the better are his chances for survival."

The surgeon shook his head and rose. "Do you have any

questions?" he compassionately asked, and he added, "I also have a son fourteen years old and I know how you feel."

Shirley and Raymond merely shook their heads and the surgeon retreated to the surgical suite.

Two days passed without any major complications that could not be corrected by the medical staff but Howie still hovered between life and death. His condition continued to be extremely serious and he was totally sedated so that he should not feel the pain and torment of his unbelievable injuries. But the doctors made a decision—send him immediately to Galveston. Procrastinating was not helping him.

So, two and a half days after the tragedy, Howie was transferred to the Shriner's Burn Center in Galveston where Shirley was given a room adjacent to Howie's where she could live while he was hospitalized—and she was told that Howie would be there for many weeks and probably many months—and the nurse added "if he survives."

That afternoon, after Howie was brought to Galveston, fifty miles from Houston, one of Shirley's friends called me and told me what had transpired. Toby and I usually went to Galveston every sixth week for an evening in order to have dinner with our son, Scotty, who was a Resident in Ophthalmology at the University of Texas Medical Branch. After concluding the phone call, I told Toby that we would go to Galveston that evening so that we might see Shirley, Raymond, and Howie—in addition to having dinner with our son, Scotty.

We only spent about an hour with Scotty at which time he told us that he had examined Howie's eyes as the Resident on duty when Howie had been brought to the hospital, and, luckily, the flames had not damaged his eyes. "But," he sadly added, "he was burned on eighty-nine percent of his body."

At 8 P.M. we went to the hospital. A nurse directed us to Howie's quarters. The nurse instructed me to put on a gown and mask in order to keep the room sterile when entering Howie's quarters, but Toby decided to remain in the hall.

Howie was lying on his stomach and was wearing only a skimpy loincloth to cover his genitalia. My first gaze at him indicated only raw flesh, from the soles of his feet up to the middle of his back. The only "normal" part of his body seemed to be his head that did not have any burn marks from the flames.

"I'm here to help all of you in any and every way possible," I softly whispered to Shirley as I hugged her in that strangely lit room. It was difficult for me to understand why they kept the room as if it was noontime in July in Galveston with the sun emitting a maximum of its rays, but that is the way the room was always kept whenever I visited Howie.

Howie looked as if someone had painted him red and black. Part of his body looked as if it was red as a steak in a butcher shop while the remainder looked as if the chef had forgotten to remove the steak from the grill. It was close to black.

Shirley wept bitterly as I held her and attempted to inject a handful of comforting words, but what words can be considered "comforting" when one's son is tottering and reeling between life and death, and one does not know what the word "life" will mean for him if he survives this tragedy?

After about fifteen minutes of holding Shirley's hands and talking to her, we walked toward Howie's bed where I recited a prayer for his recovery and return to a normal life. "Amen," Shirley responded as I concluded my petition to God.

"I'd like to sit next to Howie's bed," I commented to Shirley as we walked away from his bed. "I'd like to talk to him. I know he's very heavily sedated and does not respond to our comments, but I know he hears us, maybe not entirely, but at least partially."

I hesitated for a moment and then continued, "I remember when my son Michael was hurt and in a coma we would constantly speak to him—but there would be no response. But when he came out of the coma and was eventually able to speak, he told us about many of the things we had said to him. True, some of them sounded distorted and contorted but he was able to understand and repeat to us about sixty percent of the material that we had attempted to convey to him."

Shirley applied a Kleenex to her eyes as she wiped away additional tears. "Rabbi, would you mind if I sit in my room and talk to Toby while you talk to Howie? It hurts me to sit here and watch him immobile and not responding. My heart is pounding and my head is throbbing. I haven't left him for almost three days. I think I'm dying together with Howie."

"Shirley, never give in and never give up," I emphatically but softly stated to her as I conjured up a compassionate look and once again held onto both of her hands. "If Howie sees optimism and hope in your eyes, he'll always make progress. But if he sees pessimism and hopelessness in your eyes, he'll start sliding backwards. Even if you have to wear a mask in his presence, smile and indicate hope, confidence, and faith. Always remember that cheer breeds healing and mending, progress and recovery; depression results in dejection, despondency, disheartenment, discouragement and a worsening of one's condition. This is the time to learn that lesson." I held her close to me and hugged her. "Start wearing that mask of cheer for Howie now." Shirley kissed me on the cheek and walked off to meet Toby.

I took a chair and sat down adjacent to Howie's bed on the side where his face was pointing and began speaking to him as if the two of us were going to have a conversation. "Howie," I quietly began, "I know that you hear me. When my son Michael was hurt, he told me that he heard most of what I had told him even though he could not respond. During the next weeks, Toby and I are going to come out to Galveston to visit you—and I am going to talk to you like I'm doing now. But I can tell you now that the basic message I'm going to give you is—Never give up; Never give in."

The volume of my voice began to increase as I continued. "Always look forward to tomorrow. Remember that your situation will get better. Heaven is the place where there is loads of hope. You are a courageous young boy. You were an excellent ice skater—and that's what you're going to be again."

It was impossible for me to know whether I was merely fantasizing or truly prognosticating the future, but I felt that I was obliged to inject in him a spirit of hope, a confidence for a better day, and an aspiration for good health.

"Let me tell you a story," I continued as I moved my chair closer to his bed. "This story is about another young boy who found himself in an equally difficult situation. He name was Tom Dempsey."

For a moment I waited. I guess I was expecting a miracle, for Howie to open his eyes and say, "Rabbi, go on with your story." However, no miracle occurred , so I went on. "Tom was born with only half a right foot and a deformed right arm. His classmates would continually make fun of him, but his father would always tell him, "Don't listen to those bullies. You will achieve whatever goal you set for yourself. Yes, you have a handicap but if you make up your mind to overcome that obstacle, you will achieve your goal. Just never say the word 'can't', 'I can't do it.' It is a word of hopelessness, pessimism, despair, and discouragement—and you don't need that."

Again I hesitated. I do not know what I was really expecting but when nothing again happened I simply went on. "When Tom was thirteen he told his father, 'I want to join the Boy Scouts,' but the Boy Scouts had told him 'You can't. We have a ten mile hike three weeks from Saturday and you can't march ten miles.'

"But Tom's father responded, 'The word 'can't' is not in my son's vocabulary. Tom will be present at the hike—and he will make it.' "

I felt as if I was talking to myself but I remembered what my son Michael had told me, "Dad, even though I was in a coma, I heard about sixty percent of what you told me."

I therefore went on, staring at Howie's eyes that seemed to be focused on me. "Tom's father therefore took Tom to a friend who was a shoemaker and that man made a special shoe for him that allowed him to march those ten miles. His first hurdle had been conquered.

"Then Tom told his father that he wanted to play football but he could not run like the other boys. So his father said to him, 'Why can't you be the kicker, the punter?' which sounded good to Tom. But again there was pessimism, despair, and dashed hopes. The high school football coach told him, 'You only have half a foot and a deformed arm.' But again Tom's father went to his friend the shoemaker, and again he made him a special shoe that enabled Tom to kick as well as the other high school students."

For a second I thought I heard a comment from Howie and I put my ear closer to his mouth but it was only a groan indicating his pain, not a response to my story.

So, once again I went on. "Tom was good at kicking on the gridiron. He continually repeated to himself, 'Never give in; never give up,' whenever anyone would say to him, 'You only have half a foot and a deformed arm.' But eventually he received a contract from the San Diego Chargers—but it did not last long. The coach suggested to him that it would be better for him if he left football.

"But the phrase 'can't do it' was no longer in his vocabulary. So he applied for the position of punter with the New Orleans Saints. The Saints' coach did not even want to give him a tryout when he was told that he only had half a foot and he saw his deformed arm. But Tom begged, begged, and begged until the coach relented—and the coach was pleasantly surprised when two weeks later Tom kicked a fifty-five yard field goal in an exhibition game. The coach immediately gave him a contract, and that season Tom scored ninty-nine points. Everyone was happy."

It seemed to me as if I had to get used to a unidimensional conversation, but once again I continued. "But, Howie, Tom's big moment came on November 8, 1970, when his team, the New Orleans Saints, was playing the Detroit Lions before 66,000 fans. Unfortunately, the score was 17 to 16, with Detroit in the lead. Yes, New Orleans had the ball but it was on its own 28 yard line, and there was only enough time left for two plays, at most."

I, myself, was now deeply engrossed in the story, and I enthusiastically proceeded. "The first play was a gain for New Orleans for seventeen yards. The ball was now on the New Orleans forty-five yard line, only fifty-five yards from a touchdown and victory. But it was obvious to one and all that New Orleans needed a miracle—no, a super miracle—to gain the fifty-five yards for a touchdown. Everyone was whooping it up, shouting and screaming, 'It can't be done.' Scores of people began leaving the stands in order not to be caught in the masses that would soon be simultaneously leaving when the final whistle was blown. Everyone 'knew' that New Orleans was going to lose."

Again I thought I heard a sound from Howie but it quickly became obvious to me that it was not a response to my story but once more an indication of pain, in spite of the heavy sedation. So, again, I resumed my story. "But to everyone's surprise, the New Orleans Saints' coach did not call for a 'Hail Mary' play and hope that one of his men in the End Zone would catch the ball and score a touchdown. The chances of that occurring was even slimmer than winning a lottery. But the coach cried out at the top of his voice, 'Dempsey, get in there and kick a field goal.'

"Everyone on the New Orleans team stared at the coach as if he had lost his mind, as if he believed that voodoo could achieve the impossible for his team. The ball was on the New Orleans forty-five yard line and the kicker had to place the ball eight yards behind the line of scrimmage to clear the hands of the defensive team. That would place the ball on the New Orleans' thirty-seven yard line, sixty-three yards away from the goalpost.

"But the previous longest successful field goal attempt had been achieved by Bert Rechichar of the Baltimore Colts—but that had only been a fifty-five yard field goal, eight yards shorter than that which Tom was being asked to achieve."

I looked at the door and I could see Toby signaling me to come out to talk to her and Shirley but I motioned to her to wait because I was in the midst of my story with Howie. Again I continued. "But deep in his heart Tom said to himself, 'I *can* do it. My father told me that if I wanted to do it bad enough, I *could* do it.'

"Meanwhile, the trickle of people leaving the stadium had turned into a flood. They were not even looking any longer at the playing field. They were merely searching for the exits. They *knew*. They were *positive* that the game was over and Detroit would be the victor.

"The referee shouted, 'Play ball,' and the ball was snapped by the New Orleans center."

My eyes once again focused on Howie. Even though I had related this story many times, I always became tense when I came to the climax of the story. Once again I hoped for a response from Howie, but none came forward. So, once again I persisted. "Tom kicked the ball. It was a good kick and it went—went—went—and went. The referee at the goal post raised both his arms. It was a field goal—one that everyone thought was impossible to achieve, but I guess they forgot to tell the ball. New Orleans had defeated Detroit 19 to 17."

I was on a roll. I felt as if I had pierced Howie's impervious armor even though he did not respond. "Here was a football player with half a foot and a deformed arm who had done what everyone told him he could not do. But he did not listen to them and therefore he made the impossible the possible, the unattainable the attainable. Instead of listening to the pessimism and negative comments of his friends telling him what he could *not* do, Tom listened to his father who had always told him, 'If you want hard enough to do it, you *will* be able to do it.'"

I then pursed my lips, breathed in heavily, and concluded, "Howie, Louis Brandeis was an American Supreme Court Justice. Remember his words. He once said, 'Most of the things worth doing in the world have been declared impossible before they were done.'"

Then I arose from my chair, leaned down toward Howie's bed, and dogmatically declared to him, "Howie, I'm your rabbi. With your determination to get better and all of us helping you, you *will* get better and you *will* eventually get back to the hockey rink. We're all pulling for you. All of us together will get you better."

I had merely been talking to him but I was emotionally exhausted and I was perspiring. Again, I looked down at Howie. There was absolutely no response and no movement. All I could see was that red, raw flesh and black charred flesh—and I could vividly surmise the sharp pain that it represented.

It was not easy looking at him. He was a young boy who had as yet not even begun living but now he was hovering between life and death. His entire future was a gigantic question mark. The only time I had seen flesh like his was in a movie, for a fleeting moment, but never on a live human being. It was debilitating and nerve-racking, mentally exhausting and emotionally fatiguing.

Tears filled my eyes as I left his room to meet with Toby and

Shirley. Toby had had a good effect on Shirley. She had related to her how we had struggled with Michael when he had been shot and left for dead, how we had refused to give in or give up but constantly helped and aided him—and he beat the odds. Shirley, I think, felt that she was speaking to a woman "who had been there," who had experienced a similar trauma but had refused to capitulate. It gave her the strength to face another tomorrow.

We told Shirley that we would return every few weeks and visit with her and Howie—and this became our schedule for many, many months. We would have dinner with our son, Scotty, then we would go to the hospital before returning to Houston.

As the months flew by, I would always sit at Howie's bedside and tell him stories of people, animals, and incidents where the impossible had become the possible, the hopeless had become the hopeful, and the unthinkable had become the thinkable.

For months and months there was no reply. Howie underwent skin graft after skin graft and they always kept him heavily sedated.

I remember once being in his room about 9:30 P.M. when a therapist was working with his legs, attempting to move them at the knees so that the muscles would not atrophy. But as soon as the therapist manipulated his leg a shrill cry came forth from Howie. It was heaven-piercing. Even under maximum sedation the pain and torment must have been overwhelming. My heart literally broke for Howie as I felt helpless and powerless to help or aid him.

The weeks passed into months and Scotty could not meet with us as often as previously because his studies monopolized his time. Our trips to Galveston became fewer and fewer—more sporadic than regular. However, Howie was making progress. It was truly a miracle. The doctors at the Burn Center were truly "miracle workers." I kept in touch with Shirley by phone and she would regularly relate to me each minute detail of Howie's physical and emotional growth.

About two years after Howie's accident, I was conducting

our Early Shabbat Prayer Service (E.S.P.) at 6 P.M. on a Friday evening in the Sanctuary and my sermonette was about miracles. I was relating how our legends tell us that when the Israelites left the slavery in Egypt, three thousand three hundred years ago, they found themselves pursued from the west by Pharoah's army and blockaded on the east by the waters of the Red Sea. They were stuck. They could not go forward and they could not go backward. The Israelites therefore began praying and pleading to God. They were cemented in their tracks. The inevitable was obvious—the mass destruction of the Jews.

However, one man, Nachshon, the son of Aminadav, arose and cried out, "I don't know about you, but this is *not* the time for prayer or shouting to God. This is the time for action. I'm going to jump into the sea and start swimming to the other side. If I make it—good. If I don't—then at least I made an attempt. But I will not stand by helpless and impotent and wait for my destruction. Remember—God helps those who help themselves"—and he jumped into the water.

At first, I told the congregation, no one moved, but a few minutes later a handful began jumping into the water as they saw Nachshon making progress. Then it became a flood of people entering the water, and then, according to our legend—a miracle occurred. God split the sea for the Israelites and they walked through on a dry path—all because of one man, Nachshon, who had great faith in himself.

And I concluded by saying, "Don't scoff or mock at miracles. *We* make them happen. If *we* have great faith in ourselves, the impossible *can* become the possible."

And as I uttered those words I looked at the door of the large Sanctuary and I could not believe what my eyes saw. It was Howie in a wheel chair. His hands were still covered with bandages but he had a big grin on his face.

Immediately I proclaimed to the congregation, "We have a miracle in our Sanctuary this Shabbat," and I quickly descended from the pulpit and semi-jogged toward Howie and his parents. "Howie," I proudly stated as I kissed him on the brow, "you are my miracle. Come up with me to the pulpit and let me publicly bless you there."

However, Howie shook his head indicating his reluctance to fulfill my wish. "When I can walk up the steps to the ark under my own steam, that's when I will willingly and gladly accept that blessing. Until then, *my* miracle is not complete." He was adamant in his contention and nothing that I could say could budge him from his stance. But I respected him for his unyielding stance. *He* had suffered. *He* had struggled to get back to where he was now. *He* was entitled to choose the time when he would come to the front of the synagogue for a blessing.

Quickly, I returned to the pulpit and concluded the Service.

Six months later, while once again conducting the lively 6 P.M. E.S.P. Service on a Friday evening, I saw the rear door of the Sanctuary open just before the *Adone Olam* hymn marking the conclusion of the Service. The door opened wide and I could see a woman and a man pushing a wheel chair into the Sanctuary. I stared at all of them and it quickly became apparent that Shirley and Raymond were the pushers and Howie was in the chair. But this time I noticed that there were no bandages on Howie's hands—but he was still in the wheel chair.

I allowed the Service to end as I normally did, by asking everyone present to greet those standing in front of them, behind them, to their sides and to introduce themselves to those whom they did not know.

After the final benediction I quickly descended from the pulpit and maneuvered my way toward Howie; however, he and his parents had begun to move slowly toward the pulpit.

"Howie, you don't have any more bandages on your hands," I exclaimed with glee and joy. "It's obvious that you're making great progress."

Howie's parents smiled as if they were affirming my comment but Howie ignored my statement and interjected his own. "Mom, Dad, push me to the pulpit." It was as if he did not see me or hear me. However, I quickly followed the three of them until they arrived at the pulpit.

It was then that Howie turned toward me. "Rabbi," he announced with eyes staring directly at me, "six months ago I told you that I did not want your blessing in the Sanctuary until I could personally walk up to the ark—not be carried up, but walk up all by myself to the ark where we keep the Torahs [biblical scrolls containing the five books of Moses and written on parchment]. I counted those steps when I was here six months ago—ten from the Sanctuary to the pulpit and an additional six from the pulpit to the ark. For six months those steps were burned in my mind and I've been working on climbing steps since then. It's not easy for me yet to climb steps. It hurts. It hurts like heck. But I've been working hard for the past six months and I want to try it now."

Shirley and Raymond had tears in their eyes but Howie had determination and resolve written all over his face. Before anyone could say a word, Howie braced himself, stiffened his arms, and pushed himself up to a standing position.

I automatically stretched forth my arms to help him and to brace him. "Rabbi," Howie instinctively grumbled, "I told you before, I've got to do it myself. Please step aside."

I looked toward Shirley and Rayond and their response was apologetic but direct, "Rabbi, let him do it. This has been one of his goals for a long time."

"Take the wheel chair away from me," Howie directed his father. Tension, strain, and stress were written all over his face but determination was equally inscribed on his countenance. His steps were erratic and spasmodic but Howie was now climbing his Mount Everest. He was like Edmond Hillary, slowly but surely inching his way "to the top", each step a painful and agonizing experience—but he refused to stop.

Congregants who had been talking amongst themselves and had delayed leaving the Sanctuary saw Howie's struggle and about thirty of them slowly meandered toward the pulpit encouraging him to continue and to go forward. Everyone could hear Howie's grunts and groans as he held onto the banister with his right hand to ascend the ten steps from the Sanctuary to the pulpit. When he finally reached the pulpit there was a spontaneous outburst of applause from the congregants who had remained.

Beads of perspiration now covered Howie's forehead but he did not bother to stop and catch his breath or momentarily rest. He merely raised his head, stared at the twenty-foot parochet (curtain covering the ark) as if it was the top of his Everest, and he plodded on.

However, there was no railing from the pulpit to the ark. There were merely six steps. As Howie lifted his right leg to place it on the first step, all could hear and see his distress and agony. Most congregants watched him grimace and some called out, "Rest a moment," but Howie acted as if he heard nothing, as if he was there all by himself. He merely trudged on. His youth was his energy and his innocence was his perserverance.

On the fifth step Howie tottered. Raymond and I instinctively began to quickly ascend the steps to help him, but Howie commandingly cried out, "Don't help me. I can do it myself. If I fall, I'll pick myself up."

A woman standing in the Sanctuary, tensely watching Howie, cried out, "May God help you reach your goal."

Howie's head was now totally soaked in perspiration. He was so close, yet so far. His hands were shaking and his legs were unsteady. But in a final burst of energy he ascended the sixth step. A quickly expanding smile overtook his face. It was like the powerful rays of the sun penetrating thick, dark clouds. Howie raised his head toward the ark and cried out, "I made it. I made it. I made it."

Raymond, Shirley, and I quickly scrambled over the steps and embraced Howie, while those in the congregation came up on the pulpit and shouted "Mazal tov," "Congratulations," "You are terrific."

Howie was exhausted but I quickly opened the ark and held onto Howie as I prayed, "Three thousand years ago King David proclaimed [Psalm 118:24], 'Zeh ha-yome asah Adonai, nageelah v'nismechah vo,' 'This is the day that God has made, we will be happy and joyous in it.'

"This evening, on this Shabbat, O God, Howie has returned to life. Yes, these steps tonight are merely his first steps, but it is a sign for the future—total recovery. Howie was knocked down, but he refused to stay down. With the help of his parents, his doctors, his friends, and You, O God, Howie has progressed along the road of recovery—and will keep on moving in that direction until he is totally recovered. This is truly a day of happiness and joy."

I looked at Howie as I prayed and I could see tears in his eyes. "O God," I continued as my eyes were focused on the Torahs in the ark, "in the Bible we are told how the Prophet Elisha was told by a woman from Shunem that her son was very sick. Everyone had given up hope. They even said [II Kings 4:32], *'Met,'* 'The boy is a goner.'

"But the mother refused to accept this depressing and disheartening news. She immediately went to Elisha and wept. 'He is my only child. He is only a baby. He is an innocent child. I can't have any more children. Please help me.'

"And the Bible tells us [II Kings 4:33-34] that Elisha stretched himself across the child—his mouth on the child's mouth, his eyes on the child's eyes, his hands on the child's hands, and *'Vayitpalel el Adonai,'* 'He prayed to God.'"

I breathed heavily and continued, "And then, the unexpected occurred. The child sneezed, his color came back to his face, his body began to move, and Elisha smiled and cried out to the child's mother [II Kings 4:36], *'S'ee v'naych,'* 'Take your child. He will be fine.'"

I continued to hold onto Howie as I noticed tears gushing forth from Shirley's eyes. "Howie," I resumed, "you are our modern-day boy of the Shunemite woman. You refused to give in or give up. The odds were against you. Everyone was pessimistic about your prognosis. But your parents, your doctors, your therapists, your friends—and your God were always there in your corner. They were always fighting your battle with you and for you. They were always saying, *'Gom zu ya'avore,'* 'He shall overcome this problem.'

"Howie, every day we recite in our prayers the words of King David [Psalm 20:2], *'Ya'oncha Adonai b'yome tzarah,'* 'May God answer you and help you and aid you in your day of trouble', and that was our continual prayer for you since the moment you were hurt.

"Today, our prayer for you is, 'May God help you make progress every single day. May you go from strength to greater strength. May you get better and better, stronger and stronger, healthier and healthier. May we soon see you running up these steps to the ark. May God's blessings always be upon you."

As soon as I said those last words and lowered my voice, everyone cried out *"Amen!"* Almost every woman had tears in her eyes and many men were likewise damp-eyed.

Howie leaned over and kissed me on the cheek, and with several tears in my eyes, I dogmatically decreed, "The two of us, with the help of your father, are going to walk down the steps to your chair." Howie did not argue. He was almost totally fatigued and exhausted.

We all embraced at the foot of the pulpit—Howie, Shirley, Raymond and I, and even the congregants who had remained also embraced Howie and his parents and said to him, "May God bless you," and "Mazal tov." There was now not a dry eye amongst all of us, especially when I briefly told the congregants what had happened to Howie.

As the months flew by, Howie continued to make progress after undergoing additional plastic surgery procedures. Six years after his accident, Howie had graduated from high school, had visited Israel, and was working on the West Coast. His hope was to eventually marry, have a family, and enjoy a normal life.

• • • • •

1) Someone once asked James J. Corbett, the world's heavyweight boxing champion, what was the most important thing a man must do to become a champion. He replied, "Fight one more round."

2) The Duke of Wellington said that the British soldiers at the Battle of Waterloo were not more brave than Napoleon's soldiers, but they were more courageous only five minutes longer. That made the difference between victory and defeat.

—Author unknown.

Don't Ever Give Up!

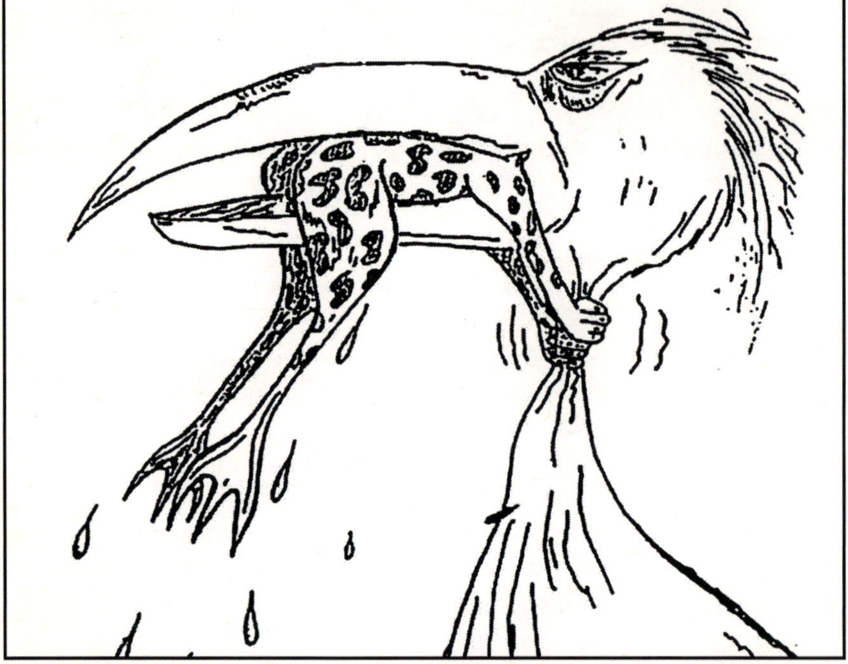

Persistence Pays Off

A CHAMPION

Never Gives Up

CHAPTER 4

Don't Make Split Second Decisions

It was about fifteen years ago, about a month before Rosh Hashanah when rabbis begin seriously thinking about their sermons for the Jewish New Year.

I was reading a book by Rabbi Jack Riemer and Professor Nathaniel Stampfer that was entitled *So That Your Values Live On—Ethical Wills And How to Prepare Them.* It was an extremely interesting book because it contained the words of approximately seventy-five Jewish men and women who penned their thoughts to their families before they passed away.

Most people usually have their lawyers do this. They meet with them in their offices and dictate to their attorneys how they want their shares of stock in IBM, Ford, General Motors, American Express, Weingarten Realty, Motorola, General Electric, Pfizer, Microsoft, and Amgen distributed amongst the members of their family. They usually also indicate a number of charities that should be financially remembered upon the death of the benefactor. So, too, properties owned by the one making out the will, money closeted in his banks, or bonds held in his safety deposit boxes are also pinpointed for specific distribution. Wills are financial documents that are itemized point by point by the head of a family while he is alive so that there should not be any arguing or fighting, quibbling or quarreling amongst family members after his death. The will is supposed to indicate what the head of the family felt and wanted and not what his inheritors felt and wanted from their "Good Samaritan."

However, Riemer and Stampfer indicated that Judaism preached that "the most precious thing we leave behind when we die is not our property; it is our legacy of *values* and *beliefs*. . . . Those who write ethical wills—often parents writing to their children, or grandparents to their grandchildren—try to sum up what they have learned in life, and to express what they want most for, and from, their loved ones. . . . Ethical wills are windows into the souls of those who write them."

Rabbi Riemer and Professor Stampfer suggested that in addition to Financial Wills prepared in lawyers' offices we should also personally prepare Ethical Wills in the recesses of our own homes. They suggested that at least four copies should be prepared: one should be kept by the one preparing this document, one should be mailed to that person's lawyer, one should be given to the eldest child, and one should be sent to one's rabbi.

I was literally mesmerized by this subject and I was additionally hypnotized by this idea of "Ethical Wills" when I read the one written by Sam Levenson that was included in the Riemer-Stampfer book.

"Sam Levenson's Ethical Will and Testament to His Grandchildren and to Children Everywhere" initially appeared in *Woman's Day* magazine in its May 3, 1977 edition. Levenson had enjoyed a checkered career. He had been an extremely popular Spanish teacher at Tilden High School in Brooklyn, New York, but was best known as a humorist and comedian who appeared nationally on radio and television. Levenson also authored a number of books and also starred on his own TV program, "The Sam Levenson Show". Most of his work focused on the family and how to raise children. He was the Dr. Spock and Dr. Dobson of the 60's and 70's.

Levenson wrote to his grandchildren and to children all over:

> I leave you my unpaid debts. They are my greatest assets. Everything I own—I owe.
>
> 1. To America—I owe a debt for the opportunity it gave me to be free and to be me.
> 2. To my parents—I owe America. They gave it to me and I leave it to you. Take good care of it.
> 3. To the biblical tradition—I owe the belief that man does not live by bread alone, nor does he live alone at all. This is also the democratic tradition. Preserve it.
> 4. To the six million of my people and the thirty million other humans who died because of man's inhumanity to man—I owe a vow that it must never happen again.
> 5. I leave you not everything I never had, but everything I had in my lifetime: a good family, respect for learning, compassion for my fellowman, and some four-letter words for all occasions: words like "help," "give," "care," "feel," and "love."

I therefore decided to speak on the first night of Rosh Hashanah on the subject, "Have You Yet Prepared Your Will?" I told my congregants how ancient rabbis prepared Ethical Wills to guide their families in the moral direction that they hoped they would follow. They attempted to guide them on the ethical roads of life that would face them after these rabbis passed away.

I therefore prepared a card and asked our porters to include one in every *machzor* (holiday prayer book) that was put in the book holders in front of each seat.

The questionnaire contained questions concerning pre-funeral preparations, the funeral service, the *Shivah* services (services conducted for seven days at the home of a mourner after the funeral service), and the recitation of *Kaddish* (mourner's prayer) recited by the children of the deceased (for eleven months) and other close relatives (for one month). The questionnaire was quite detailed and even contained questions as to whether the parents preferred their children to remain at the grave as the casket was lowered and whether they favored being buried in traditional shrouds or in a suit or dress.

However, at the end of the questionnaire I intentionally left blank a third of the large card suggesting that those returning the cards to me include some personal comments to their children, coming from the depths and recesses of their hearts and souls, just as the rabbis wrote to their children years ago: how they should treat their husbands/wives, how they should raise their children, how religion should be an influential dimension in their lives, how they should spend time with their families, how they should smile more and frown less, how much the parents loved their children, and how their children had made life meaningful for them. I told my congregants that they should inscribe these words if they were important to them, and to indicate to the family, if they so desired, that on many occasions they wanted to talk about these subjects with their children but never could muster the courage, backbone, or resolution to initiate such discussions because they felt these subjects were too delicate and would precipitate ill feeling if a face to face conversation was launched. These cards, I proposed, would afford an excellent opportunity to convey thoughts and feelings to their children that were profoundly important to them but were difficult to articulate.

I actually felt that the sermon was successful because within the next two weeks I received more than two hundred completed cards which I read and had my secretary file.

However, about four weeks after I preached that sermon, after all the holidays (Rosh Hashanah, Yom Kippur, and Sukkot) had been concluded, I received a phone call from a congregant. He spoke softly but deliberately.

"Rabbi Segal, my name is Gerald Schneider*. I am a member of your congregation, but, unfortunately, our paths have not crossed on many occasions."

He hesitated for a moment and then continued as I sat back in my soft chair behind my desk. "We met only when my son was Bar Mitzvahed seven years ago and my daughter was Bat Mitzvahed five years ago."

"How can I help you?" I commented in order to make him realize that I was listening attentively to his words.

"Well, Rabbi," Gerald went on, "I debated with myself for

the past four weeks whether I should call you, and last night I decided that if one has a problem he should expose it and not hide it. Exposed problems can be cured. Hidden problems merely fester and become worse."

I did not know where this conversation was leading but I told him that I agreed with the philosophy just stated.

"Well, Rabbi," Gerald went on again, "I want you to know that I *am* a member of your congregation but the only time I attend services is on Rosh Hashanah Eve and Yom Kippur for *Kol Nidray* [a moving and emotional prayer recited and chanted on Yom Kippur Eve]. I love the music, I enjoy your sermons, and I must admit that those two services are uplifting, but, as I intimated, religion is not my cup of tea. Two services a year are enough for me. I belong to the synagogue because of my wife—from whom I am now divorced—and my children. Religion is not that important to *me*."

It was quickly becoming obvious to me that Gerald had a problem in regard to the synagogue and he was now going to expose it to me. I thought that he was going to tell me that some children sitting near him during the services were noisy, or he had forgotten his tickets when he left his home and an usher asked him to enter through the school entrance to verify that he was a member, or, I even felt, that he was going to tell me that he had erred for so many years and now wanted help and assistance to properly be guided so that religion and religious practices could be more meaningful for him. But my spontaneous judgment and my analysis were faulty and erroneous.

"Rabbi," Gerald sighed heavily, "I told you that I only attend services twice a year. I want you to know that I expect to get something positive from those two investments of time. I want to walk away from those experiences with food for thought, a smile on my face, a concept of optimism, or an idea for confidence in life."

Again Gerald breathed in heavily. The sigh was obvious and audible. "But, Rabbi, what did *you* do on Rosh Hashanah night? *You* spoke about death and sadness. *You* spoke about burying a beloved one and writing a will—even though it was an Ethical Will. *You* spoke about weeping and mourning.

"Rabbi," Gerald went on in a more accelerated pace, "I wanted to leave the sanctuary with a smile on my face but you made me exit with a frown on my face. I wanted to leave the congregation holding the hands of my son and daughter. But you made me so upset with your depressing talk about death that as I left the sanctuary I merely tore up the card you asked your congregants to mail back to you, the one that was in my prayer book."

Again Gerald hesitated and I attempted to jump in and tell him that more than two hundred cards had been returned but it quickly became obvious to me that this was merely going to be a one way conversation, from Gerald to me. He was not interested in my comments.

And again Gerald began. "Rabbi, I lost my father thirty-five years ago, just before my Bar Mitzvah. That was a traumatic blow to me. I was raised only by my mother. I was an only child. And my mother is hale and hearty today living in Los Angeles, and all *you* did for me on Rosh Hashanah eve was to make me think of her as dead or dying. That was a blow below the belt. You should have spoken about calling her every week, and not discussing her funeral. I couldn't sleep that night. In fact, I called her as soon as I returned from services just to make sure she was OK."

Gerald continued on for the next five minutes adding criticism upon criticism and vitriol upon vitriol.

During a brief hesitation, I again attempted to interject a comment, struggling to explain why I had chosen that subject for my sermon, but Gerald was totally oblivious of my words.

"Rabbi," Gerald once again began, "my son told me not to make this phone call, even though he agreed with me. He told me that he was pulverized simply thinking of his grandmother dying but I decided that I had to get this subject off my chest because my daughter informed me that she had sent your card to my mother in Los Angeles and had informed her about your sermon. She said that she thought that it was better to face the future head high than hide one's head in the sand."

Again Gerald breathed heavily and again he went on. "I was so upset and upended by her action, but since my mother never commented to me about it when I made my regular Sunday evening call to her, I just let it go."

"But, Rabbi," Gerald commented to me with deliberation and obvious reflection as it sounded to me that he was concluding his call, "I feel duty bound to tell you that your sermon on Rosh Hashanah eve was the worst sermon I ever heard. You did not elevate me; you dropped me. You did not raise me up; you depressed me. I'm truly sorry to have to tell you this but I feel it is as much for your good as for my good."

Gerald went on for another thirty seconds and concluded by saying, "I like you as a human being, Rabbi, but in regard to your sermon on Rosh Hashanah—you goofed."

Gerald then said "Goodbye," but he never gave me an opportunity to explain my actions. However, I felt that no matter what I would have said to him he would not have heard. His ears were attuned to a different frequency. His "receiver" was not going to be attentive to anything I said.

I must admit that his words weighed heavily on my mind and conscience. I tried so hard to speak about a subject that I felt most people ignore because it is uncomfortable. This subject was usually discussed after someone died, and so often the children would say to me, "I wonder what my dad would want us to do." But by then it was always too late.

Gerald's comments bothered me for about a week, but like everything else, time causes most dark clouds to dissipate, scatter, and disappear.

I must admit that sporadically and intermittently I would think of Gerald's comments, especially when I was going to speak about delicate and controversial issues, and that was quite often, but I would not allow his words to cast the veto vote. A sermon was not a sugar pill to cause masks of smiles to constantly appear on congregants' faces. A sermon, I felt, should be a call to action. If a rabbi did not have the courage to say what was in his heart, I felt, he should not be on the pulpit.

Two thoughts have always guided me in regard to my sermons. One was a comment by Ralph Waldo Emerson, the nineteenth century American poet and essayist, who said, "If you have an important thought in your mind, have the courage to say it and bring it to fruition."

The second comment was stated by L. Kenneth Wright who preached the belief that "a good attitude is like cork—it can hold you up. A poor attitude is like lead—it can sink you." Do not worry about singular and individual negative comments. You will never get one-hundred percent of the people to agree with you. That is an impossibility, a goal that is impractical.

But a little more than a year after Gerald called me to criticize my sermon my secretary buzzed me and said that there was a long distance call for me from a Gerald Schneider. It took me a few moments to recognize the name and place it in its unappealing context.

"I wonder what I said now," I said to myself as I shook my head in wonderment and my hands became slightly damp. But I picked up the receiver, smiled as if Gerald could see me, and in a congenial and pleasant tone stated, "Gerald, it's good to hear from you again."

The voice on the other end of the line was extremely subdued and somber. "Rabbi," Gerald semi-whispered, "I hope you remember me."

"Of course, of course," I assured him.

"Well, I want you to know that this call was difficult to make."

Now, I was positive that he had another complaint. I had not seen him in the synagogue during the past High Holidays that had been celebrated four weeks earlier and our telephone conversation had occurred a year ago. Our paths had not crossed during the past year. "What did I do this time?" kept running through my mind.

Gerald continued in his suppressed manner of talking. "Rabbi," he went on, "as hard and as difficult it is to say, I feel I must say it."

"Get it out, get it out," I said to myself. "The suspense is painful."

And then Gerald said it. “Rabbi, I called to apologize.”

As he hesitated, as was normal for him to do, I thought that I had misunderstood his statement or I was merely dreaming. “I couldn’t hear you Gerald,” I abruptly mused. “There must be something wrong with our connection,” I fibbed.

This time Gerald’s voice was much stronger. “Rabbi, I called—to apologize.”

“What’s the apology for?” I queried, as I became more and more curious.

“Rabbi, I’m apologizing for lambasting you and scolding you so harshly last year about your sermon concerning writing an Ethical Will.”

Instinctively I parried, “Gerald, that’s not necessary. You said what you honestly felt. Everyone doesn’t have to agree with me. I merely ask them to listen to me. This is America. Everyone has the right to believe what he wants to believe and even to say what he wants to say. There is no need, Gerald, to apologize.” But I must admit that I felt good hearing his words even though I did not know what precipitated them.

“Rabbi.” Gerald stumbled on, “this is not easy for me to say. Please just listen. Don’t say anything. Just let me talk. It’ll make it easier for me.”

“OK,” I quickly responded.

“Rabbi.” Gerald began again, “last week my mother died.”

“I’m sorry,” I instinctively commented.

“Rabbi, again I ask you, please don’t make any comments. This is not easy for me. You know I’m a tough lawyer and I don’t like to lose cases. This one I obviously lost because I was very foolish.”

I did not know to what he was referring but I said nothing.

“Rabbi, as I said, last week my mother died. She was only sixty-nine and supposedly in pretty good health. But she had a severe heart attack and when they called us from the hospital in Los Angeles she was already dead.

“My son, daughter, and I immediately flew to California to prepare for the funeral, but I must admit that I was at a total loss as to what to do. As I told you, my father died years and years ago, before my Bar Mitzvah. I didn’t remember the protocol, procedure, or anything. I know I should have called you but I was totally confused and bewildered. Where do I start? What should I do?

"I expressed my confusion and perplexity to my children. I wanted to bury my mother according to *her* wishes, but I had never uttered the word 'death' in her presence and she had never mentioned it to me.

"We were sitting in my mother's apartment but my mother had been placed in the hospital morgue until I could give them final instructions. And as my daughter was meandering about my mother's bedroom looking at the pictures that she had on her wall and dresser, my daughter called out, 'Dad, look what I found on Grandma's dresser.'

"I quickly entered the bedroom and I saw my daughter holding an oversized card. It was the card that *you* had handed out a year ago for your Rosh Hashanah speech and that my daughter had mailed to my mother—and I quickly noticed that all the blank spaces had been filled in by my mother in her own handwriting."

I was going to make a comment but I quickly remembered his instructions: "Don't say anything." So I remained totally still.

"Rabbi, I read the entire card, from top to bottom. In a sense *you* were speaking to me.

"'First, call me or the Assistant Rabbi or another rabbi—but contact a rabbi immediately for ritual advice or for a meeting.

"'Then choose a Funeral Home to do the burial. Then, if you are in a hospital, ask the nursing staff on your floor to release the body to that Funeral Home. Then, call the Funeral Home to make an appointment to speak to them.'"

Again Gerald waited for a moment in order to catch his breath.

"Then you had all these questions for my mother to complete—and she did. Her answers were so different from what mine would have been, probably because religion was important to her but it is almost meaningless to me."

I squirmed as I heard his comment—but I said nothing. "She indicated that she wanted to be buried in a simple wooden casket, wearing the simple, inexpensive traditional shrouds, and she wanted the Jewish Burial Society to have its women wash her and dress her according to the ancient Jewish tradition. I must admit, Rabbi, I would have done none of these for my mother and neither would my children have had these rituals performed for her.

"But then, as I read on, I saw in her handwriting the following words: 'I would prefer to have my son and his children remain at the cemetery for the lowering of my casket into the ground before they recited the mourners' *Kaddish,* [prayer for the dead], but I feel that this would be too traumatic for them. If so, I suggest that they recite the *Kaddish,* leave the cemetery, and the rabbi will remain for the lowering of the casket. I do not want to force my personal beliefs on my son and grandchildren. I do not want to traumatize them—if they are squeamish.'

"I continued to read her words: 'I would feel so good if my son would recite the *Kaddish* for the entire year, as is traditional, but I do not want to ask for the impossible. I would even feel satisfied if he would recite the *Kaddish* once a week for the year, but, again, I do not like to ask favors of people that make them feel uncomfortable. Therefore I merely request of him to recite the *Kaddish* for me whenever he feels the urge to do that.'"

Gerald went on and on, indicating how his mother had personally filled in the blank spaces to my questions, and he always concluded his statement by adding a postscript: "I never realized that these rituals were so important to her. Had my daughter not found the card none of her wishes would have been fulfilled."

For an extended moment there was silence. I thought I had lost the connection but then I heard Gerald take a heavy breath again as if he was experiencing great emotional pain.

"Rabbi," Gerald commenced again with a quivering voice that intimated that he was finding it difficult to hold back tears, "my mother then had attached to your card with a paper clip a blank sheet of paper that had a specific message for me and my children, that you had suggested. It was an Ethical Will.

"My mother wrote, 'Gerald, you were very bright since the time you were a small child. Your mind was far ahead of those of your contemporaries. And I gave you everything because I felt you had been cheated in life—your father died when you were only a youngster. I therefore had to act as both your mother *and* your father. Therefore, I spoiled you. I never said 'no' to you. Your wish was my command—and now I know that that was a mistake.

"'However, you always gave me pleasure. You excelled in school and received honors galore at your High School and College graduations. Then, in Law School you were on the *Law Review,* received highest honors at graduation, and received a prestigious job before you went into private practice.

"'You were my son, the successful lawyer, and that was my internal energy for many years. You were my sun, my moon, and my stars. You were my heartbeat and my lungpower. I lived vicariously through you.

"'And when you married Suzanne*, I was truly in seventh heaven. And when the children were born, I was walking with God.

"'But Gerald, something happened. I guess too many people patted you on the back. Too many people told you how god-like you were. Too many people convinced you that you were above everyone else—and you began to change. You began drinking, and drinking heavily. You began experimenting with drugs. You began spending more and more time away from your home, wife, and children, and your pretty secretary began telling you how extra-special you were. In a short period of time you were having an affair with her and your marriage was floundering on the rocks.

"'Gerald, Suzanne was your gold mine, your heaven, your paradise, but you abandoned her for a temporary delight who eventually deserted you when she saw how you were accelerating your use of alcohol and drugs.

"'Gerald, Suzanne was the best thing you ever had—better than all your high school, college, and Law School awards. She was better than your law practice and all your colleagues because she truly, honestly, and sincerely loved you. She would have remained with you under all conditions but you always insulted her, humiliated her, and degraded her.

"'I loved her like a daughter but you tossed her aside like an old, battered doll. That is why I was happy when, after your divorce, I heard that she had moved to another state and remarried. I wish her the best of luck. She is an extra-special woman and the mother of your children—and the best thing you ever possessed. You ignored and lost your greatest asset in life.

"'However, I now fear for my grandchildren, Adam* and Bonnie*. What kind of model are you presenting to them? Adam sees you drinking and drinking, and still getting involved with drugs, and I fear that he will follow in your footsteps, if he has already not embarked on that route. And Bonnie, I fear, will find it difficult to fall in love and trust men because she has personally seen how her father abandoned her mother for another woman and had an affair while still married to her mother.

"'I love my grandchildren and I fear for their futures because *you* are presently not guiding them on the proper road of life.

"'Yes, I know that your generation calls my generation a 'bunch of old geezers' and 'fuddy duddies', but I wonder whether your generation with its alcohol, drugs, divorces, and infidelities is really a happy generation. I think not.

"'In Judaism, we have one day a year, *Yom Kippur,* when we come before God and say, 'O God, I have sinned. I want to change my way of life'—and God listens. Gerald, this is *your Yom Kippur, your* day of inner scrutiny, *your* time of personal reflection. Don't let it slip through your fingers. You've already lost Suzanne. Don't lose Adam and Bonnie. This is your time for change.

"'After your father died, the only thing I wanted, my greatest goal in life, was your happiness—and that is still my greatest goal. But you will only achieve it if you look hard in the mirror and reflect on your present actions.

"'Abandon your drugs, liquor, and loose women. None of them will bring you happiness.

"'Spend time, quality time, with your children. They are more important to you than your clients.

"'I have tried my best for you all my life. It is obvious that I was not always successful. Now the ball is in *your* hands. Don't drop it. Don't fumble it. Do what is proper and what is right.

"'God bless you, my son.'"

There was a long pause after Gerald concluded reading to

me his mother's Ethical Will. I could hear Gerald softly sobbing. It was obvious that he was attempting to hide from me his sensitivity and emotions. But, then, he began again.

"Rabbi, my mother was speaking to me from the grave. She truly loved me. She really sacrificed her life for me. She was a very pretty woman, and after my father died she could have remarried but she did not do that because she did not think that a second husband would love *me* as much as my father loved me. So, she lived a lonely life until she recently died."

Again there was a brief pause and again I heard Gerald breathing heavily. "Rabbi, I called to apologize, to apologize strongly, for being a fool last year and criticizing you for your sermon about death and Ethical Wills. Your wisdom was my foolishness. I ask you to please, please accept my apology."

"It isn't necessary," I quickly replied. "We all act hastily at times."

"But I want you to know one thing," Gerald barged in. "I'm going to do my best to change my way of life. My mother was right. Success, money, honor, and glory all went to my head and I lost so much. Liquor, drugs, gambling, and loads of women will never bring me happiness. All I really have left now—if I still have them—are my children, and I don't want to lose them."

Gerald's voice became stronger and stronger. "Rabbi, I was a fool in many ways. To you, I apologize, I apologize, I apologize." Again there was a momentary hesitation and Gerald concluded with a surprising, "God bless you," and he hung up.

My heartbeat was accelerating and the palms of my hands were damp but I must admit that I felt great satisfaction that I had *possibly* helped Gerald. A small card handed out at a Rosh Hashanah service had *possibly* been the combination to open the lock for a better life.

Three years later, Gerald called me again. He was now living in another state and practicing law there. His son was in Law School. His daughter was in college. However, he called me, he said, to tell me that he had abandoned liquor, drugs, and womanizing and had met a lovely and loving young widow whom he hoped to marry. He told me that he purposely called me to share his good news because I was the cause of his turn around in life.

His call truly made my day—and week.

• • • • •

"There are no hopeless situations;
There are only men who have grown hopeless about them."

—*Clare Boothe Luce (20th Century writer and Congresswoman)*

CHAPTER 5

Terror In The Bayou

It was a very beautiful spring day in Houston, warm but not muggy. The sun was shining brightly but no one was perspiring. It was Sunday morning and our Religious School was filled with youngsters and I was addressing a group of 12-year-old students about the forthcoming holiday of Passover that was almost upon us.

At this particular session I was asking them questions about the holiday. The first five students coming forth with the correct answers to each question would receive Hershey bars as rewards and prizes. The atmosphere was electric. All the boys and girls, almost 40 of them, wanted to walk away laden with chocolates.

I had covered all the material with them during the previous two weeks. They merely had to recall that which I had taught them.

It was difficult keeping them in their seats. They were jumping up and down shouting out the correct answers. Even the girls, who normally were much more placid and tranquil than the boys, were fighting tooth and nail to win those Hershey bars.

"Who was the first man to jump into the Sea of Reeds when Pharaoh was pursuing the Israelites after the Exodus?"

"Why is Moses' name only once mentioned in the *Haggadah* [booklet recited at the Passover meal recounting the Exodus from Egypt]?"

"Why do we drink four cups of wine at the Passover Seder [meal] and fill a fifth cup with wine, label it the 'Cup of Elijah,' open the house door, and *not* drink from this fifth cup?"

"Why do we eat hard boiled eggs dipped in salt water before we begin the Passover meal?"

"What is the meaning of the *Chad Gadya* story related at the end of the *Hagaddah* that tells of a goat eaten by a cat, who is eaten by a dog, who is beaten with a stick, that is consumed by a fire, that is extinguished by water, that is gulped down by a cow, who is slaughtered by a butcher, who is taken in death by the Angel of Death, who is finally defeated by God?"

The youngsters were not only winning the Hershey bars but some were even eating them during the quiz. "Go faster, faster," some of the super-winners were shouting. They wanted to go home with their pockets laden with chocolates.

But before I could pose another Passover question, a high school student who regularly volunteered in the school office on Sundays, brusquely entered my classroom. "Rabbi," he loudly called out without waiting to be recognized. "There's an emergency call for you in the office from the police SWAT Team." His eyes were wide open and it was obvious that he was extremely tense. "They say that there's a girl in the bayou," he cried out in a nervous outburst, "and she says that she's going to kill herself unless *you* come over quickly."

The young students began to laugh because they thought he

was playing a joke on me. It was the beginning of April and "April Fools' Jokes" were the norm for the week.

But immediately after the young boy's outburst the school secretary entered my room with a serious visage upon her face. "Rabbi," she whispered in my ear," "I'll take over your class. The police have a serious situation on Chimney Rock and North Braeswood, in the bayou. One of our members' children is in the bayou, holding a scissors to her throat and threatening suicide unless *you* come to see her *now.* The SWAT team is there but they can't get too close to her out of fear that she'll harm herself. Go now, and I'll take your class," she implored me as her eyes broadened with fear.

My twelve year old students still thought it was an "April Fools' Joke" and it was difficult for the secretary to silence them or even quiet them, but I gave her a list of additional Passover questions and instructed her to give two Hershey bars to those answering the questions correctly. This suggestion acted like an antidote to the noise problem, and I quickly left.

The name of the student was still unknown to me. All I knew was the location of the incident, and when I arrived within a half block of the bayou I could see at least one hundred spectators milling about and staring into the bayou. Quickly, I found a parking spot and rapidly walked over to the bayou.

However, I was abruptly stopped by a policeman. "No one is permitted beyond the yellow markers," he gruffly informed me as he stretched forth his arms indicating that he was serious about his decree.

"I'm Rabbi Segal," I spontaneously replied. "I received a call from the SWAT team to get here immediately."

The officer without delay apologized, took me by the arm, and escorted me to a police sergeant standing directly above the bayou.

The sergeant was quickly informed that I was the Rabbi Segal they were anticipating and he immediately briefed me about what was happening.

However, while he was talking I looked into the bayou. Two officers were standing on the eastern incline of the bayou while another two were standing on the western incline, on dry land.

Between them, in the shallow but murky water, up to her knees, was a young woman. It was difficult to see who it was because her back was toward me. She was speaking in a most agitated and quivering manner to two of the policemen on one side of the bayou while the other two policemen, who were behind her, were attempting to inch up on her, grab her, and then remove the scissors from her hand.

However, she turned around abruptly. "Get away from me, you devils," she began shouting at the police as she placed the scissors even closer to her neck. "If you do that again, I'll plunge the scissors into my throat."

The policemen docilely apologized. "We were only trying to help you get out of the bayou." They spoke with softness in their voices. They did not want to bother or irritate or exasperate her.

"She's like a time bomb," the sergeant remarked to me while shaking his head from right to left. "You don't know what'll cause her to explode."

However, when she turned around, I recognized her. It was Gayle Fishman*. Her parents were members of my congregation and I had officiated at her Bat Mitzvah, Confirmation, and Hillel High School graduation. She had been a student in my Religious School classes for two years. She was about twenty-three years of age and I remembered very vividly how during the past Rosh Hashanah holiday she had approached Toby and me, and Toby had remarked, "That girl is stunning. She looks like Marilyn Monroe," and I had agreed with her. She was then truly very attractive and beautiful.

But now, in the bayou, her face was tense and stiff. Her eyes looked glassy and transfixed. "Where is Rabbi Segal?" she began to shout. "I want to see him. He is the only one who can rid me of the Devil. He is the only one in this world who can fight the Devil and beat him. Where is Rabbi Segal?"

I could not believe what my eyes were seeing and my ears were hearing. I had known her for at least fifteen years and never once had I experienced such a violent reaction on her behalf. She was always the prettiest girl in her classes and she always had a warm and broad smile on her face. No one had ever told me that she had any emotional problems. On the contrary, once she had even scheduled an appointment with me to show me the musical she was writing "for Broadway." She had placed on my desk about thirty pages of text and had sung two or three songs for me—and they were not bad. In fact, they sounded pretty good and pretty lively. They were very melodious. "That is my goal in life," she confided in me, "to become a writer of musicals that will be produced on Broadway"—and I had wished her well.

I waited for a briefing from the SWAT officer, but before he spoke to me about what he wanted me to do Gayle's father approached me. "We've got a difficult situation," he nervously informed me. "Gayle has had psychiatric problems since she was about eight years old. However, her Psychiatrist always gave her medication and that always brought her back to normal. But when she does not take the medicine, she has outbursts. Luckily, she has always been willing to take her medicine except for two times, and that is when we had trouble. In fact, those two times we had to have her committed to the Houston Community Psychiatric Center*. But after about two weeks, she was always back to normal. I believe that she has again neglected to take her medicine and that's why she's reacting this way."

This information truly surprised and shocked me. I thought that I knew her quite well. I had officiated at so many of her religious ceremonies and all I had seen was a creative young girl and young woman who seemed to have musical talent. She truly looked like someone who could eventually migrate toward Broadway or Hollywood, but I guess that outer looks are often deceiving and misleading. "You can't tell a book by its cover," or, as Rabbi Meir stated two thousand years ago in the *Mishnah* (*Avot* 4:27), "Don't look at the jar. Look at what is in it."

The SWAT officer then told me that the police were soon going to make a move. The longer they waited, the more dangerous the situation became. Gayle had already been in the water over two hours and soon she would become chilled. Without a second's warning she was capable of stabbing herself and inflicting a serious or even a fatal wound to herself.

"Rabbi," the officer authoritatively announced, "she thinks

she's being attacked by the Devil or a group of Devils and she believes that you are the only one who can help her. If you're willing, I'd like you to walk down the incline to the bayou—where the officers are now standing—and occupy her attention with conversation. She'll probably be happy to see you and begin asking you some questions. Just answer her questions, and if she stops talking, you begin to talk to her. As soon as her attention is on you, the officers toward her back will rush into the bayou, grab her, and remove the scissors from her hand. She'll be quickly disarmed. It will only take a handful of seconds."

The officer looked down into the bayou to see if the situation had changed but Gayle was still in the bayou, the scissors was still at her neck, she was still shouting that she wanted to see Rabbi Segal to exorcise the Devils within her, the policemen still flanked her on both sides of the bayou, but the number of people now viewing the potentially dangerous event seemed to be increasing.

The officer grabbed my arm quite decisively and deliberately and led me toward the bayou. He did not even ask me if I wanted to participate in this "rescue." He simply took it for granted.

"We found Rabbi Segal," the officer quickly cried out to Gayle and she immediately turned in my direction; however, it seemed as if she put the scissors even closer to her throat. It was as if she felt that the officer was attempting to deceive and delude her and she was going to take no chances on being overpowered by the unknown uniformed men.

The officer pushed me slightly toward the bayou and whispered, "Start walking down toward the bayou and don't forget to keep talking to her. You talk and we'll do the action."

For a moment I hesitated but a second mild nudge catapulted me on my way.

I slowly began walking down the incline toward the waters of the bayou. The incline was muddy because it had rained all the previous evening but I ignored the mud that was accumulating on my shoes.

"Hello Gayle," I weakly and innocuously called out to her. "It's Rabbi Segal—your teacher—your rabbi—and your friend." I had a wan and weary-looking smile on my face.

She turned toward me and began to squint—with the scissors now even closer to her throat. "I don't have my contacts on or my glasses on. You sound like Rabbi Segal," she brayed at me, "but you don't look like him." She hesitated momentarily and fumed again with frustration. "Are you really Rabbi Segal or are you merely one of the Devil's henchmen?"

Another forced smile quickly appeared on my face. "I'm really Rabbi Segal," I meekly replied. "Don't you remember when you showed me the text for your Broadway musical and sang several of the songs for me? They were terrific."

The scissors no longer was touching her throat. My words seemed to partially tranquilize her and the scissors now seemed to be about an inch from her throat.

But before I could say another word the scissors was back to her throat. "You're trying to fool me. You're *not* Rabbi Segal. You're an impostor. You're an impersonator. You're a masquerader. You're wearing a mask, and the mask is the face of Rabbi Segal."

I smiled even more broadly and lamely and said, "How can I prove to you that I *am* Rabbi Segal? Shall I preach to you the sermon I gave last Friday night?"

"No, no," she shouted and shot back at me as her face became more and more taut.

"What would you like me to do for you?" I implored her. "Your wish will be my command."

"OK," Gayle blurted out. "Give me the following information that only Rabbi Segal would know."

"What is it?" I beseeched her.

Her eyes were now squinting at me but staring directly at me. I did not look to the right or the left because I wanted Gayle to concentrate on me. However, my peripheral vision allowed me to see the two SWAT officers on the other side of the bayou inching up toward her.

"What are the names of Cantor George Wagner's children—and how many children does he have?" Gayle shouted at me. "Only Cantor Wagner, his wife, and Rabbi Segal know the answers to those questions. You're obviously not Betty; you're also obviously not Cantor Wagner," and she began chuckling as she made her last comment. "But are you Rabbi Segal—or one of the Devil's henchmen with a mask on?"

I smiled with assuredness and confidence. Cantor Wagner and I had already worked together for over fifteen years. Toby and I had had dinner at his home and he and his wife had been guests for dinner at our home on several occasions.

It was obvious to me that I had to drag out my reply in order to give the SWAT officers enough time to reach her. As soon as they stepped in the waters of the bayou she would hear them and no one could say what would then happen.

I therefore commenced speaking loudly and slowly. With self-assurance painted all over my face I began. "Cantor Wagner has four children—two boys and two girls. His first child is a girl; the second one is a boy; the third one is a boy; and the fourth one, the youngest one, the caboose, is a girl." I was smiling happily and joyously as I stated that response.

It was my feeling that such a light-hearted reply would bring a smile to Gayle's face and tranquility to the tension, but the opposite was true. "Don't play games with me," Gayle barked at me. "Give me the names."

"Of course, of course," I quickly responded. My heart was no longer beating quickly. I was coasting home. The SWAT officers were almost near the water's edge.

I then began again. "Cantor Wagner's oldest child is Rebecca, a very beautiful young woman."

"Don't give me any descriptions," Gayle angrily cried out. "All I want is the names."

"Steve is his second child," I rapidly continued, and I could see the first officer quietly and noiselessly entering the murky waters of the bayou.

"Then Cantor Wagner's third child—who was adopted—is Jeremy," and even though Gayle warned me not to elaborate concerning information about their personalities I quickly added, "and you must admit that he was an angelic child as a youngster."

I could see that Gayle's face was once again becoming tight as a drumhead so I resurrected another smile and continued on as I noticed that both of the officers' feet were now in the water.

"The fourth child," I went on, "was also adopted. It was a girl and she was nine years younger than Jeremy and she was in my son Scotty's class because they were born in the same year, 1968." The smile on my face was now plastered all around my head—360 degrees. "Her name is—," but nothing came into my head and nothing came forth from my lips. My head was blank. There was only hesitation. This was impossible. I knew her name just as I knew *my* name but my mind at that moment was as bare and void as a brand new chalk board that is brought into a classroom.

I therefore shook my head and tried to start again. The smile was no longer on my face, not even a weak one. "Her name is—" but again nothing came forth.

However, the response was speedy and rapid. Once again Gayle began to shout. "I knew you were an impostor. You work for the Devil. You're *not* Rabbi Segal. He would have known the answer to that question. You're wearing a mask to appear like Rabbi Segal but you're the Devil or one of his henchmen."

Immediately she turned around and saw the SWAT officer not more than twenty feet away from her. "Get away from me. Get away from me. Get away from me or I'll kill myself," she bellowed and shrieked at the officer, and he quickly retreated.

The SWAT officer who had originally spoken to me immediately grabbed me by the arm and took me back to the top of the bayou. "Sorry you didn't know her name," he disappointedly huffed. "In ten more seconds we would have had her."

Then it hit me like a bolt of lightning. I freed myself from the arm of the SWAT officer, turned toward the bayou, and shouted and yelled, "Gayle, Cantor Wagner's youngest child is named Elyse. It's Elyse. You spell it E-L-Y-S-E. I merely forgot it for a moment."

I thought a smile of gratefulness, success, and appreciation would appear on Gayle's face. All the spectators shouted "Hooray" and began applauding. The grim faces of the onlookers were converted into smiles, but a shout came forth from the bayou from Gayle, "You're *not* Rabbi Segal. Someone gave you the answer."

"No, no," I attempted to argue with her. "I swear to God I'm telling the truth. I merely forgot her name for a moment. I'm Rabbi Segal, your teacher, your rabbi, your friend."

But my moment had come and gone. I could see the scissors being brought closer to her neck. "Get away from me you liar," she shouted again, "Don't make it worse than it is. I hate and detest liars, and that's what you are—Mr. Devil."

The SWAT officer quickly directed me around the corner away from Gayle's sight. "I don't think she should see you now," the officer apologetically advised me. In her eyes, *you* are now her opposition, her nemesis. Just thinking of you could possibly push her off the deep end. We don't want to take any chances."

I stopped in front of my car and he sympathetically added, "Go home or go back to your synagogue, but don't worry. We'll get her. There'll be a short moment when she'll be off guard either in front of her or in back of her and in that fleeting moment we'll disarm her and quietly take her to the Houston Community Psychiatric Center where a doctor will see her. However, you did your best."

The officer hesitated for a moment, shrugged his shoulders, exhaled heavily, and added, "Unfortunately, you went blank at the crucial moment. Certain times in life we only get one chance to succeed."

About three hours later, I received a call from Gayle's father. Gayle was now in the Houston Community Psychiatric Center. A swarm of gnats had invaded the bayou and had encircled her. She attempted to swat them and disperse them for about half a minute. Her arms were flailing and thrashing about from side to side and up and down, and during the brief intervals that her mind was concentrating on the gnats she momentarily dropped her scissors. In that flashing instant, before she could retrieve the scissors, the four SWAT officers standing on both sides of the bayou rushed toward her, overpowered her, subdued her, restrained her, and pulled her forth from the bayou.

She was shouting, "You are the Devil, the Devil, but I will not let you destroy me and conquer me." But the police quickly immobilized her hands, put her in a squad car, and took her to the Houston Community Psychiatric Center where physicians quickly sedated her.

Her father asked me if I could visit her that day but I asked him whether that would be smart or logical. While in the bayou she had vociferously labeled me "The Devil" when I could not identify Cantor Wagner's youngest child. Her father agreed that today might be premature, but he added that the Psychiatrist had stated that by Friday she would probably be starting on her "path to recovery." She had always considered me one of her mentors and role models. She had always looked up to me as a guide in her life. "Friday will be good," he finally agreed.

I concurred and visited her on Friday. It took quite a while to get permission to actually see her because she was in a locked ward and I had to go through a metal detector before gaining entrance to her section. In fact, I was obliged to check my Swiss knife that I always keep with me.

However, when I entered Gayle's ward, she ran toward me and quickly embraced me. "Rabbi, why are they keeping me here?" she pathetically asked. "Rabbi, why am I being held against my will? They tell me that I had to be pulled out of the bayou. Rabbi, you know that I'd never go into that dirty and filthy water. They say I was screaming about the Devil. Rabbi, I'm Jewish. We don't believe in a Devil. Why are people lying about me? Why are they trying to keep me away from my family?"

I released her hands from around my neck and walked her over to a couch. She continued to ask question after question and would not wait for an answer or a response.

I spent about an hour with her, just holding her hands and listening to her, until an attendant approached us and sympathetically interjected, "Gayle, the Rabbi has to leave now. You've got a session with your therapist now. It's eleven o'clock. He's got to go now."

Gayle was not happy with this decision but I arose, told her that I would be back again, gave her a hug, and was escorted to a locked door which an attendant opened for me.

Gayle spent six weeks at the Houston Community Psychiatric Center but then was released. But in the interim, as the years have gone by, she has been hospitalized on and off at least once a year—and I have always visited her. In the hospital her face has always been taut and tense, stiff and strained. However, out of the hospital she has always reverted to her sweet and pleasant countenance, speaking to me about her musical and how she hoped to have it produced some day on Broadway.

Even though many years have gone by since the bayou incident I have always asked myself, "Why did I forget Elyse's name at that crucial moment?" True, I realize that even if I had remembered her name Gayle would have been hospitalized; however, it is difficult for me to accept the fact that my error caused her to eventually be rushed by the SWAT team rather than slowly approached by them and escorted out of the bayou.

We all carry our personal baggage on our shoulders.

• • • • •

"There are those who can achieve eternity in one hour [and also those who can lose it in one hour]." Talmud, *Avodah Zarah* 10 b

CHAPTER 6

The Lamb Becomes The Lion

It was the spring of 1943 and I had just turned fourteen. I was concluding my freshman year in high school, a private religious school called Mesivta Rabbi Moshe Abraham.* The school was located in the Brownsville section of Brooklyn and was housed in a six-story former bank.

Unfortunately the school was not initially built as a high school and even when it was renovated to be a school the architect merely removed the bank facilities and "updated" it so that it was now a building with rooms. The teachers were told to improvise and do the best they could.

I remember the "gymnasium" very well. It was the basement of the former bank—a long room with a twenty-five foot ceiling. I remember the height of the room very well because in that room was the only permanent gym equipment—a rope that had been attached to the ceiling. And I distinctly recall how the burly gym instructor had barked at me on the first day of gym, "Segal, climb that twenty-five foot rope." The only other equipment we had in the gym were mats that we used for tumbling and wrestling.

However, in order to enjoy more extensive gym facilities our gym instructor would take us to the Blackman Street Park* which was only two blocks from our school. There, we could use the chinning bars, handball courts, baseball field, and all the other equipment; however, that park could only be used when we had pleasant weather. But if it rained or snowed, or it was cold, or we were experiencing other forms of inclement weather we would be obliged to return to the school basement.

But I remember this particular spring day very well. It was early in May, the sun was shining brightly, the thermometer registered in the low nineties, and into the basement came two young men.

The first one was about five foot six and he wore thick glasses through which he continually squinted. He looked chunky, as if he weighed about 170 pounds, but it was really difficult to tell since he was wearing a double breasted suit jacket and a baggy pair of pants from a different suit. Both the jacket and the pants looked as if they needed a good pressing. He also had on a white shirt, not buttoned at the top, and he was not wearing a tie. However, over his white shirt, which looked as if he had been wearing it for at least three days, he wore a large *arba kanfose* (a serape-like rectangular shawl with a hole in the center that fit over the head, and onto whose four ends were attached fringes, *tzitzit,* as described in Numbers 15:37-41; most Orthodox Jews wear this garment *under* their shirts but some extremely Orthodox Jews wear them *over* their shirts), and his head was covered by a broad-brimmed grey fedora hat. It seemed as if he was about twenty-four or twenty-five years of age but again this was difficult to tell because he had a four or five day growth of beard.

His friend, however, was about six foot one, clean shaven, handsome, and he wore a sweater and dungarees. He was about nineteen years old.

As all the twelve students of our freshman class lined up in the basement, the young man wearing the baggy pants and jacket spoke softly. It was actually difficult to hear him in that oversized basement that the school had labeled a "gym".

"Young men," the disheveled and rumpled young adult informed us, "unfortunately, your regular gym teacher, Mr. Greenstone,* cannot be with you today. His wife is ill and he had to take her to the hospital. However, I have been appointed his substitute for the day. My name is Rabbi Avigdor Samuelson*. Normally I teach Talmud at the Ner Yitzchock Yeshivah*; however, our class is off for the day—so, I've been appointed your gym teacher." He smiled sheepishly as he made his pronouncement as if he could not believe that he was now a gym teacher, and a universal grimace enveloped the students as they, too, obviously could not believe that this young man had been appointed to lead them for the day in their gym activities.

But Rabbi Samuelson turned to the young man who was with him and continued, "I'd like you to meet Yitzik*. He's my student at the Yeshiva and I must admit that he's very good." Yitzik momentarily blushed and Rabbi Samuelson patted him on the back. "Since we're free today from the Yeshiva, Yitzik said he'd join me and help me as a gym teacher. He's good when it comes to athletics. You should see how good he is in Punch Ball. He can hit it two sewers." Rabbi Samuelson thought that his comment would bring forth a spirit of enthusiasm on behalf of the students but the twelve of us merely stood as statues thinking, "When is this period going to be over?"

Rabbi Samuelson slapped Yitzik's back and loudly pontificated, "Let's all go to the Blackman Street Park. It's nice outside and we won't have to choke in this damp and musty room—and we'll all be able to play something because of all the equipment there."

The rabbi waited for some movement but no one budged, so the rabbi was the first through the door shouting, "Follow me," and immediately the twelve were running toward the park and its equipment while Rabbi Samuelson and Yitzik followed behind.

When the rabbi arrived at the park everyone was already engaged in some game. Four (including myself) were playing handball on the handball court, six were playing basketball (two teams of three each), one was on the chinning bar, and one was on the parallel bars.

The rabbi smiled joyously and rapturously as he and Yitzik

arrived at the park. . "Keep on doing what you are doing," the rabbi called out to the twelve of us. "I'll tell you when the period's over—in another forty minutes." And as a postscript he added, "Enjoy yourselves; enjoy yourselves."

Yitzik went off to the other end of the parallel bars and began working out on the bars. He was quite good and he was able to do a set of twenty dips on the parallel bars. I had previously never seen anyone do so many at one time.

However, Rabbi Samuelson merely sat in the sun on a bench, removed his jacket, took a book of *Tehillim* (Psalms) from his briefcase, and audibly began reading in Hebrew (Psalm 1:1) *"Ashray ha-ish asher lo halach ba-atzot resha'im* ... [Happy is the man who does not walk in the council of the wicked ...]." But he was *shokling.* His body was vibrating from side to side as he was reading and his hand was also locomoting from side to side. He had started from chapter one of the Book of Psalms and it was obvious that his goal was to continue until the end of the period, even though he realized that he would not be able to complete all one hundred fifty of David's psalms.

Everyone seemed happy. The twelve boys were informally doing what they wanted to do; Yitzik was increasing the size of his biceps and triceps; and Rabbi Samuelson was obviously communicating with God.

The Blackman Street Park was in an area primarily habituated by families of Ukrainian descent and, unfortunately, there had previously been shouting matches and even fights between Ukrainian and Jewish teenagers. At times it was extremely discomforting and distressing being in the park because hordes of local youngsters would taunt the Jewish boys from the Mesivta, but when Mr. Greenstone was present there was no problem. He was tall and massive, burly and muscular, and the Ukrainian youngsters did not want to tangle with him.

I do not know why, but the Jewish history in regard to the Ukrainians was never the best. In fact, it was often pretty bad. In 1648, Bogdan Chmielnicki led an uprising of Cossacks and Ukrainians against *non-Jewish* Polish landowners but approximately two hundred thousand *Jews* were killed. In 1903 and 1905 there were more pogroms against the Jews in Kishinev, and between 1918 and 1920 Cossacks once again went on a rampage and massacred one hundred and fifty thousand Ukrainian Jews. Now, in 1943, rumors were circulating in the United States that the Nazis were exterminating Jews and some Ukrainians were aiding the Nazis as concentration camp guards and also as police rounding up Jews.

Unfortunately, the Ukrainian teenagers were not pleased with the Jewish students being in Blackman Street Park, on "their turf." In fact, they were offended. They did not want us near "their" park and there always seemed to be friction when Mr. Greenstone was not present. None of the Mesivta boys wanted to go there when Mr. Greenstone was not present.

My handball partner, Sam Miller*, and I were elated. We were beating our opponents eighteen to seven. We only had to win three more points. We were truly on a roll. We had made the last eleven consecutive points. Nothing seemed to be able to stop us.

All of a sudden, two really big locals walked on the court. In my eyes and in Sam's eyes each one looked like Gargantua. Both were well over six feet two inches tall and each one weighed over two hundred pounds. They were well muscled and spoke roughly and gruffly. "Hey Jew boys, get off the court," one barked as he stood in the middle of the court with his hands on his hips.

I stared at him hoping that I could reason with him. "The game's almost over. We only have to get three more points. You can challenge us then. We're going to be the winners."

They were in their early twenties, and both laughed heartily as I spoke. "Get off the court quickly, Jew boy," he once again growled. "We don't want to play the winner. I'm going to play my friend." He hesitated for a brief moment and then brusquely blurted out, "Get off the court now or I'll break your little Jewish [expletive] head."

I rapidly, but silently, recited a prayer asking God to see to it that Mr. Greenstone quickly returned but immediately realized that that was a *berachah levatalah,* a meaningless prayer. Mr. Greenstone was in the hospital with his wife. He was *not* coming. All we had was Rabbi Samuelson who was *davening* (praying) and his Talmud student, Yitzik.

What could I do? The two toughies standing in the middle of our handball court were clenching their fists. It was obvious that no logical argument was going to cause them to change their minds. They were prepared to physically throw us off the court.

I therefore did the only thing that I could do—I told the other three to join me in relating to Rabbi Samuelson that we could not conclude the game because of the two hooligans who had commandeered and forcibly seized the court.

Rabbi Samuelson was now well into his *davening* from the book of Psalms. He was still *shokling* and vibrating (Psalm 30:6), "*Ba-erev yalin beh-chee, v'la-boker reenah* . . . [In the evening weeping comes, but in the morning there is joyful song . . .]." He was oblivious of everyone and everything around him. He was totally immersed in his own world, having a heart to heart talk with God.

I thought it was fruitless telling Rabbi Samuelson. What was he going to do? But I wanted to be marked present for that day's gym period, and if I told Rabbi Samuelson that I had not completed my game he probably would have marked me "absent."

So the four of us quickly approached the Rabbi. "Rabbi Samuelson," I embarrassedly softly spoke to the Rabbi, "There are two very big guys who just kicked us off our court. We can't finish the game. What do you want us to do?"

Rabbi Samuelson did not even miss a beat. He merely continued on with David's Psalm (Psalm 30:11), "*Shema Adonai v'cha-nay-nee, Adonai heh-yay ozayr lee* . . . [Listen to me, O God, and be gracious unto me, O Lord be my helper now . . .]." However, while he was *shokling* and looking into his book of Psalms, he blurted forth toward us, "Who was on the court first?"

"*We* were," I immediately and enthusiastically replied.

The Rabbi closed his book of Psalms, stood up as the now

strong wind made his *arba kanfose* and *tzitzes* flutter in the wind, and smilingly said to us, "Come boys, I will go talk to these young men. I am sure they are reasonable young men and will listen to logic."

He stared at the four of us and began talking to us before proceeding to the handball courts. "Boys," he proudly declared, "our Judaism is straightforward about this case. It's a black and white case, not even a gray one. It's called *hasagass gevull* [taking over someone else's property]. The Bible is very clear about this law. It says in *Devarim yud tet, yud dalid* [Deuteronomy 19:14], *"Lo tasig gevul ray-acha,* one is not permitted, in fact, *prohibited* to take over a neighbor's property." A broad smile now blossomed all over his face. "If it belongs to a neighbor and you want to use it, you must first ask permission. If he grants it—OK. But if he rejects your request, you may not use it. It is *prohibited,*" and again he emphasized the word "prohibited." "That's what the Bible tells us."

Once again he looked at the four of us and triumphantly exclaimed, "Let's go. Let's settle the matter. You don't have much more time for your gym period."

The Rabbi lay his book of Psalms on the bench, put on his rumpled jacket as if this was going to be an official meeting of leaders of two titanic corporations, walked over to the handball court (followed by the four of us) and with an affable smile on his face courteously addressed the taller of the two antagonists. He was at least eight or nine inches taller than the rabbi and probably a minimum of forty pounds heavier than him. Rabbi Samuelson was obliged to incline his head upward to look into the eyes of his adversary. The Rabbi walked onto the court and stood not more than two inches from his opponent.

My heart was now racing. "Was Rabbi Samuelson crazy?" I thought to myself. "These two guys had muscles on their muscles. They spoke with such anger in their hearts as if they ate nails for breakfast and glass for lunch." I breathed heavily and thought, "Maybe I should have let bygones be bygones and forgotten about the handball court. I don't want Rabbi Samuelson bloodied or even killed because of a stupid handball court." However, as I looked about I noticed that Yitzik had left the parallel bars and was now slowly sauntering over to the court where the Rabbi was attempting to talk to the two who had commandeered the court from us.

"Excuse me, sir," the Rabbi addressed the two as his smile widened broader and broader. "I think a mistake has taken place between the two of you and my four students."

The two burly Ukrainians stopped bouncing the ball that they shared, grimaced, and the one standing closer to the Rabbi grunted, "Who the [expletive] hell are you, you four-eyed [expletive]?"

The Rabbi ignored the ignoble and base comment and merely continued. The smile on his face remained the same as if he had not heard any of the foul and insulting comments. In fact, Rabbi Samuelson stretched forth his hand and continued, "Let's shake in friendship and start all over again with warmth in our hearts and friendship in our souls."

However, the tall Ukrainian forcefully pushed the Rabbi's hand away from his and continued to berate him. "You Jewish [expletive], get the hell off my court before I break your Jewish [expletive]."

The Rabbi seemed to be deaf. The smile was still on his face. "Gentlemen," the Rabbi once again continued, "I feel positive that the two of you are church-going young men and the Bible is important to you. If so, I know that your religious leader has taught you the biblical law of *hasagass gevull,* that one is *prohibited* to take away from another person property that belongs to, or is used by, the latter. One is not permitted to use force, or power, or might to overpower an individual and take what is rightfully someone else's."

Rabbi Samuelson looked at the t-shirts being worn by the two strong-looking young men. To the one standing abreast of him, the Rabbi said, "I see that your name is Gregory," and he turned toward the second one and added as a postscript, "and your name is Leo. Very fine names. The embroiderer did an excellent job putting your names on your shirts.

"However, back to the problem at hand," and the Rabbi's smile was still as ebullient as before. "The handball court belongs to these four young boys. They were playing on it prior to your arrival and their game was as yet not concluded. Also, you will notice at the side of the court is a sign that says, 'One hour maximum playing time,' but they were on the court no longer than twenty minutes."

The smile quickly evaporated from the Rabbi's face. "Therefore, Gregory and Leo, I would appreciate if you would vacate the premises so that the boys might conclude their game. I have a feeling that they should be finished in about five minutes because we have to get back to school." The smile quickly reverted to the Rabbi's face as he once again extended his hand in friendship and camaraderie.

Gregory and Leo merely stared at the Rabbi as if they did not know what to do with him, but Rabbi Samuelson continued as his hand remained outstretched waiting for a similar expression of friendship. "Gentlemen," the Rabbi resumed, "please do not forget the biblical law to which I referred. Let us be friends. Let us settle this minor problem amicably."

However, Gregory once again forcefully shoved the Rabbi's hand away. "You Jew [expletive]," Gregory roared. "If I hear one more word from you—just one more word from you—I'll smash your head."

The Rabbi, however, refused to remain silent. A pathetic look came over his face as he retracted his hand, but he continued, "But Gregory, biblical law is biblical law. God gave it to us. You don't want to break God's law, do you?"

A rage overcame Gregory. "I warned you before that I'd break your [expletive] Jewish [expletive] if you continued bothering me." Meanwhile Leo was laughing as if he was about to burst his britches. It was as if he had seen this scene before and knew what the result was going to be. "I'm going to break you in half, you [expletive] Jewish [expletive]."

The smile was no longer on the Rabbi's face and neither was the pathetic look of compromise now on his face. "Why do you continually refer to my religion in such a derogatory manner when I am merely trying to get you to follow God's command?" Rabbi Samuelson was obviously attempting to stifle and tranquilize Gregory's temper but it seemed that he was losing the battle. "Let us sit down together for a moment," the Rabbi rebounded while once again resurrecting his smile. "Let us talk this over peacefully and in friendship," and again the Rabbi extended his hand toward Gregory.

I was standing about ten feet behind the Rabbi and I felt that we had reached the point of no return. Gregory was going to obliterate the rabbi—and it was all my fault. I should have gone to the chinning bar or the parallel bars, forgotten about the remainder of the handball game and allowed Rabbi Samuelson to continue *davening* from his *Tehillim.* Now his blood would be on my head. Both Gregory and Leo towered over Rabbi Samuelson. Rabbi Samuelson looked like a grasshopper standing before a dinosaur.

I heard a noise behind me and again I turned abruptly and noticed that Yitzik was standing no more than five feet from my left, slightly behind me.

"That's it," Gregory raged, and his right hand shot out toward the Rabbi's face with the speed of a bullet and the power of a locomotive. I felt as if I was watching Joe Louis in his second fight with Max Schmeling. It was going to be a quick knockout with plenty of blood—and all because of me and a meaningless handball court.

The four of us shouted in fear. It was a simultaneous shout of disbelief. Who could believe that a handball game would result in a trip to the hospital? Rabbi Samuelson was such a peaceful and lovable person. All he enjoyed doing was *davening* and studying and teaching Torah.

Into my mind quickly appeared the name "Lutheran Hospital." It was the closest one to the park and I knew that that was where we would take the Rabbi to the Emergency Room.

However, to my utter shock and to Gregory's utter surprise, Gregory's powerful fist never reached the Rabbi's face. As soon as Gregory began throwing his punch, the Rabbi sidestepped the punch by moving to his left, beyond the trajectory of the punch. However, while he was defusing Gregory's punch, the Rabbi grabbed Gregory's lethal right arm and threw Gregory over his right hip. It all took place in less than a second. It was like a flash of lightning and the Rabbi was screaming at the top of his lungs, *"Shema Yisra'el, Adonai Ehlohaynu, Adonai Ehchad.* [Hear O Israel, the Lord is our God, the Lord is one.]" He kept repeating and repeating it as he threw Gregory to the cement floor of the handball court and as Gregory sounded forth a cacophonous din of pain. The Rabbi's *arba kanfose* was covering Gregory's face but Rabbi Samuelson quickly brushed it aside and instinctively placed his right arm over Gregory's throat.

Gregory began gasping for breath and there was a small trickle of blood coursing down from his head where it had hit the pavement.

Leo instinctively quickly prepared to attack the Rabbi from the rear but Yitzik angrily bellowed, "You touch him and you're a dead man," and Leo quickly backed off as he noticed Yitzik's clenched fists.

Meanwhile Rabbi Samuelson was still screaming—screaming at Gregory—but his words were now different, not words of anger, wrath, and fury, but words of sorrow, grief, and sadness. "Please forgive me. Please forgive me. I didn't mean to lose my temper. *Ich bett m'cheelah.* [I ask for your forgiveness.] *Seloch lee; m'chal lee; kapper lee.* [Forgive me; excuse me; pardon me.]"

Rabbi Samuelson was petitioning Gregory in three languages—English, Yiddish, and Hebrew—for forgiveness, but of course Gregory could not reply. Rabbi Samuelson's arm was still pressing down on Gregory's throat. In fact, Gregory's face was turning colors and his eyes were beginning to bulge. A few seconds earlier, Gregory's arms were flailing in all directions but now they were limp.

Yitzik speedily grabbed the Rabbi and shouted, "Rebbe, Rebbe [My teacher, my teacher], let go of him, let go of him. He's out. He's finished. He's *kaput.* You're going to kill him if you don't let go."

Yitzik could not pull the Rabbi off Gregory but all of a sudden Rabbi Samuelson shook his head as if he had come to his senses and rapidly removed his arm from Gregory's neck. Gregory began coughing and sputtering. He attempted to raise his head but was unable. His eyes merely stared in disbelief at the Rabbi as Leo apologetically softly spoke to Yitzik, "I'll take him home."

However, Rabbi Samuelson shook his head. "No, Leo. Let's take him to the Lutheran Hospital. It's only five blocks from here."

Yitzik motioned to Leo and instructed him, "Run quickly to Pitkin Avenue and flag down a cab. I'll pay for it. I want to make sure that Gregory is not hurt."

Rabbi Samuelson's smile was once again resurrected as he pointed to Gregory. "I think Gregory and I are going to be good friends. In fact, I feel that he's going to help me when I bring my classes to the park. He's got a lot of potential and I think we can help each other."

Gregory gurgled up a slow "Yep, yep, yep" as the Rabbi continued. "Gregory, the Bible says, 'Love thy neighbor as thyself.' I want to be your friend. God created *both* of us. We are really relatives. I love you and I want you also to love me." Rabbi Samuelson hesitated for a moment and then added, ""Please Gregory, please." Once again Gregory gurgled, "Yep, yep, yep."

The color was now returning to Gregory's face and his eyes were no long bulging. Rabbi Samuelson grabbed Gregory under the arms and helped him up. Gregory still could not speak and it was difficult for him to remain erect. However, the Rabbi and Yitzik led him toward a bench as they awaited Leo's return with a cab.

Rabbi Samuelson once again picked up his Bible, held it before Gregory's face, and spoke softly. "Gregory, let me teach you something from my Bible, which is your Bible too. Christians call it *The Old Testament* but they still consider it holy. In Leviticus 19:18 it says, as I told you before, 'Love your neighbor as yourself'; however, I did not tell you the end of that sentence. It ends with the words, *'Anee Adonai,'* 'I am God'. The rabbis asked, 'Why does it say, 'Love your neighbor as yourself' and then it says, 'I am God'? Why doesn't it say, 'I am God; Love your neighbor as yourself'? And the rabbis replied by saying that the 'neighbor' is mentioned before 'God' to teach us that love of neighbor, love of your fellow human being, love of your fellow man is even more important than your love of God.

"Gregory, I am *your* neighbor. Gregory, you are *my* neighbor. Let's not fight with each other. Let's love each other."

Gregory was still overwhelmed. He could not move. All he could do was reply, "Yep, yep, yep." With this comment the Rabbi kissed Gregory on both sides of his face. Rabbi Samuelson was exultant and elated. "Gregory, God is now happy. Two people who did not know each other an hour ago, two people who may have previously had negative feelings toward each other, now love each other. Gregory, *ich hoff oz Gott vet dich benshen,* [I pray that God will bless you]." And again the Rabbi kissed Gregory on both sides of his face.

A few minutes later, Leo returned with a taxi, and Leo, Gregory, and Rabbi Samuelson went to the Lutheran Hospital Emergency Room where the Rabbi wanted Gregory to be examined. The Rabbi meanwhile told Yitzik to take care of his class and to see to it that they returned safely to school.

When the cab left, all twelve of the boys pounced on Yitzik. "Was it a miracle from God that Rabbi Samuelson knocked down Gregory? Was it like the days of the Maccabees when God helped the Jews so that the few could beat the many and the weak could trounce the powerful?"

Yitzik laughed heartily. "Sit down boys," he instructed the twelve as he pointed to several benches that were close to each other. We quickly squeezed onto two benches as Yitzik began.

Yitzik's face was now serious and he sat down on the ground in front of the two benches. "Rabbi Samuelson is probably the best *Rebbe* we have at the Yeshiva [Theological Seminary]. He tries to bring Judaism to life and I remember very vividly his lecture a year ago when he spoke on the subject, 'God Loves Those Who Help Themselves.'

"He told us that the Talmud in *Pesachim* page 64b says, *'En somchin ol ha-ness,'* 'One does not depend on miracles.' When something has to be done, don't say, 'I'll pray to God and He'll do it for me.' No! Learn how to do it yourself and do it."

Yitzik looked about to see if the boys were listening to him and it quickly became apparent that he had captivated their attention.

"Rabbi Samuelson therefore told us," Yitzik proceeded, 'Never forget the words of King Solomon. In the book of *Mishley* [Proverbs], chapter 20, sentence 29, King Solomon stated most emphatically, *'Tiferess bachurim kochom,'* 'The beauty of young men is their strength.' Develop your muscles every day after you've completed your Torah studies.

"Rabbi Samuelson therefore told us to learn to protect ourselves. The Nazis are killing Jews every day in Europe and we are helpless—and no nation is volunteering to help us. He therefore told us that we should never forget the Maccabees. They fought for Jewish rights and for Jewish freedom. They should be our Jewish heroes—in addition to the rabbis who gave us the Talmud and *halachah* [Jewish law].

"'Every week,' Rabbi Samuelson said, 'another boy from the Yeshiva is beaten up by a local thug and called 'a dirty Jew', and what do we do? We either keep quiet or report it to the police, and they do nothing about it.'"

Once again Yitzik stared at the boys to see if they were still attentive and it was quickly obvious to him that they were still captivated by his comments.

"Well, what did *he* do?" one of the boys cried out.

"Yeah, yeah," several other boys called out. "What did *he* do?"

"Well, he decided to take the bull by the horns," Yitzik continued, "and three years ago he enrolled in a Karate class at a gym, and for two hours a night, six nights a week, except Shabbat, he practiced Karate with a master instructor. And during that time he earned a Black Belt. In fact, he worked one night a week as an instructor and he is still an instructor one night a week. Kim Fu*, the head instructor of the school, stated that Rabbi Samuelson was the best student he ever had—and he is the only student that he ever had who always wears a *yarmulke* [skull cap], and it almost never falls off his head.

"Rabbi Samuelson can smash boards with his hands or feet and he can do likewise with cement blocks. He is powerful and strong, and he also works out regularly on the chinning bar, parallel bars, and with weights. He may look *shoompidik* [like a weakling] but he's really 'Mighty Rabbi.'

"However, his goal is never to hurt anyone. His goal is merely to subdue his opponents and make them his friends.

"Rabbi Samuelson usually quotes from the Bible or the

Talmud when he wants to emphasize a point, but I remember so very well how he once quoted the words of a famous American president, the twenty-eighth president of the United States, Woodrow Wilson, who said, 'Friendship is the only cement that will hold the world together.'

"Rabbi Samuelson told us that that idea of President Wilson was preached by the rabbis more than fifteen hundred years ago. He told us that the rabbis said, *'Ay-zeh-hu geebor sheh-b'gee-borim . . . zeh-hu sheh-oseh sone'o o'havo,'* 'Who is the strongest of the strong? He who can convert an enemy into a friend' [A.D.R.N.23].

"That is why Rabbi Samuelson was so upset when he pulverized Gregory.

"Boys," Yitzik called out as he rose, "It's time to get back to school. If any of you is interested in the Rabbi's program, call me at home," and he gave the students his phone number.

As we walked back to the Mesivta one of the boys cried out, "Do you think Rabbi Samuelson is the *mashi'ach* [Messiah]?"

• • • • •

"Friendship is like a Treasury: you cannot take from it more than you put into it."

—*Benjamin Mandelstamm*

Chapter 7

"I Don't Want To Go To Hebrew School"

My first association with school was a negative one.

I remember it very well. I was about four-and-a-half years of age and my parents registered me in the Kindergarten of P.S. 144 in the Brownsville section of Brooklyn. My mother escorted me to my classroom that had an additional thirty-one students, and she gave me a big kiss. "Yankee [my Yiddish name]," she said as she gave me a big and a tight and a loving hug, "you will love kindergarten. You have the best teacher in the school, Miss Armstrong*. She loves children and she's going to love you. I'll pick you up at 3:00 o'clock when your class is over."

With that pep talk my mother directed me into the classroom and toward the teacher who took my hand. The other children were already seated since my mother was ten minutes late bringing me to class.

Miss Armstrong, who was about sixty years of age, had never been married and was as skinny as a string bean, took my hand and rapturously proclaimed, "Children, we have one more student in our class, Jackie Segal. Let's all say 'Hello Jackie Segal.'"

And like a group of lemmings they all called forth, "Hello Jackie Segal."

I was not even five years of age but I felt embarrassed being the center of attention. I wanted to run out of the room and hide in a closet.

And then Miss Armstrong proclaimed, "Where shall we put our Jackie Segal? The room is very crowded. Let me see." She held her index finger to her chin as if in deep contemplation and then announced, "There is still one seat open toward the rear of the class. Jackie Segal, that will be your seat." Then Miss Armstrong pointed in the direction I was to go. "Jackie, go sit in that seat," and she pointed to what was to become my seat. "On your right is Alice Billingsley*, and she pointed to Alice, a heavy-set redheaded girl. "Say 'hello' to Jackie, Alice," Miss Armstrong instructed Alice—and that is exactly what Alice did. "On your left is Myrtle Chilton*. . . . In front of you is Ellen Foley*. . . . And in back of you is Rosemarie Symcox*. . . ." And to all of the girls Miss Armstrong pointed her index finger and instructed them to greet me—which they did. Then she concluded, "You may now go to your seat, Jackie Segal."

However, I hesitated and did not budge. Miss Armstrong gave me that same instruction again, and once again I did not move. The smile was now erased from Miss Armstrong's face and she gave me a gentle shove in the direction of my seat. "Jackie, she pedantically instructed me, "when I say something in this class, you do it. There is no maybe, perhaps, possibly, perchance, or anything else. You do it." She looked at the class and bellowed, "Class, am I correct?" And like little robots they all replied, "Yes, Miss Armstrong," and with that exclamation of approbation, the teacher once again gave me a polite prod in the direction of my seat. I pouted but I went.

Miss Armstrong told us how lucky and fortunate we were to live in the United States, and then she asked each student where he or she had been born. Almost everyone said "Brooklyn," even though one said New Jersey and one little girl who spoke with a funny accent said "Atlanta".

Miss Armstrong pointed in my direction and remarked, "Jackie Segal, are you Jewish?"

"Yes," I meekly replied.

"Were you born in Poland?"

"No" I naively answered. "I was born in the Unity Hospital on St. Johns Place. I never heard of that Poland Hospital." I even added as a postscript, "Whenever my mother takes me past the Unity Hospital she always points to a window in the hospital and tells me that I was born in that room."

Miss Armstrong merely stared at me, so I added, "Haven't you heard of the Unity Hospital, Miss Farmstrong? It's next door to the Commodore Movie House. My mother takes me there sometimes on Friday afternoons."

Miss Armstrong's eyes opened widely. "Jackie, my name is Armstrong and not Farmstrong and I'm glad you were born in Unity Hospital."

My teacher taught us several songs and we played several games—the boys with the boys, and the girls with the girls. But during recess I was encircled by Alice, Myrtle, Ellen, and Rosemarie. It seems that they were all friends, lived near each other, and I heard one say, "That Jackie is cute."

However, I sulked because I wanted to play with the boys but they did not want to play with me. "Who are you?" they all seemed to be saying. The only ones who wanted to play with me were the girls.

At dinner that evening, my parents smiled and beamed, smirked and laughed. "Yankee, how was your first day at school? You have such an excellent teacher, Miss Armstrong."

However, I growled, "I ain't going back to school."

"Why?" my mother queried with surprise written all over her face.

"They put girls all around me," and I stared my mother straight in the eye and emphatically declared, "I don't like girls."

Both my father and my mother attempted to rationally explain to me why I had to go to kindergarten, but my ears were closed to all arguments and my mind was sealed in regard to all explanations. "I don't want to go to kindergarten. I won't go to kindergarten. And I don't like girls."

And you will not believe it. But that was the only day I attended kindergarten. My parents allowed me to bamboozle them—and I spent the remainder of that year just playing with friends in the street but not attending kindergarten.

However, the next fall my parents enrolled me in the first grade of the Yeshiva Rabbi Zalman Baruch*, a Jewish Day School one block from our home. This was an all boys school from grades one through eight. It was a dual track form of education—religious and secular. The students would study Hebrew, prayer book, Bible, Talmud and other religious subjects from 9 A.M. to 3 P.M. The traditional public school curriculum would be covered from 3:30 P.M. to 6:30 P.M. from Sunday through Thursday. Friday, school was in session from 9 A.M. to 1 P.M.—only for religious subjects.

The first grade Religious School curriculum was primarily the study of Hebrew and the teaching of the prayer book in Hebrew.

My first grade secular school teacher was a lovable and kind Mrs. Pinsker*. She always had a smile on her face and a kind and complimentary word on her lips. Mrs. Pinsker was about thirty-five years old, about five-foot tall, and about one hundred and sixty pounds in weight—but all the children loved her and all the students made great strides in her class.

However, our Hebrew teacher was Mr. Eisenboim* who was also short, about five foot four inches tall, but who never had a smile on his face. He had a pointed goatee which made me think that I had seen him in the zoo and he never had a complimentary or commendatory comment for any of his students.

During the first day of the second week of school, the school secretary called my mother and told her to come immediately because I was constantly crying and disturbing the class. Mr. Eisenboim was terribly upset because he could not teach his class. He told me to leave his class and stand in the hallway until I could control myself but that only exacerbated the problem. I was now gushing tears.

My mother quickly went to the school and listened as Mr.

Eisenboim excitedly denounced me as a "troublemaker" who was destroying his class. She had to take me home where she made me a cup of hot chocolate and called my father into the kitchen to discuss the problem. (My father ran his business of manufacturing sports vests from our house.)

My parents listened to me as I told them how Mr. Eisenboim frightened me. He was always angry, shouting, and critical of all. If he did not like a student's demeanor, he would strike the student over the knuckles with an old hanger. I was scared, petrified, and terrified. When I told him that I had to go to the bathroom, he barked at me stating that it was too early. "No one goes to the bathroom before 11 o'clock." I told my mother that I thought I was going to wet my pants. In fact, my exact words to my mother as my eyes became damp and oozy were, "I thought I was going to pee in my pants."

My parents listened with their ears but also with their hearts. My mother then put me on her lap, hugged me, kissed me, and told me that everyone had to go to school. I had already missed kindergarten—but first grade was obligatory for all.

My mother then attempted to bribe me. "I'll take you to the movies every Friday afternoon if you return to school."

"No, I'm scared."

"I'll buy you an ice cream every day after class."

"No, I'm scared."

"I'll take you on the rowboats at Prospect Park every Friday afternoon after school."

"No, I'm scared."

My mother breathed in heavily and in exasperation shook her head and asked, "Yankee, what can I do for you that will get you back to school like all the other boys? You are the only one of all the boys who doesn't'want to go back to school."

I hesitated for a moment, stared my mother in the eyes, and with tears cascading down from my eyes replied in anguish, "You stay in school with me in my class, in Mr. Eisenboim's class. I won't be scared of him then."

"Preposterous," my mother chuckled.

But my father quickly interjected his thought. "Birdie," he softly but persuasively commented, "why don't you do it for a few days? I'm sure Mr. Eisenboim won't mind. I'm positive that after a few days Yankee will gain self-assurance, get used to Mr. Eisenboim, and then ask you to leave the class." My father hesitated for a moment and then added with a smile on his face, "Birdie, try it, you may like it."

I was then asked to go into another room but I heard my parents discussing this subject. My mother's voice was no longer subdued. I could hear her strongly questioning my father, "Are you crazy?" But he remained tranquil. "It will only be for a few days. He'll get used to his teacher, the school, the students, the studies and he'll be perfect. This is all new to him. We should have insisted that he attend kindergarten last year, but it's too late now.

"Birdie," my father added again, "try it, you may like it."

I could hear their voices oscillating—getting louder and lower, stronger and softer—but then both my parents came into the room where I had gone and my mother, with a warm and loving smile on her face, said, "Yankee, I'm going to tell the teacher that I'll sit in class with you for a while until lunch time. Let's see how that works out."

I jumped on my mother, hugging and kissing her. Now I knew that Mr. Eisenboim could not terrorize me.

My mother informed my teacher of her intentions and it was fine with him. At least, that is what he told her. My mother began this project with the goal of leaving after one week but because of my prodding, complaining, weeping, and squeaking she remained in my class for the *entire year.* Later in life, when I was married, my mother would tell me that that was the way she learned Hebrew and mastered the prayers in Hebrew. When she was a child, Jewish girls never attended Religious School. Therefore, Hebrew was a totally foreign language to her. Yes, she had attended Sabbath services with her father as a child but all she knew were the tunes that were chanted at the synagogue. She did not know an *aleph* from a *bet* (an A from a B). However, during *my* first year of school, *she* learned an appreciation for the Hebrew language, and Judaism became more meaningful to her.

But when the second grade was about to begin, she put her

foot down. "No more sitting with you in class. You don't want to be called 'baby' by all your friends." I had no alternative, so I grumpily and surly acquiesced to her demands.

However, I still did not like my religious studies classes. But what could I do? My mother was adamant and inflexible—she would *not* be my fellow student in grade two. She had stated that most assertively and dogmatically.

But I learned a new technique to temporarily absent myself from my religious classes. I would tell my mother that I had a painful stomach ache or I would throw up at home or at school. It quickly became apparent to me that merely complaining about a stomach ache was not sufficient to get my mother to allow me to be absent from the morning sessions; however, if I concurrently threw up, my mother would take me out of class if it happened at school or allow me to miss the morning session if I threw up before leaving for school.

It appeared to my parents to be a cyclic malady because at 3 P.M. I *always* returned to my normal status and would go to the afternoon sessions to study the secular subjects. The "ailment" merely appeared during the morning and early afternoon hours when the religious studies subjects were in session.

My parents eventually thought that I was suffering from a recurrent ailment and often took me to my mother's cousin, Dr. Sam Nussbaum*, who lived in Manhattan and had his office in his home. By specialty he was a dermatologist but he was my mother's cousin, so, during the days of the Depression, we used him as our physician for all medical problems—including pediatrics.

Dr. Nussbaum on many occasions told my parents that he could find no medical reason for the habitual cramps or the throwing up, and after a while he informed my parents that he thought that I was a "malingerer." I was using phony and fraudulent excuses to get out of Religious School. And the proof of the pudding, he assuredly stated, was the fact that I never had those pains and I never threw up after 3 P.M. However, my parents refused to listen to him. Their young and adorable Yankee could not be that conniving and conspiring. So, Dr. Nussbaum would prescribe a tonic that would always help, *after 3* P.M., and my parents would feel that my medical needs were being satisfied.

This technique was often employed by me throughout grades two and three to "legally" be absent from religious classes. However, late in the third grade semester, when school was preparing for vacation, when I had just turned eight, I once again cried "Fox."

I had a *Chumash* (Bible) test that morning and I was totally unprepared. Therefore, already at 7:30 A.M. I began whining and weeping, "Mama, it hurts me badly. I can't stand it. It's killing me." And to add drama to my problem I shouted, "I'm going to throw up"—and I ran to the bathroom—and did.

My mother, of course, came to my rescue, put a cold wash cloth to my head, and appeased me with soothing words. "Go lie down. You'll stay home this morning. I'll give you some hot soup."

But when she walked out of my room I could hear her talking to my father. "Henry, this is it. This doesn't stop. We've got to get to the source of the problem immediately. There may be something really wrong with him. I'm calling Dr. Nussbaum right now."

My father merely stretched forth his arms in desperation and whispered, "Make an appointment for this morning."

My mother called immediately but was told by Mrs. Nussbaum, who was also the doctor's secretary, that he was out of town and would not be back until the next morning or, at the earliest, late that evening. However, she said, Dr. Hirschman*, a young doctor who was a surgeon, was covering for Dr. Nussbaum, and she suggested that we call him immediately.

Hesitancy was not a characteristic of my mother and she at once called Dr. Hirschman who told her to bring me over as soon as possible. Before I knew it, I was in the car and my parents were driving me to the Lower East Side in Manhattan to the People's Hospital*, a small hospital of about one hundred beds—at most.

We were shown into an examining room at the hospital and Dr. Hirschman entered about five minutes later. He was young, handsome, and well muscled. He probably lifted weights at night and he also had a captivating smile.

The doctor put me on the examining table and began to question me. He still had a warm smile on his face.

"Where does it hurt?"

"In my stomach," I immediately replied.

"Point for me the exact place where it hurts."

Dr. Nussbaum had always asked the same question, so I gave the same reply. "On the right side of my stomach."

Dr. Hirschman pointed to a position directly to the right of my belly button but I told him, "Lower."

His finger went lower and lower until I said, "Yes, there."

However, I noticed that Dr. Hirschman no longer had a smile on his face. In fact, his face was quite serious.

"How strong is the pain?"

"Very strong."

"Is it very strong or very, very strong?" he queried me.

Dr. Nussbaum had never asked me that question so I now had to invent additional descriptions for my ailment. "It's very, very painful." And then I began to invent a whole new story. "It's killing me. I don't think I can stand it another minute. It's like knives punching into my side. It does it, then stops, then starts up again. I always know it's coming back," and I also produced tears in my eyes.

Dr. Hirschman prodded my right side in all directions and occasionally I would grimace and cry out "Ouch!" I always made sure to indicate my severe pain when he pushed on the exact same area on my right side; however, each time my cry of "Ouch" became stronger and stronger. I could see that my mother's facial muscles were extremely taut and my father appeared about to faint. My hope was that Dr. Hirschman, too, would merely say, "He's got a temporary stomach ache. Just give him two teaspoons of this tonic and he'll probably be fine by one or two o'clock this afternoon."

My face appeared wan and pained, but internally I was jumping with joy and glee. Dr. Hirschman motioned to my parents and they walked to the corner of the room where there were three chairs. "We'll be back in a moment," he whispered almost silently to me as he moved to the corner of the room to join my parents. But when he sat down with them, his demeanor became quite serious. Yes, they moved an additional ten feet away from me and their voices were subdued but I could still hear their conversation.

"I think he's got an appendix that's about to rupture," the doctor sympathetically informed my parents. "Every time I touched his side, he'd scream." He hesitated for a moment, looked into my mother's eyes, and again continued. "I don't think we have time to take blood tests and wait for the lab results—if we want to prevent peritonitis."

My mother's face turned ashen white, my father was on the verge of swooning and collapsing. "What makes you say that?" my mother inquired with a motherly gasp.

"Well, he's got all the symptoms of a bad appendix. He has severe abdominal pain and he indicated pain and tenderness each time I touched the lower right-hand part of his abdomen. Even when I applied slight pressure he shouted. That's a sign of an inflamed appendix. He also felt warm when I touched him and you told me he threw up this morning. You also told me he didn't eat this morning, probably because he had no appetite."

Dr. Hirschman momentarily hesitated again, moved his chair closer to my mother's chair, and held her hands. "We're playing around with an obviously swollen appendix that has the potential of perforating or rupturing—and that's very dangerous. If that happens, the contents will be released into the abdomen and this usually will cause peritonitis." Dr. Hirschman once again hesitated, squeezed tightly on my mother's hands, and slowly added, "And that can be fatal," and he emphasized the word "fatal."

My father exuded a breathy "*Oi vey,* [Woe is me]," and my mother bit down on her lower lip and in a voice just above a whisper asked, "When do you think you have to operate?"

"Right now!" was the unemotional and calm response that came forth from the doctor.

My mother spoke for a minute to my father who had tears in his eyes and quickly gave her consent. Dr. Hirschman went to the nurse's station and informed the nurse to get two orderlies to prepare me for the surgery.

This new doctor was *not* going to give me my usual tonic.

He was going to make an incision in my side; he was going to cut me and take out something called "an appendix." He was obviously a violent man even though he looked so gentle and mild. But what could I do? I was caught between a rock and a hard place. If I refused the surgery they would definitely know that I was a phony. If I allowed them to take me to surgery then I would be paying an extremely astronomical price to stay out of Religious School. What should I do?

As my mind fluctuated and vibrated between admitting my fabrication or going to surgery, the die was cast. The two orderlies entered the room and began wheeling the gurney toward surgery as my mother held my hand and kept repeating, "Everything will be fine. Everything will be good. Dr. Hirschman will fix you up so that you never have a stomach ache again." My father walked beside my mother and wiped tears from his eyes.

I was cornered. I had painted myself into a corner of the room from which I could no longer exit without being exposed as a liar, fabricator, and a raconteur of tall fables. I was stuck—so I said nothing and allowed them to wheel me into surgery. I did not want my mother to know that I had fooled her all this time in order not to attend Religious School classes. Yes, I had to pay a high price for my secret, but to me it was worth it. Maybe after that surgery I could still continue my charade—the surgery was *not* successful.

I could see the doctor scrubbing his hands with soap and putting on a white gown. Time was running out on me. Beads of perspiration appeared on my forehead and a nurse wiped them off, patted my head, and sweetly commented, "You'll be OK. You'll be OK."

The doctor was still scrubbing as one of the orderlies began pushing my gurney into the surgical room. Now, it was not only my forehead that was wet but the palms of my hands were similarly damp.

All of a sudden, the swinging doors of the holding room for the patients awaiting surgery opened and in barged Dr. Nussbaum, my mother's cousin. He was obviously angry and exasperated. "Those stupid fools made a mistake. The meeting is *next* Wednesday, not today," he cried out with rage and fury. "They ought to fire that secretary." He hesitated momentarily and shouted, "In fact, they ought to fire the president of that committee. The stupid fools, they made me waste my entire morning."

Then Dr. Nussbaum looked around the room and saw my mother, and once again he cried out, "Where's Dr. Hirschman? They tell me that my cousin's son is here for SURGERY," and he shouted the word "SURGERY". "Who the heck ordered that? He's *my* patient."

Dr. Hirschman kicked the swinging door allowing him to enter the Waiting Room. He shook his head, breathed heavily, and addressed Dr. Nussbaum, "I guess I'll have to wash all over again, but, Dr. Nussbaum, this boy is suffering from what I believe is an inflamed appendix and I feel that if we wait any longer it will burst—and then we'll have a lot of trouble. I have always believed in the old motto, 'A stitch in time saves nine.' Operate now and you won't have to worry about peritonitis tomorrow."

Dr. Nussbaum banged down heavily on an examination table. "Dr. Hirschman," my mother's cousin barked, "have you ever seen this kid before? I've been seeing him regularly for almost three years. He's an actor *par excellence!* He should be given an Oscar for dramatics. He's better than Edward G. Robinson or Frederick March. That kid can bamboozle everyone, especially doctors. He doesn't need surgery. He needs *ah potch in der toochiss* [a swat over the backside]. That kid needs an appendectomy now like I need brain surgery now." His voice kept getting more and more thunderous as he spoke.

"He simply does not want to attend the Hebrew part of his Yeshiva [Jewish Day School]. He's merely a phony, a fraud, a fake, a sham." Dr. Nussbaum stared Dr. Hirschman directly in the eyes and whispered as a grin spread over his face, "He's a little brat who has been driving his parents crazy."

Dr. Nussbaum then turned toward my mother, grabbed her by her hand, and walked toward the operating room. Simultaneously, he also grabbed Dr. Hirschman by his hand and kicked the swinging door of the Operating Room inwards. By the fright on my face, he knew that I had heard his shouting and ranting. My perspiration, I knew, was no longer because of the anticipated surgery but rather because of Dr. Nussbaum's wrath.

Dr. Nussbaum smiled at me, took the sheet off my body, and with kindness coating each word softly said to me, "Yankee, I'm going to examine you."

He then pushed his index finger into the right side of my stomach—and I shouted because I had heard Dr. Hirschman say that that was one of the signs of appendicitis.

But he smiled deeply at me and commented, "Yankee, Dr. Hirschman only gave you half of the examination. He forgot to examine you on the left side," and immediately his index finger prodded me on the left side of my stomach.

No one had told me anything about the left side—so I made what I considered was an educated guess. To myself I said, "The appendix is probably all over my stomach. So if hurting on the right side is a sign, hurting on the left side is probably also an additional sign." So I cried out in pain and anguish, misery and agony, as he stuck his finger in my left side. My mother thought I was being tortured. I could see her grimace, twist, and distort her face.

Dr. Nussbaum walked out of the room pulling Dr. Hirschman after him. "Now do you believe me that he's a phony? He'll scream in pain no matter where I touch him as long as he thinks that will get him out of school."

Dr. Nussbaum stroked his chin and squinted his eyes. "I think I've got it," he pontificated to a wordless, silent, and completely embarrassed Dr. Hirschman. "This kid comes from a very Orthodox home. I think I'm going to bamboozle him rather than have him bamboozle me."

Dr. Nussbaum and Dr. Hirschman remained out of the room for ten minutes, then they returned.

Dr. Nussbaum stared at me. His face was very serious. "When will you be eight," he interrogated me.

"I was eight last month in April," I replied with tears in my eyes, "the 18th of April."

"That means that you are eight years and a little more than one month. You still have time."

I raised my eyes and hesitantly asked, "What do you mean that I still have time?"

"Well, the medical journals state that your sickness has never lasted in children more than eight years and two months. That means that by June your sickness should be over." But he then sympathetically stared at me and added, "However, if it is not over by eight years and two months, then—" and he broke off his conversation. "I'd rather not go on."

I gawked at the doctor and demanded, "What does happen if you're not cured by eight years and two months?"

"I'd rather not discuss it," he responded as his eyes moved upwards. "But" he added, "I'm going to tell your mother not to send you to Hebrew anymore in the mornings this semester. You'll start Hebrew again next year, after the summer. By that time you'll be perfect—no more pain—no more hurt—no more sickness. Otherwise," and he stared penetratingly straight through my stomach, "we'll have to send you to a surgeon in Chicago who does only very serious surgeries." But a smile quickly reappeared on his face, "But I know that by September, when school starts again, you'll be perfect."

He grabbed both my hands, kissed me on the head, and pinched my cheek. "Be thankful that September will soon be here. You'll be back in school and you'll be perfectly healthy," and with an index finger tapping me on my shoulder he concluded, "I'm *positive* of that. No more medicines. No more tonics. No more anything. You're almost eight years and two months. Presto! You'll be as healthy as a lion and a tiger—combined."

Dr. Nussbaum did not even wait for me to reply. He merely turned around, grabbed my mother by the arm, and exited from the room.

Outside, he told my mother, "I think I scared the hell out of him."

September came along and I once again had trepidations about attending Hebrew School and Religious School at the Yeshiva. But I was now past eight years and two months.

But I had a new Hebrew teacher, Mr. Fishel*. He was about

sixty years old and a little more than six feet tall. He had a beard like the late General Grant but *always* had a smile on his face. He never was grumpy or angry, disgruntled or ill tempered. On the contrary, he was *always* jovial and happy, jolly and cheerful. In fact, the first time he saw me in the play yard he picked me up and swung me around. I could not believe that. The only time I had previously had a direct relationship with my Hebrew teacher or religion teacher was to criticize me or "bawl me out" or beat my knuckles.

The next day, Mr. Fishel even asked me to play catch with him and he produced a ball from his pocket.

The following morning, he saw me before I entered class and said, "Would you like a Tootsie Roll for lunch? My wife gave me an extra one."

I could not believe this man. He treated me like a human being. He treated me like a loving grandfather—and he was not even related to me.

One day, Mr. Fishel even challenged me to a handball game, and I quickly accepted the invitation. Of course I beat him, twenty-one to six, but he actually got six points from me. I was the best handball player in my class—but he still got six points from me—and he was my grandfather's age.

The next morning, I gave *him* a Tootsie Roll and said to him, "You truly deserve it."

One evening about a month later, Mr. Fishel made a surprise visit to our home. My parents looked surprised, "Has Yankee been acting up?" they questioned him. "Has he been sick in class again?"

"No, no," Mr. Fishel replied with an expansive grin. "He's just the opposite. I see him as a young boy with great potential. He has a sharp mind. He can be a very good student. I don't know what happened in the previous three years, but I see great years for him in the future. He has a good mind for the Bible. Not only is he a good translator from the Hebrew to the Yiddish but I think he can go much faster than the other children in the class."

My father's eyes were wide open. "Mr. Fishel, what are you actually suggesting?"

"I'd like to tutor him on Fridays and Saturdays in your house, one hour a day. It's only for two hours a week but I think it will help him enormously."

I did not even wait for my parents' reply. I merely grabbed my father's hand and implored him, "Please say 'Yes,' Daddy." Mr. Fishel had truly found a niche in my heart and my soul. He actually redirected my interest in Hebrew and religion from an extreme negative to a vibrant positive. It was not the subject. It was the teacher. It was not the curriculum. It was the means of teaching the material—with love and compassion, tenderness and a smile. Previously, every time my teacher would say *"B'ray-sheet bara Elohim . . .* [In the beginning, God created the heavens and the earth]," the first words of the Bible, I would get sick, but when Mr. Fishel said, *"B'ray-sheet bara Elohim,"* I would cry out, "What does Rashi [a biblical commentator] say on that statement?"

Every day he continued to play ball with me and give me Tootsie Rolls as rewards for quickly learning the biblical translations, and often he would grab me under the arms and swing me around.

Mr. Fishel showed me beauty in the Bible—and made me forget stomach cramps, appendicitis, and peritonitis—and even Dr. Nussbaum asked me questions about the Bible during the two times that year that my mother took me to his home for a family social visit.

The Rubicon had been crossed. A soft soul had shown me that the glass was half full and not half empty.

• • • • •

1) "A merry heart causes a healthy appearance, but a depressed spirit dries the bones."

—Proverbs 17:22

2) *"Saychel iz an aydeleh zoch"* ("Common sense is a very precious object")

—An old Yiddish expression, author unknown

Chapter 8

"I Crossed The Word 'Impossible' Out Of My Dictionary"

It was storming like in the days of Noah. The rain was coming down in buckets and Toby told me to check the streets to see if they were flooding and to also see if the waters of the rain were threatening to enter our home.

I told her to continue watching television. Yes, the rain was severe but we still did not have any flooding. In fact, cars were still occasionally traversing our street.

However, at about 9:15 that evening, I heard the two bells of our chimes. One bell meant that someone was ringing at the back door. Two bells meant that someone was ringing at the front door.

"Who is it?" Toby quickly called out.

"I don't know yet," I immediately responded. "Let me go to the door and I'll see."

Toby again speedily called out, "Don't open the door. That's the way people get robbed. They come late at night, on a rainy evening, ring your bell, and say, 'I've got a flat tire. Can I come in to call the AAA?' Jack, if he says that, tell him to wait outside and *you* will make the call for him."

I could truly hear fear in Toby's voice. I guess the many crimes of violence that we would daily read about in our local newspaper really influenced Toby—and I must admit that I probably also exacerbated the situation by always admonishing her, "If I'm not home, don't open the door for a stranger. If they have to make a call, tell them to give you the number and *you'll* make the call. If they have a message, tell them to slip it under the door." I always stressed, "If I'm not home, don't open the door for a stranger."

However, I looked through the window of our front door and I saw Stuart Finkelstein*, whom I had known since I had arrived in Houston in 1965. He graduated from our Synagogue Day School. I officiated at his Bar Mitzvah. I had been his Religious School teacher. I officiated at his Confirmation, and I conducted the service for his Hillel High School graduation. I knew him for at least twenty years and he was probably twenty-three years of age now. I knew that he was a freshman in Law School and his mind was set on becoming a criminal lawyer.

I opened the door and saw that Stuart was soaked. He obviously did not have an umbrella and he must have had the wrong address to my home because his car was parked four houses down from mine.

"Stuart, come in. You look soaked," I called out to him over the din of the rain. And to Toby I cried out, "It's only Stuart Finkelstein. He's come to visit," and I giggled innocently.

Stuart entered our house but immediately removed his shoes and raincoat. I momentarily left the room and quickly returned with a towel for him to dry his hair and I hung his coat in the bathroom.

"Stuart, come into the kitchen. I'll give you a hot cup of coffee. It's cold outside and you look frozen, and it's obvious that you're soaked."

Stuart apologetically thanked me for my courtesy and hospitality, followed me into the kitchen, and was seated at the kitchen table as I put the kettle on the stove and put a teaspoon of Folgers coffee crystals in a cup.

We waited for the water to boil but, meanwhile, I asked

Stuart, "It's pouring outside. There must be a good reason for you to be out tonight and visiting me at 9:15."

"Yes, Rabbi, there *is* a good reason for me to be here." He pathetically looked toward the stove and said, "It *is* really cold outside and I *am* soaked. I guess I picked the wrong night to see you—but I just had to talk to you."

Stuart had aroused my curiosity. What thought was running around in his mind that catapulted him into going out on this miserable and threatening evening?

I sat down next to him and inquired, "Stuart, what can I do for you—besides give you a hot cup of coffee?" The kettle began to whistle. I poured the water over the coffee crystals and put some milk and SWEET'N LOW on the table. Stuart raised the cup in the palms of both of his hands, probably to become a bit warmer, took a sip of the hot coffee, then looked up at me. "Rabbi, I came here to ask a favor of you."

"What is it, Stuart? I'll do my best to help you."

He hesitated for a moment as if he did not know how I would respond to his query.

"Ask it, Stuart," I urged him again.

"Rabbi," he slowly continued, "I'd like you to show me *your* copy of *your* Webster's 5th Collegiate Dictionary."

I blinked my eyes two or three times, hesitated again, and once more asked, "What do you want me to do?"

Without batting an eyelash, Stuart immediately responded while looking down into his cup of coffee, "Rabbi, I would like to see *your* copy of *your* Webster's 5th Collegiate Dictionary. Rabbi" he continued inquisitively, "didn't you once say that when you went to college you used Webster's Fifth Collegiate Dictionary and it was quite battered and pummeled because of the constant use you made of it?"

"Yes, that is true," I instantly replied, but for a moment I really thought that he had had too much to drink—whiskey, that is. Who would come out in the midst of this inclement weather to look at my old dictionary? Was he going into the antique business and thought that my dictionary would draw a high price? Something did not sound kosher to me.

Then, before I could rise from my chair, while he was still

holding onto his cup of coffee with his two hands, he looked up and slowly asked me, "Rabbi, do you *really* have a Webster's 5th Collegiate Dictionary?"

This query sounded even more bizarre and more odd than the previous one. So I pointed at Stuart, "Finish your cup of coffee, first. Then I'll take you into my library. I use it almost every day so I know exactly where that book is. I'll get it for you in a second."

As I arose from my chair, it seemed to me that I noticed a faint sly smirk on his face as if he felt that he had caught me in a fabrication, in a lie—even though I could not understand the logic of such a feeling. He took a deep gulp of the hot coffee, put the cup down, and rose.

I walked over to one of the two bookcases that were in my study and quickly pulled out my Webster's 5th Collegiate Dictionary. It was battered and torn, held together with scotch tape both inside and on the cover, weather-beaten and obviously still in need of additional repair. Immediately I brought the book into the kitchen, handed it to Stuart, and jokingly inquired, "Would you like to buy it from me?" But without waiting for a response I shook my head from right to left and emphatically declared, "It ain't for sale."

Stuart did not even crack a smile at my supposed humor. "May I please look at it?" he solemnly went on. His eyes were fixated on the tattered pages of the book and he sat down once again.

"Of course," I replied, as my curiosity peaked, and I handed him the book.

Stuart immediately began delicately turning the pages as if he wanted to make sure that he did not tear any of the already torn and brittle pages. However, it seemed to me that he was looking for something specific. He did not meander from beginning to end and back to the beginning. The dictionary was initially opened to about the middle of the book and Stuart then began turning one page at a time as if he was aiming and searching for a specific word. Then, all of a sudden, he stopped turning pages, his eyes began moving from the top of the column downwards, and then—his eyes no longer moved. They were concentrated on one line. They were transfixed on that one line.

Stuart shook his head. "I don't believe it. I just don't believe it," he commented as he exhaled heavily. "It's just as you said three years ago on Rosh Hashanah [the beginning of the Jewish religious year, one of the holiest days of the year]."

I raised my eyelids in amazement. I was truly dumbfounded. "What are you talking about?" I asked as I stretched forth my hands, palms up. "What did I say on Rosh Hashanah and where did I say it?" I continued as I went on in my bafflement.

Stuart breathed in heavily. "Rabbi, three years ago, on Rosh Hashanah, you stood before our congregation of three thousand people, and in your sermon said what I thought was an outrageous fib. I thought you were grandstanding before the congregation because you wanted to make a point—and therefore you said something which *I* felt was not true—but was said merely to hammer home the theme of your sermon."

I interrupted Stuart. "What was the theme of that sermon and what did you think was a lie?" The palms of my hands were still pointed upwards as if I was in a vacuum, not comprehending one iota of his conversation.

Stuart again breathed in heavily and proceeded. "Rabbi, before that large congregation you said, and I can almost quote your words verbatim, 'In my Webster's 5th Collegiate Dictionary that I've used since my college days and that I even use today, I once took a red pen and crossed out the word 'impossible' and wrote next to it in red, 'sweat more'. I did this because I believe that nothing should be impossible to you or to me. *Never* give in; *never* give up. Yes, it may take more energy; it may take more work; it may take more enterprise; but *never* give in and *never* give up. And I say the same thing to you. Go get your dictionaries right after Rosh Hashanah and cross out that word 'impossible,' and right next to it write, 'sweat more.' You will see that the impossible will eventually be converted to the possible; the unachievable will be transformed into the achievable; the hopeless will be transmuted into the hopeful; and the insurmountable will quickly become the surmountable. Make up your mind to give your maximum effort and you will see that what you previously thought was *beyond* your reach has now come *within* your grasp. Follow my lead. Cross out that one word of pessimism, 'impossible,' and replace it with that odorous phrase, but optimistic phrase, 'sweat more.'"

Stuart stared at me from behind his bushy eyebrows to see if I was going to interrupt him or make some comment, but I held back in order to hear his complete statement. "Rabbi," Stuart eventually went on, "I personally thought that you were simply being dramatic—crossing out a word and substituting for it a phrase in red ink." He shook his head and smiled. "But you *did* do it. You actually *did* do it."

With a smile on my face and with puckered lips I began, "Stuart, if I'm going to lie I'll do it before one or two people, but not before three thousand people." We both laughed heartily.

But I quickly picked up the conversation as the outline of my face rapidly changed from a smile to a grimace. "But, Stuart, why did you need the answer *tonight* in the midst of all this rain rather than tomorrow when the Weather Bureau has forecast good weather?"

Stuart leaned forward in his chair, sipped some more coffee from his cup, breathed in a lung-full of air and slowly began again—with sadness written all over his face. "Rabbi, I received some bad news today."

I inched forward in my chair as I noticed tension and stress spreading all over Stuart's face. Stuart spoke softly but deliberately as if he was not totally sure whether he should go forward—but he did. "Rabbi, as I said, I had some bad news today. My first major exam in Law School was today—and I flunked it badly."

Stuart's eyes were now directed toward the floor as he admitted to me that he had done poorly, very poorly on the exam. "In fact," he went on, "my Professor called me into his office after he returned the papers and suggested to me that I might do better going on for an MBA and dropping out of Law School. He told me that there were already too many lawyers and law was not everyone's cup of tea."

Again Stuart hesitated and again he breathed in heavily. "Foolishly, I hadn't studied very thoroughly for the exam. I thought I could get through it by the material I already knew. I hadn't studied too much in college—and I got through quite well, and I thought I could do the same in Law School.

"The Professor told me that I should give him my answer next Monday. He told me that this was the first time he had ever suggested to a student that he drop out of Law School, but my grade was so low—that it was almost subterranean."

Stuart croaked out a lame laugh at an attempt at humor but it did not evoke a response of laughter from me, so he continued. "The Professor knocked me on my backside, on my *toochiss*. No one had ever spoken to me like that before. He actually told me that he didn't think I *could* get through three tough years of Law School. His attitude was—drop it now *before* you make a big investment, time-wise and money-wise, in this career.

"Rabbi, that's why I came to see you tonight. All this happened just a couple of hours ago. I couldn't eat dinner and I knew that I would not be able to sleep.

"But your sermon was resurrected in my mind. I felt as if your words were directed toward me.

"Rabbi, can you help me," and he grabbed my hand in his hands and I beheld a teardrop in his right eye.

I held both of Stuart's hands as I moved my chair in his direction. We were almost sitting on top of each other. "Stuart," I began, "you have to answer that question yourself. I cannot answer it for you. But to answer the question as to whether you should continue in Law School, you've got to first answer two other questions."

Stuart was now looking into both of my eyes and I could clearly see that both of his eyes were moist. "Stuart," I went on, "your first question is, do you truly want to become a lawyer with all your heart and all your soul? And your second question is, are you willing to work hard and sweat profusely to achieve that goal or are you merely interested in being handed a Law degree on a golden tray?"

Stuart did not even hesitate for a moment. "Rabbi, I definitely want to become a lawyer and I'm willing to work hard for it."

The tears were evaporating and Stuart's head was now erect. "Stuart, you read me correctly when I said in my sermon never to give in and never to give up. You've encountered a big boulder in the road. Do you want to simply give in or do you want to search for a way around it, above it, through it, or below it? If you try hard enough, you *will* find a way."

We spoke for an additional hour and we both consumed two more cups of hot coffee, and when we concluded our talk, Stuart rose, pointed his index finger at me, and smiled. "Rabbi," he spoke with enthusiasm, "I'm going to cross out the word 'impossible' and write next to it 'sweat more'—and that's exactly what I'm going do—sweat more. Rabbi, I *am* going to make it. Rabbi, I *am* going to become a lawyer."

Pride truly overcame me. I felt so good. I had, I believed, changed Stuart's attitude from pessimism to optimism, from depression to hopefulness, from drowning to buoyancy, and from mental exhaustion to emotional uplift. He took his raincoat from me, gave me a tight hug, and actually kissed me on the cheek. "Rabbi," he beamed with exuberance, "you've given me another lease on life. You've rebuilt my faith in myself. I'll send you an invitation to my Law School graduation." We both laughed, and Stuart walked out into the rain. In fact, as he went in the direction of his car, he began to run and sing. I could hear him singing—"Oh what a beautiful morning, Oh what a beautiful day. . . ."

Two and a half years later, I heard that Stuart had graduated from Law School. However, the invitation to his Law School graduation must have been lost in the mail since I never received it. I was also informed that he had done well in Law School and had accepted a good position with a prestigious law firm in California.

During the next five years, I only saw Stuart very briefly on two separate occasions when he was at synagogue services with his mother on Rosh Hashanah. "I'm doing very well in California," he informed me, and I noticed that a bright smile was constantly on his face as he spoke to me—both times.

However, about a half year after I saw him the second time, his sister called me. "Have you heard the terrible news?" she asked as she wept paroxysmally. I did not know to what she was referring but before I could respond she blurted forth the story.

"Rabbi," she sobbed and whined, "Stuart's dead."

"What did you say?" I immediately asked her as I put the telephone receiver closer to my ear in order to be sure that I was hearing her correctly.

"Rabbi, Stuart's dead," his sister repeated to me. Amidst sobs and tears she blurted out what had occurred. "Stuart had gone to a Law School library to meet a client. That was the desire of the client because it was close to the client's home while Stuart's office was quite distant from the client's home. It was a messy divorce case. Stuart represented the man. However, the woman was making it difficult for Stuart's client to secure a divorce and he was meeting with his client to brief him as to what had transpired in the negotiations during the past week."

Stuart's sister blew her nose and continued to weep. "Stuart was telling his client who was very tall, heavy, tough, and rough his plans to secure the divorce; however, the man became very upset and excited, and pulled out a revolver and shot six times at Stuart. It was point blank, and he hit Stuart five times."

Stuart's sister had to hesitate as the tears were now obviously flowing like the waters of the Mississippi River—constantly and abundantly. I waited for about thirty seconds that seemed like an eternity, but again she continued. "Forty lawyers were present in the library at that time but they all fell to the floor to protect themselves or ran through the door if they were close to the exit. The librarian immediately called the police, and within five minutes the assailant was in police custody."

Again there was a brief pause as Stuart's sister caught her breath. "The police told me that Stuart was dead before his head hit the table—immediately, instantaneously."

I could not believe what my ears had heard. Stuart was gone. His dreams had quickly evaporated. A promising future had quickly come to an end.

One week later, we had a Memorial Service for Stuart in Houston and I told his family and friends of our encounter seven years earlier on a wet and stormy evening. "Stuart," I informed them, "had taught himself to throw away the word 'impossible' from his vocabulary and substitute for it the phrase 'sweat harder.' That moment in his life had caused a metamorphosis in his personality. From then on, he merely looked forward, never backward. He concentrated on the rising sun, never on the dark clouds. He listened to the rhapsodies of joy, not the dirges of gloom. He focused on the flowers, not on the thorns.

"However, because of the insanity of one man whom he had befriended and attempted to help, his entire existence was eclipsed and terminated just as it was beginning to sprout."

I prayed for him the traditional Jewish prayer that is recited at the grave of one who passes away: "May his soul be bound up in the bond of eternal life. Amen!"

• • • • •

"I am a Jew because in every age when the cry of despair is heard, the Jew hopes."

—*Edmond Fleg,* Why I Am A Jew

CHAPTER 9

Was Someone Sending Me A Message?

I was ordained in 1954 and went to my first congregation in Homestead, Pennsylvania that summer. It was a small synagogue with only ninety-two family-members; however, I liked it because it was in close proximity to Pittsburgh, just across the Monongahela River from the metropolis.

Early the next year, I received a call from a member of my synagogue, Mr. Rheingold.* "Rabbi, would you go to Petroleum Township* to officiate at a wedding for my son on May 29? It's just one hundred and ten miles north of Pittsburgh and it would only take you a little over two hours to get there. The bride lived there until she went to college and her parents still live there. Rabbi—please. My son finally found a Jewish girl to marry and my wife and I are just totally happy about this. Rabbi—please."

I quickly looked at my calendar and noticed that May 29 was blank. In fact, many of the days on my synagogue calendar were blank except for Friday nights and Saturdays when I led Services, and Sundays, Mondays, Wednesdays, and Thursdays when I conducted Religious School classes for our youngsters in the afternoons. But Sunday, May 22 was going to be the last day of Religious School for the Hebrew year 5715 (1954-1955). Therefore, beside the 8 A.M. Sunday Service that we would have on May 29, that would be concluded by 9 A.M., that day was completely free. "I'll be happy to officiate at his wedding," I quickly replied. "However, tell your son to please call me so that he and his fiancée can make an appointment to meet with me so that we will be able to get to know each other, and I will also describe to them how the service will be conducted."

When our conversation was concluded I went to my map to find Petroleum Township. Mr. Rheingold was correct. Petroleum Township was about one hundred and ten miles north of Pittsburgh and had about 17,000 people living there. However, I also went to my book of statistics pertaining to the Jews of Pennsylvania and noticed that very, very few Jews still resided in that town. Petroleum Township was on the Allegheny River and was one of the principal oil markets in the state. It contained petroleum refineries, foundries, and machine shops and was founded in 1860 when oil was discovered in that area.

Steven*, Mr. Rheingold's son, called me the next day and informed me that his girlfriend, Ellen Saperstein*, was a senior at Chatham College in Pittsburgh and both of them could meet with me later that week, at night, since she attended classes during the day and he worked during the day as a salesman in a men's clothing store in the Squirrel Hill section of Pittsburgh.

We met later that week in my office after Religious School was concluded. Steven, surprisingly, walked in before Ellen and she simply followed him in. He did not hold her hand or look at her as they walked through my doorway and into my office. "I'm Steven and she's Ellen," Steven superciliously and haughtily proclaimed as he sat down and motioned to Ellen to be seated—which she did.

As I looked at them, they superficially seemed to me to be an incongruous couple. Steven was about six foot three inches tall and his physique resembled that of Charles Atlas. He was wearing a tight-fitting polo shirt and I could see each ripple of his muscles, and his biceps and triceps were totally exposed indicating that he probably lifted weights with regularity at a gymnasium.

Ellen, on the other hand, was five foot tall, at most, and probably weighed one hundred and forty pounds—or maybe even one hundred and forty-five pounds. She was very average looking and wore a loose fitting skirt that shrouded her true, plumpish figure. However, I quickly concluded that she must be a beauty to Steven because he was going to marry her. I remembered the old aphorism: "Beauty is in the eye of the beholder." We all have different definitions of "beauty."

However, as we began to speak to each other it seemed that we were developing a dialogue rather than a trialogue. Steven was answering all of my questions and Ellen was totally quiet—even when I posed a question to her. Steven always quickly jumped in and gave the response. I believe I could have counted on one hand the number of words Ellen spoke to me at our meeting.

Steven told me that he had dropped out of school in the eleventh grade and had worked at several jobs since that time. He enjoyed working out every day at the Y.M.H.A. (Young Men's Hebrew Association) in Pittsburgh and also played semi-pro baseball during the baseball season.

As a postscript, Steven added that Ellen was going to graduate from college two weeks before their marriage and that she was a superb student in school, having majored in Biology. However, he went on, she harbored a "foolish idea" in her head. She wanted to become a doctor. Steven stared at Ellen, smiled expansively, and pointed his index finger at her, "But I changed your mind about that, didn't I?"

However, Ellen surprised me. She began speaking softly. "Rabbi, I only agreed to postpone the decision for one year, but, then, I'm going to apply to Medical School. Since I started school as a child, I've always wanted to become a doctor—just like my Uncle Irving*"

Steven rapidly rose from his chair, shook his head at Ellen, and slapped his thigh. "I thought we settled this matter last week."

He then turned toward me. "Rabbi, Ellen's dream is a fantasy. It's unreal. When we're married we're going to move to Petroleum City. Ellen's father told me that he's going to make me a vice-president of his oil company." Once again his eyes were riveted on Ellen. "What are we going to do—you'll live in Pittsburgh and I'll live in Petroleum Township? That's ridiculous."

Steven walked over to Ellen's chair, placed his hands on her arms, and with softness in his voice declared, "I've told you a million times, Ellen, I love you. I want to marry you. Both of us are going to be happy—very happy—*in Petroleum Township.*"

Ellen did not speak a word. As usual, she was silent. For a moment I thought she was going to make a comment indicating her disagreement, but before a syllable could come forth from her lips Steven kissed her and again stated, "I love you Ellen. I love you."

A teardrop slowly meandered down Ellen's face from her left eye. I looked at Steven in order not to embarrass Ellen.

"Ellen, Steven," I interjected, "maybe we ought to discuss this goal of Ellen's of becoming a physician."

But Steven once again quickly jumped in, "There's nothing to discuss, Rabbi. We already reached *our* decision." And to Ellen, Steven belligerently asked, "Am I right, Ellen?"

Several tears were now coursing down Ellen's cheeks. "Yes," Ellen responded with a heavy sigh, "you are right, Steven—as usual."

Sunday, May 29, was a beautiful day. The sun shone brightly, the birds were warbling and trilling, the flowers were blooming in full splendor, and there were no clouds in the sky. The wedding was scheduled for 5 P.M. in the Veterans of Foreign Wars Hall in Petroleum Township, and even though Mr. Rheingold told me that it should only take me a little more than two hours to get to Petroleum Township I decided that I was not going to take any chances. I decided to leave at 2 P.M., three hours before the scheduled wedding ceremony, in order to take care of all contingencies, in order to cover all bases. I believed strongly in Murphy's Law—"Anything that can go wrong will go wrong."

At 2 o'clock, I put my *Madrich* (Rabbi's Handbook), *Tallit* (prayer shawl), and *Ketubah* (Hebrew marriage license) on the back seat of the car and began my trip to the wedding.

The trip was uneventful as I drove at about sixty miles per hour through the Pennsylvania landscape and listened to classical music over the radio. However, when I was about twenty miles past Butler the car suddenly began to wobble and shake. Instantly I knew that something was wrong, so I quickly slowed down and pulled off onto the soft shoulder of the road. I opened the door and began to circle the car but it was staring me straight in the eye as soon as I turned to my right. My left front tire was flat.

"Darn it," I inwardly shouted to myself, "this is a heck of a time to have a flat." But I knew that I had a good spare tire and it was full of air since the gas station attendant had checked it for me Friday afternoon.

I had not passed a gas station in quite some time and I did not know how far it was to the next station, so I decided to change the tire myself. I whispered to myself, "God helps those who help themselves."

The equipment to change the tire was in my trunk and within two minutes it became obvious to me what had to be done. I removed my jacket and set out to change the tire. It was not really difficult. In fact, it was quite simple and within forty minutes the tire was changed and I placed the flat tire and the equipment back in the trunk. "It will be nip and tuck," I said to myself, "but I think I'll be just in time for the wedding. I'm so glad I left early."

Now I was driving only fifty miles per hour. I was being extra-cautious. I did not want to take any chances. But when I was about ten miles past Clintonville and listening to a sonorous and bombastic presentation of Wagner's *Die Walkure,* the car began to wobble and shake again. I could not believe it, so once again I pulled off the road onto the soft shoulder and opened my door to determine what had gone wrong this time. Once again it was staring me right in the eye. The left front tire, the one I had just put on the car, was flat.

Fear and anxiety quickly overtook me. What was I going to do? A car only holds one spare tire—and that one was flat. I was ten miles from Clintonville. I would have to hitch a ride back to town with the flat tire, fix the flat, return to my car, and then continue on to Petroleum Township. My hands were actually shaking, beads of perspiration were all over my forehead, and my shirt was soaked as I removed this second flat tire.

Few cars passed me going south in the direction of Clintonville. I was frustrated and tense, soaked to the bone and breathing heavily. But then, after waiting almost twenty minutes a farmer in a pickup truck stopped, told me to throw the tire in the back of the truck, and off we went to Clintonville. Luckily there was one gas station open but the owner told me that his mechanic was off on Sunday. "Come back on Monday," he authoritatively bellowed at me. However, when I told him that I was a clergyman, that I was supposed to officiate at a wedding in Petroleum Township, and that I was late for the ceremony, he quickly called his teenage son from his house behind the station and emphatically told him to fix the flat. The boy griped. "I've got a date with my girl friend," he implored his father. However, his father was adamant. "Wilson*, this man's a clergyman. He's a Jewish minister, a holy man, and a man of God. He has to unite in holy wedlock two children of God." The gas station owner then howled at his son, "Fix that damn tire and fix it quickly. I told you that he's going to unite two people in holy marriage, not like so many others I know who run off into the bushes."

The young boy said something under his breath but went off to fix the flat. The gas station owner then turned toward me and excused himself for losing his temper and using strong, "improper language."

It took about fifteen minutes to patch the tube and fix the tire. But just as the boy was turning to return to their home his father called out, "Wait a minute. This preacher has to get back to his car. Take him back."

The boy protested quite vehemently but his father shot back, "I *said* take him back to his car and I *meant* take him back to his car." The father momentarily hesitated, then added, "Your girl friend lives on the way to his car. Why don't you pick her up and then drive him back. You'll kill two birds with one stone."

I thanked the father munificently and asked him what I had to pay him; however, his eyes opened widely and in a soft congenial voice responded, "There is no charge. I never charge a minister for labor done on his car. I only charge them for parts. You only had a small patch and some glue. Go and do God's work and spread the word of God wherever you go."

Once again I thanked him profusely and off I went in the pickup truck to my stranded car with his sixteen-year-old son. However, we first picked up the boy's fourteen-year-old girl friend who looked at least seventeen. She was very pretty and very physically mature. As she came out of her home wearing a captivating smile and an off the shoulder blouse, Wilson quickly implored me, "Could you please do me a favor? Could you please sit with the tire in the back of the truck? My girl friend doesn't like to crease her skirt and it will be very crowded if three sit up front here."

"Of course," I replied as I smiled at Wilson. His girl friend jumped into the front seat of the truck, gave Wilson a big kiss, and off we went to my car. However, I do not think that she was really worried about creases on her skirt because I noticed she was sitting almost on his lap with her arm around his shoulder—but I was thoroughly thankful that they were taking me to my car.

In fact, when we arrived at my car I was totally surprised when Wilson asked me, "Would you like me to change the tire for you? I'll do it very quickly and it'll only cost you five dollars."

I told him to go to it and in five minutes I was back on the road. But my watch glared at me. It was now 6 P.M. I was already one hour late for the *Chuppah* (marriage ceremony) and I still had close to an hour to Petroleum Township.

I prayed to God as I drove at forty miles per hour, "Please, O God, no more flats. What happened today was like being hit twice in one day by lightning or winning the Irish Sweepstake. It never happens—but it happened today, to me. O God, were you sending a message to me? Were you trying to tell me something? If so, what is it?"

My body was soaked with perspiration caused by tension even though I was not wearing my jacket. I felt as if I was swimming in sweat.

Then, as I was about two miles before Petroleum Township, at exactly 6:50 P.M., I noticed that the colored lights of a local police car were flashing their multicolored message to me. "O God," I once again said to myself, "what did I do now? I wasn't speeding; I wasn't driving on the wrong side of the road; I didn't throw any trash onto the roadway. O God, what did I do this time?"

I pulled off the road onto the soft shoulder and awaited the arrival of the policeman. I was not perspiring any longer. Now I was gushing perspiration from all parts of my body. My handkerchief was super-soaked because of the many times I had wiped my brow, my face, my arms, and my hands.

The officer approached my car and before I could even ask him what had precipitated his stopping me, he put his two hands on the rim of my window and asked, "Is your name, by any chance, Rabbi Segal?"

"Yes," I replied, with trepidation that was obvious from the tone of my voice. "What did I do?" I continued as I was now inundated with anxiety and sweat because I envisioned what was probably happening at the Veterans of Foreign Wars Hall. As I closed my eyes I saw three men holding shotguns: the groom, his father, and the bride's father. I could also envision the bride and her mother wielding pistols—all of them shouting, "Where is that rabbi?"

An overflowing smile quickly appeared on his face as he cried out, "Follow me. The bride and groom are going bananas. They think something happened to you. And the organist told me that his fingers are already bleeding from playing 'O Promise Me' for the past two and a half hours. Stay out of his ornery way. He may be an organist but he's a tough character."

The policeman quickly walked back to his car, once again began flashing his colored lights, put on his siren, and called out to me, "Follow me. I'll take you directly to the V.F.W. Hall"—which he did.

When I entered the V.F.W. Hall I noticed that the clock was sounding its chimes and the hands of the clock were on the seven and the twelve. The wedding was supposed to have started two hours earlier.

All eyes were focused on me. I was quite disheveled: my jacket was rumpled; my pants no longer had a crease in them; my hair was unkempt; and the groom looked violent.

Quickly I attempted to tell the groom and his parents and his future in-laws and the bride, who were all standing close to each other, about my two flat tires, but no one, except the bride, seemed to be listening to me.

"Rabbi, let's get the show on the road," the groom angrily pontificated. "I want to get married." However, I noticed that Ellen was silent even though her mother was weeping and her father was indicating his agreement with Steven.

I breathed in heavily and to the groom I whispered, "I need five minutes in the restroom. I want to wash up, comb my hair, and look presentable." I did not even wait for a reply. I merely walked toward the sign saying: "Gentlemen."

Within a few minutes I was out, we signed the necessary documents, and at 7:15 P.M. I began the ceremony and twenty minutes later declared Steven and Ellen husband and wife. Steven kissed his bride but I noticed that there were tears in Ellen's eyes, which I concluded were tears of happiness. The organist began playing "Hold That Tiger" for the recessional and Mr. Saperstein* cried out, "There's plenty of food and plenty of drinks for everyone. Have a good time." And all the two hundred or more guests began moving to the buffet line and the bar.

I remained at the reception until about 8:30, shook the groom's hand, kissed the bride, wished them all well and told them that I would love to see them again if they ever came to Pittsburgh. By that time, everyone seemed to be in a good mood, so I left.

About nine months later, in February, I received a call from Ellen. She was in Pittsburgh and stated that she could meet with me in a half-hour, if I had the time. I was merely preparing a sermon so I told her to come over.

She walked into my office, but it seemed to me that it was

a different Ellen. No longer did she have a dour and sullen look on her face. Now, she was smiling and beaming. No longer was she about forty pounds overweight. Now, she had a svelte and lithe figure. No longer did she walk with her head bent to the ground. Now, her head was raised high as if she was prepared for, and looking forward to, encountering the future. I was truly overwhelmed. Was this the same girl at whose wedding I had officiated last May?

Ellen sat down and after several introductory pleasantries she recounted for me what had transpired during the past nine months.

"Life was never good for me with Steven, from day one," she calmly confessed to me. "Steven really did not marry *me.* He married the *vice-presidency of my father's oil company.* He was never interested in me. He actually loathed me. I was short, heavy, and *not* good-looking. Right after our honeymoon he actually told me so. He said that everyone had to pay a price to get ahead and I was the price that he had to pay to advance economically in life."

The smile was no longer on Ellen's face. Now, she was serious and somber. "I felt that I had been used and abused. Therefore, I made a decision. No longer would I live simply to make my parents happy—so that they could say that their 'lovely daughter' was married. Now, I decided, I was going to live to make Ellen happy.

"Therefore, right there and then I told Steven that I was going to sleep in a different bedroom and I was going to see a lawyer about a divorce. He didn't love me and I didn't love him. I told him that eventually we would only make each other miserable."

Ellen hesitated for a moment but then continued. "I also decided that I was going to change myself. I would become a leader, not a follower. I always wanted to become a doctor—so I would become a doctor. I wanted to look pretty like the other girls in high school and college—so I decided to get a physical trainer at a Health Club to shed my extra pounds. I also decided to see a Cosmetic Consultant to help me look better, and I was recommended to a woman who helped me choose clothing that would look good on me as I slimmed down and toned up my muscles. It wasn't easy but I think it was worth it."

I smiled and shook my head as if in wonderment. "You look stupendous. You look terrific." But my smile quickly dissolved and disappeared as I continued. "But I'm sorry that your marriage has fallen apart."

"But I'm not sorry," Ellen quickly interrupted me. "The whole marriage was a farce. There was no truth, no sincerity to it.

"Yes, Steven is angry now because my father fired him as soon as I told my father that I wanted a divorce and he could not change my mind. My parents pleaded with me but I emphatically stated, 'No!' Steven quickly moved to California where he is now selling clothing again but he keeps calling and telling me that it will cost my father 'a pretty penny' before he grants me a divorce. But I think that our lawyers have resolved that problem even though my father has agreed to pay a hefty sum to get me free again."

Ellen sat back in the chair, smiled once again, and went on. "I came here to tell you that I've been accepted in Medical School for the class that's beginning this summer." Her face beamed with satisfaction as she told me of her acceptance to Medical School. She looked like a little girl who had written the word "Daddy" for the first time.

I rose from my chair, held her two hands, and kissed her on the cheek. "You are terrific. I'm really proud of you."

But Ellen motioned to me to allow her to go on. "I don't know if you remember in detail what happened at my wedding." I raised my eyelids indicating that I was not sure where she was leading me, so she went on. "You entered the Veterans of Foreign Wars Hall looking like you had just run a marathon. You tried to give an excuse—you had *two* flat tires, you said, something that is very, very, very rare. You were very apologetic but no one was listening to you. Everyone in my family and Steven's family was angry—you were two hours late. *My* folks were really mad because they wanted me to be a married woman as soon as possible. They wanted this wedding on and over as soon as possible. They were not interested in any reasons for it being delayed."

Ellen twiddled with her watch that was on her left hand but once again went on. "But I listened attentively to you and said to myself, 'I wonder if this is a sign from God. God is trying to tell him not to go to the wedding, not to officiate at the wedding, not to legally unite us as husband and wife.' But I never believed in extraterrestrial communications coming from the heavens, so I brushed it off."

Ellen shook her head as if it was difficult for her to believe what she was going to say. "But now that it's nine months later I really believe that you *were* receiving a message—'Don't go.' But I want you to know that I believe that this cataclysm of a marriage was the best thing that ever happened to me. It made me change my direction in life and change my life itself. I probably would have been sixty pounds overweight now, and not forty. And I have the feeling that I would *not* have gone to Medical School because my self-esteem and self-pride were subterranean. The trauma with Steven snapped me out of my lethargy and mental sluggishness. Rabbi, thank you for officiating at my wedding even though *you* had to overcome the trauma of two flat tires and I had to overcome the trauma of getting married and living a false life. That marriage opened my eyes to reality."

Ellen rose from her chair. "Rabbi, it's getting late. I merely came here so that you would know what happened to me. But that's all in the past. The future is before me. Yes, the marriage *was* painful but I'm glad that in spite of the two flat tires you made the wedding and set me on the path of a meaningful future—to become a doctor; get married to someone who will love *me,* not my father's money; and have children with someone I will be proud to say, 'This is my husband, the father of my children.'"

Ellen quickly shook my hand, kissed me on the cheek, and was gone.

Ten years later, my wife, Toby, and I and our children went to McKeesport, Pennsylvania, to visit Toby's parents. McKeesport is only about eight miles from Pittsburgh and as I was walking in Squirrel Hill, the Jewish section of Pittsburgh, on a Sunday afternoon, I noticed a good looking young woman accompanied by a handsome man walking with a child about five years old and also pushing a baby carriage with a child of about one in it.

As we approached each other, she looked familiar to me but I could not place her. However, as we came still closer she cried out, "Rabbi Segal, Rabbi Segal," and ran toward me. She took me by surprise and introduced herself as Ellen and asked me if I remembered the two flat tires. I was literally taken aback by this encounter. I had not thought of her in the past decade after leaving Pennsylvania and moving to Oregon, New York, and then to Texas.

But Ellen was full of glee and joy, bliss and delight, and as we stood in the middle of the street she introduced me to her husband and children and told me that she was a pediatrician in Pittsburgh. She and her husband were deeply in love, she added, and her children, she went on to say, were her wealth and her treasures.

And as a postscript she informed me that she had heard from Steven five years earlier when he had called her. He had told her that he was still living in California, was married, had two children, and was the vice-president of a construction company even though he knew almost nothing about the construction business. The girl whom he married had been raised in California and had gone to Chatham College in Pittsburgh, Ellen's alma mater. Ellen added with a blossoming smile on her face, "Steven asked me if I had known his wife, Marjorie Wiesenfeld*, who was a senior at Chatham when I had been a freshman. However, I told him that I did not know her. But three months later, I received a letter from him wishing me a happy birthday and I noticed that it was written on corporate stationery where his name was listed as 'vice-president'. But I also noticed that the name of the corporation was 'Wiesenfeld Builders Inc.' and was located in a small town about two hundred miles north of Los Angeles. Below the name of the corporation was the statement, 'Builders of Shopping Malls in twenty-six states.'"

Ellen was now laughing heartily. "I wonder if the rabbi at

Steven and Marjorie's wedding had *three* flat tires going to the *Chuppah* [wedding ceremony]? I'll bet Marjorie weighs close to two-hundred pounds and her father and mother are now happy that she has a wedding ring on her finger and has two chidden."

We spoke for another five minutes and then Ellen's husband reminded her that they were already a half-hour late for a party with three other young couples. Once again, Ellen kissed me on the cheek and she and her family departed.

As they left, I silently prayed, "I hope Marjorie doesn't awake one morning and say, 'I always wanted to be a lawyer. Why have I spent the last ten years merely eating chocolates and accomplishing nothing?'"

• • • • •

Your task . . . to build a better world," God said.

> I answered, "How? The world is such a large,
> vast place, so complicated now, and I so small
> and useless am, there's nothing I can do."

But God in all His wisdom said, "Just build a better you."

—Author Unknown

CHAPTER 10

The Most Vulgar Four Letter Word In The English Dictionary

It was early in March when I received a call from Dr. Priscilla Dunkins*, the Headmistress at the Trafalgar School* in Houston. The school was a private school running the gamut from Kindergarten through grade twelve.

"Rabbi Segal, it's good to speak to you again," Dr. Dunkins blissfully intoned. "It must be at least two years since we last spoke."

Dr. Dunkins continued for about another minute asking me about my "darling and gorgeous wife" whom she had met at a reception at the Israeli Consulate and then she asked me about my "marvelous synagogue" that she had visited for a *Bar Mitzvah* for one of the students of her school.

"Is there any way I can help you?" I interjected as Dr. Dunkins rambled on.

"Well, now that you asked," the Headmistress conceded, "I believe there is a way you can help me."

Dr. Dunkins hesitated for a moment and then began to describe her problem. "We have sixty-nine students who will be graduating from our high school this year, but now that they have taken the S.A.T. tests and submitted their applications to college they no longer are motivated to study. They merely come to class and ignore their teachers. Their attitude is: 'We don't have to pass another test. Our grades have already been sent to our colleges. So, why study?'"

Again Dr. Dunkins hesitated for a moment but then immediately resumed describing her plight and dilemma. "Rabbi Segal, I would like to invite you to speak to our seniors and motivate them to be active in class again. That's what they need—motivation. I heard you speak to the *Bar Mitzvah* boy in your synagogue about the importance of helping others, not merely thinking of himself. By the look on that boy's face, you motivated him. I felt that he was ready to begin a crusade to help the underprivileged."

I attempted to tell Dr. Dunkins that the boy's eyes were aglow and he was smiling broadly because it was his *Bar Mitzvah,* a very special day in his life. Friends and relatives had come from afar; he had chanted the service extremely well; he had been very articulate in presenting his talk; right after the conclusion of the service we were going to enjoy a hearty luncheon—for the entire congregation; and that night, his parents were hosting a lavish dinner for about two hundred guests at the Double Tree Hotel, to which Dr. Dunkins had also been invited. That is why he was beaming and that is why he was radiating confidence and self-assurance. It was not I who had motivated him. It was the spirit of the weekend that had enheartened him and inspired him.

However, no matter what I said, Dr. Dunkins would not take "No" for an answer. Her ears were closed to my protests. She merely continued on with a flood of panegyrics about my ability to motivate people.

So, after listening to her for several minutes I gave in and agreed upon a date during the next week for me to address the sixty-nine seniors.

I arrived at the Trafalgar School five minutes before my scheduled talk and I was greeted by a smiling Dr. Dunkins and several of her administrative associates. We quickly went to the large auditorium where I was to address the students and I noticed that in addition to the students there were also about seventy-five adults present. Dr. Dunkins informed me that they were students' parents and teachers who had come to hear my talk.

After a glowing and commendable introduction that was more fitting for a eulogy at a cemetery than for a group of bored students at a posh high school for wealthy teenagers, I noticed that almost all the students had their heads reclining on their arms that were on their desks. They were totally oblivious to my presence.

I walked toward the front of the room where Dr. Dunkins had previously been standing and in my normal speaking voice I simply said, "Good morning, students."

However, not one student responded to my exclamation of greetings and no one budged from his, or her, position of calcification on the desk. It was as if I was in a morgue or a mortuary. I quickly turned toward Dr. Dunkins and in her forced smile I could read extreme embarrassment and discomfort.

Therefore, I once again turned toward the students and shouted, "Good morning, students," enunciating each word slowly. The results were immediate. Heads were lifted from the desks, eyes began blinking, and sixty-nine pairs of eyes were quickly focused on this intruder, this interloper, who had had the gall and effrontery to waken them from their lethargy and drowsiness.

I had their attention for a moment and I knew that I was going to quickly lose it unless I dropped a "bombshell" in their midst. So, with a smile of contentment written all over my face I asked the students to simply do three very brief things for me. Firstly, I asked them to take out a piece of paper and put it in front of them.

I could see anger and resentment written all over their faces. "We don't know this rabbi and we don't want to know him. Who invited him here anyway?" However, in the midst of grumbling and whining they slowly followed my instruction and each student put a sheet of paper in front of him or her.

Then, with a warm grin on my face I asked each student to take out a pen or pencil and put his or her gender—male or female—in writing at the top of the page, and I added, "You don't have to write out the entire word. You may merely place an 'M' or an 'F' at the top of the page," and I quickly and pedantically added, "Please don't copy from your neighbor." To this last comment about a dozen students let go with a slow, "Ha-ha, Ho-ho," and one student raised his hand and asked, "What do you write if you're both F *and* M?"

I could see Dr. Dunkins internally raging, a number of parents placing their hands over their eyes in disbelief that this question had actually been raised, and still more parents smirking in obvious uneasiness and discomfort. The students, however, broke out and exploded into convulsions and hysteria, and it took about fifteen seconds for them to settle them—but at least, now, I knew they were alive.

I did not remonstrate or castigate the questioner. With a straight face I merely replied, "That young man or young woman should write an M in the right hand, top part of the paper and should also write an F in the left hand, top of the paper." Once again there was an outburst by the students. They had thought I would easily become bothered and upended and flustered but the opposite had occurred. I had merely rolled with their punches and joined them in their jocular response.

The momentum existed and I did not want to lose it. Therefore, I quickly said, "I want you to write just one more thing on that page." I shook my head from right to left as if I was not sure whether my next request was a proper one or an improper one, and then I went on. "I have a feeling that many of the parents and members of the staff may feel offended and slighted by this request—but I feel it is necessary. I merely ask for their indulgence, forbearance, and patience."

I looked all around the room. Dr. Dunkins had doubt and puzzlement written all over her face and the parents and staff looked as if they were asking themselves, "What's this guy up to?"

As the students stared at me and as the adults did likewise I once again added a comment of propitiation, appeasement, and conciliation. "Please forgive me if I offend any of the parents, staff, or students. My next request is made with no malice aforethought. It is merely stated to help me in my talk."

I could now see several beads of perspiration on Dr.

Dunkins' forehead, but I went on. "Students, on your papers I want you to now write only one word. That word should be the most vulgar, the most obscene, the most disquieting, the most vile, the most foul, the most lewd, and the most vomiting four-letter word that you know. It must be a four-letter word—really disgusting and obscene. It should not be a five-letter word or a three-letter word. It must be a four-letter word."

The students initially began looking amongst themselves. They obviously did not believe what their ears had heard and one bellowed forth, "Do you really mean this?"

"Yes," I strongly replied as I saw and heard smiles and snickers, laughter and giggles erupting among the students as they wrote their four-letter words on their papers.

However, I also noticed that perspiration had now quickly enveloped Dr. Dunkins' entire forehead. She quickly approached me and whispered, "Rabbi, is this really necessary? You're embarrassing the parents and teachers. We have to rise above the students, not lower ourselves below their level."

It was also obvious to me that the parents in the audience were now talking amongst themselves and I was quite positive that the women were not exchanging cake recipes.

I turned to Dr. Dunkins and whispered, "You asked me to motivate them. Please let me go on while I have their attention. At least we all know now that they are breathing."

Once again, I turned to the students. "Don't copy from your neighbors," I instructed them, and again there was an eruption of laughter. I went around the room collecting the papers and then stood in front of the blackboard.

"Maybe I really shouldn't do this," I sighed as I picked up a piece of chalk, "but I am going to write *my* most vulgar, obscene, disgusting, vile, foul, lewd, and vomiting four-letter English word on the board."

I could see tension, stress, and strain written all over the adults' faces. Then I raised my chalk and wrote quickly in large letters, "CAN'T," and shouted, "'CAN'T'—that is the most vulgar, obscene, disgusting, vile, foul, lewd, and vomiting four-letter word in the English language. You've got to eliminate that vulgar word from your vocabulary. You CAN do anything you really want to do and is of interest to you. Never give up. Cross that word 'CAN'T' out of your dictionaries."

Immediately, I could hear sighs of relief from the parents and faculty, but I could simultaneously hear statements of disbelief from the students. "You must be kidding;" "You're joking;" "You're pulling my leg."

But I had their attention and I went on to speak to them for about a half-hour about the importance of never accepting defeat but *always* giving one's maximum to every effort undertaken. I attempted to do this by citing examples.

One of the illustrations that captivated their attention was the one in which I asked them, "Tell me who this is. I'll tell you twelve things about his life. *You* tell me who you think it is when you think you know his name.

#1 He failed in business in '31.
#2 He was defeated running for the legislature in '32.

I had the attention of the students but most of them were merely contorting their faces as if to say, "Who's he talking about?" But I went on.

#3 He failed again in business in '34.
#4 His sweetheart, his fiancée, died in '35.

A handful of random answers came forth from the students but none were even close. So, again, I continued on.

#5 He had a nervous breakdown in '36.
#6 He was defeated in a political election in '38.
#7 He was defeated in his run for Congress in '43.

Sporadically, as I reeled off one clue after another, wild guesses were again shouted forth by the students but I continually told them, "Sorry," and after each attempt at an answer I would go on again.

#8 Once again he was defeated in a run for Congress in '46.

#9 If that was not bad enough, he lost again in an attempt for election to Congress in '48.
#10 He then ran for a Senate seat but lost in '55.
#11 Then he ran for the vice-presidency but lost in '56.

One young man rose quickly and triumphantly from his seat and cried out at the top of his voice, "I know it. I know it. It was Estes Kefauver. He ran with Adlai Stevenson, the second time Stevenson ran on the Democratic ticket—and they lost. I got it. I got it. I learned it in my American history class last semester."

Almost all of the students began shouting and whooping it up and bellowing their congratulations and compliments to this student, but one short student wearing thick glasses grimaced, pointed his hand at the student who had called out the answer, and softly commented, "That's ridiculous. Kefauver did not fail in business and his fiancée did not die and he did not have a nervous breakdown.

All eyes were quickly concentrated on this one student and then on me. I smiled and remarked, "That young man is correct," and again I went on.

#12 He once again ran for the Senate but lost in '58.

Students' heads were shaking indicating that they did not have the foggiest idea of whom I was talking. Then I smiled and said, "It should be obvious that this man was born under a black cloud. However in *his* vocabulary and in *his* English dictionary the phrases 'I give up,' 'I give in,' or the word 'CAN'T' did not exist."

Immediately, several students cried out, "Who was it? Who was it?"

I smiled again and replied, "I think you'll guess it now. He was the sixteenth president of the United States."

At once, seven or eight students cried out, "Abe Lincoln, Abe Lincoln."

"That's right," I cried out in response. "Lincoln never saw the glass as half empty. He always saw it as half full. Lincoln never concentrated on the thorns on the stem. He always focused his eyes on the rose."

I added a few more examples during my half-hour talk and often I engaged several of the students in a dialogue. When the talk was over, at least a dozen of the students approached me and told me how much they enjoyed the talk. Several even asked me to come back again.

Even Dr. Dunkins and a number of the parents, with smiles plastered all over their faces, approached me to congratulate me. Dr. Dunkins even added, "You had me scared for a few moments," and all the parents laughed and chuckled in agreement.

After all the adults left, I began looking through the papers the students had submitted to me. Sixty-eight of the papers had written on them the same word. It was the four-letter word that I thought they would write. Only one of the sixty-nine papers had written on it "CAN'T," in big capital letters.

I then noticed that one student had remained in his seat while all the other students had gone off to their next classes.

His eyes were squinting but his head was focused on a book in front of him on his desk, *All Quiet On The Western Front* by Erich Maria Remarque.

"Aren't you going to be late for your next class?" I inquired, even though I merely posed that question to begin a conversation.

"No," he replied as he opened his eyes widely and stared at me. "I have a study period now."

"I see you're reading *All Quiet On The Western Front*. I also read that when I was in high school."

"This is the third time I've read this book," he answered.

"Why have you read it three times?" I asked as I raised my shoulders and eyelids indicating a lack of understanding.

The senior breathed in heavily before answering as if implying that any person with common sense could understand that Remarque was an extra-special author. "Remarque's works are very realistic. In this book he clearly describes, with deep compassion, the suffering and the courage and the comradeship of the common soldiers—not of the High Command but of the common soldiers. He himself was a soldier during World War I and he wrote of his personal recollections of that bitter war. In a sense, it's the German *Red Badge of Courage*. He describes war as General Sherman described it, but most people only remember the last words of Sherman, not his first words."

He then stared at me as if his gaze was piercing me. "Rabbi, do *you* know Sherman's first words before his famous statement, 'War is hell'?"

"No, I don't," I replied as I shook my head in embarrassment.

The young man snorted, "Well, neither does anyone else in my class and I would swear that neither does my teacher—because it's not in our textbook."

There was a five-second pause and he said nothing more and merely arose to leave. So I asked him, "What else did Sherman say?"

"I'm glad you asked," the student commented with a big grin on his face. "Sherman made his 'War is hell' statement fourteen years after the end of the Civil War. But preceding that statement were his words, 'I am tired and sick of war. Its glory is all moonshine. It is only those who have neither fired a shot nor heard the shrieks and groans of the wounded who cry aloud for blood, more vengeance, more desolation.' It was after that introduction that Sherman said, 'War is hell'."

I shook my head in appreciation of his comment.

Once again he began walking toward the door but he abruptly stopped. "Rabbi," he again stated as he turned his head toward me, "Did you ever read *The Road Back* that describes the miseries of postwar Germany and its returning soldiers after World War I? It's the sequel to *All Quiet on the Western Front*."

"No," again I replied, shaking my head from right to left.

"I think you'd enjoy it," he emphatically stated with a healthy smile on his face as if he had just checkmated me.

"And, by the way," he continued, "I'll bet all but one of the papers you collected had written on them the obscene word that you expected to get and only one had written on it the word 'can't'."

I smiled, pointed my index finger at him, and softly stated, "*You* were the one who wrote 'can't'?"

"Of course," he answered as the words began to cascade from his lips. "These kids live for only one thing—to have fun, fun, and more fun. If they did not get an assignment they would never open a book. They live for parties and cars, good times and vacations, sex and money, and almost all their parents give in to their every whim and fancy. They call me a 'nerd' because I like to read books and go to the symphony and opera."

Again he hesitated for a moment and I quickly interjected, "What about *your* parents? Do they want you to always read books and go to the symphony and opera or would they rather you also socially associate with your classmates?"

The young student merely stared at me as if *I* had said an obscene word or phrase and he walked toward the door saying, "I'm late for my next class. I must admit that I enjoyed your talk—even though I don't think it'll have any effect on those whom you addressed," and he quietly exited the room.

I was quite confused because he had just told me that this was his study period and now he had left me because he stated that he was late for his next class. The two statements did not synchronize with each other. However, I had a meeting at the synagogue in forty-five minutes and I was not going to become Sherlock Holmes to quickly unravel his contradictory comments.

As I was leaving the school, Dr. Dunkins once again saw me. "Rabbi Segal, once again I want to thank you for a most inspiring talk. Even if you only touched the soul of one of our students, to make him or her more serious about their studies, that would have been satisfactory. Thank you again, and I think you moved several of the students."

As I shook her hand again and began to depart, Dr. Dunkins called out, "One moment, please," and she approached me again. "I saw you talking to Edward Hubbert* one of our students, who remained back as all of the other students left the room." She shook her head as if indicating confusion. "He's a very bright boy but socially he does not mix with any of the students. We've tried and tried but the kids don't seem to want to be with him and he obviously does not want to be with them."

I shrugged my shoulders as if I too was confused. "We were having an interesting conversation about the author Erich Maria Remarque," I commented, "when I merely asked him about his parents, and quickly that was the end of the conversation."

Dr. Dunkins' head swiveled on her shoulders as if to indicate that I had committed a faux pas. "Rabbi Segal, Eddie's father was a First Lieutenant in the army and was sent to Vietnam just after Eddie was born." Dr. Dunkins hesitated for a moment, then proceeded. "His father was killed in Vietnam."

I noticed that Dr. Dunkins rubbed her eye. At first, I thought she had a speck of dust in her eye but it quickly became obvious that she was wiping away a tear. "It was not easy for his mother to raise Eddie. She married another army officer about three years later and he truly accepted Eddie as his own. But, unfortunately, after being married to him for about four years he was killed in a military training accident. That truly unraveled not only Eddie's mother but also Eddie. And then, to add insult to injury, Eddie's mother was killed in an auto accident about five years ago when she was returning from a vacation in Austin. A drunk driver broadsided their car, hitting it on his mother's side. She was dead before they could get her to the hospital while Eddie was barely scratched—but he saw his mother killed before his very eyes.

"That was the third major trauma he experienced in his short life. Now he lives with his mother's brother and his wife, his uncle and aunt. But they don't get along very well. Eddie loves culture and education while his uncle, he told me, enjoys sports, gambling, and whiskey. It's not a good match. However, thank God for his aunt. She attempts to be a tranquilizer between Eddie and his uncle. We gave him a full scholarship and that's how he attends our school."

Once again Dr. Dunkins rubbed her eyes but this time she used a handkerchief.

"Eddie is very bright," she continued, "but his social growth has been stunted by those three major tragedies. Unfortunately, eighteen year old teenagers, both male and female, do not have patience to help their peers who have experienced such major problems. Most of our students come from well-to-do homes and life has been handed to them on a silver platter. Eddie, unfortunately, has been confronted with obstacle after obstacle on *his* road of life."

A smile quickly appeared on Dr. Dunkins' face. "However, I hope that next year when he goes to college, and he has received a full scholarship to Tulane as a pre-med student, that life will change for him."

Dr. Dunkins looked at her watch and broadly opened her eyes and mouth as if exasperated. "Rabbi, I'm already five minutes late to a meeting. I must leave. Thanks again for the talk," and she quickly departed.

As I left the school building and entered the parking lot I was surprised to notice Eddie standing there reading a paperback. He looked at me and half-whispered to me, "Rabbi would you mind if I called you to make an appointment to speak to you."

An overjoyed smile enveloped my face. "Of course, Eddie, of course. Here is my card. Please call me. Let's talk." He put the card in his pocket and off he went, back into the school building.

As Eddie disappeared into the building I thought of the Talmudic statement (Sanhedrin 37a), *"Kol ha-me-ka-yem nefesh ah-chot . . . k'eelu ke-yem olam malay,"* "He who saves one life . . . is as if he has saved the entire world."

• • • • •

I met a little maid
    A rosy burden bearing;
"Is he not heavy?" I said
    As past me she was hurrying.
She looked at me with grave, sweet eyes,
    This fragile little mother,
And answered in swift surprise:
    "O, no Sir. He's my brother."

—*Author Unknown*

Chapter 11

"What's OK For Me Is Not OK for You"

When I arrived at Beth Yeshurun Congregation in 1965, my Senior Rabbi, Rabbi Malev, informed me that on Thanksgiving Day our congregation was to be part of a group of churches and two synagogues in our area that annually participated in a non-denominational Interfaith Thanksgiving Service.

Almost all the ministers, priests, and rabbis in our area, long ago had agreed that the one-hour service would primarily be a patriotic service indicating our thanks to the United States for giving liberty and freedom, opportunity and independence to all those living within its shores regardless of religious beliefs, places of origin, gender, size of one's bank account, or the extent of one's education. We wanted to sing loudly and proudly, "My country, 'tis of thee, Sweet land of liberty." We wanted to express our thanks for the benefits that had been heaped upon us by our nation for living in this land.

Every year, the service would be conducted in a different house of worship, generally two years in a church and one year in a synagogue. The reason for this was obvious—Jews were a small minority in Houston, about one and a half percent of the population, even though most of the Jews of Houston were located in our Meyerland area and environs.

When this program was initially created, I was told, all the clergy agreed that the prayers recited and the music played and chanted would be supervised by a small committee. A Catholic, a Protestant, and a Jew would oversee the selections submitted so that only those that could be used in all churches and synagogues would be part of the program. No one was to be made uncomfortable by participating in, or attending, these services.

One year, I was put in charge of the program because the program was to be held at Beth Yeshurun, and the selections were made quite quickly. A rabbi was chosen to give the invocation, several patriotic statements were to be read by different clergymen, a Protestant minister was to deliver the main talk, the Beth Yeshurun Cantor, Cantor Wagner, and his choir were to chant patriotic hymns, and the benediction was to be pronounced by a Protestant minister. Afterwards, Beth Yeshurun was to host a coffee, punch, cookies, and cake reception.

Thanksgiving Day was sunny and cool and the 11 A.M. service was very well attended. Almost every seat in the sanctuary was occupied. Approximately one thousand came to this service—both Jews and Christians.

Cantor Wagner and his choir were excellent. They sounded as if it was Yom Kippur because he had about two dozen in his choir and they sang as if they had practiced for two months. So, too, the readings were most apropos and the speaker's talk was entitled, "What America Means to Me." He told how his parents had migrated from Eastern Europe to the United States after World War I where their income was barely enough to support them with food on the table and a roof over their heads. But in the United States "a miracle" occurred. Even though his parents did not speak English when they arrived, his father went to night school, learned to speak English, found employment in the construction industry, supported his wife and three children, and eventually he did something that neither he nor his parents had ever dreamed of. He sent all his children to college. One became a lawyer, one a teacher, and he became a minister. He praised the United States as a nation where dreams could be realized, hopes could be fulfilled, and everyone could worship God as he saw fit. When he concluded his talk he received an ovation that lasted almost two minutes. He had unified the congregation that consisted of worshipers of many religions. He stressed what united us, not what divided us. He emphasized what we had in common, not what separated us. Smiles were apparent on the faces of the vast majority of the congregants.

Then, the congregation was asked to rise for the benediction, and the minister, Rev. Don Wadsworth*, came to the lectern as the Holy Ark was opened by the President of our congregation exposing the thirteen Torahs (the parchment scrolls containing the five Books of Moses) and the beautiful artistic mosaic of the Burning Bush under which was the Hebrew inscription (Exodus 3:2), *"V'ha-sneh ay-neh-nu oo-kul,"* ("The Bush was not consumed").

Rev. Wadsworth bowed his head and pontifically intoned: "O God, Thou who rules over the heavens and the earth, creator of the universe and humankind, today in the United States is Thanksgiving Day—and we are truly thankful. We are thankful for all the blessings that you have heaped upon us—blessings of family and friends; blessings of good health and soundness of mind; blessings of being able to support ourselves and send our children to college; blessings of being able to worship You and pray to You in any language that is understandable to us and in any church or synagogue that is meaningful to us; blessings of enjoying love from our wives, husbands, and children, and being able to reciprocate that love to them; blessings of being able to travel all over our nation, all fifty states, and be welcome in all of them as Americans; blessings of having jobs or professions that enable us to make a living and support our families. O God, we are truly blessed—because we live in the United States of America.

"O God, there is no other country like our country; there is no other nation like our nation.

"Therefore O God, we pray to You that our nation will always remain strong and will always be the bulwark to grant freedom and liberty to all who live within its borders. May we always turn toward You, not only when the sun is shining but also when the clouds are dark. May You always be beside us, to walk with us, support us, and encourage us throughout our lives, and may we always be devoted to You no matter what our circumstance may be."

Rev. Wadsworth hesitated for a moment, lifted his bowed head so that he now looked out into the congregation, raised his hands toward the heavens, and in a booming voice proclaimed, "We pray in the name of Jesus Christ our Lord, Amen."

Many Amens and Hallelujahs echoed forth from the congregation but they were not as numerous as the Amens and Hallelujahs that had been heard after the conclusion of the prayers and statements made by the previous clergymen. It was obvious that at least half of the congregation had not responded, was mute, silent, and even aphasic to the minister's final benediction.

The service was quickly concluded and I invited the entire congregation to the reception in our auditorium. A flood of people ascended the steps to the pulpit to congratulate our speaker and also those who had participated in the service. However, I noticed that those who extended complimentary comments to Rev. Wadsworth were almost exclusively Christian. I only saw one Jew shaking his hand and complimenting him.

When almost all had left the pulpit, I approached Rev. Wadsworth. "I think the service was an excellent one and was well accepted by those who attended," I commented to him.

With a broad smile of satisfaction, he shook his head in agreement. "You are absolutely correct." He put the copy of his prayer in his pocket and was about to descend from the pulpit to join the congregants at the reception.

"Do you think I could get a copy of your benediction?" I matter of factly asked him.

His smile broadened even more widely. "Of course, Jack," was his response. "In fact," he added as he handed me his copy of his prayer, "you can have my copy. I have a carbon copy in my office."

"Thanks," I replied, and I quickly opened it to peruse it, but at the end of the prayer I noticed that the words "We pray in the name of Jesus Christ our Lord" were not present.

"How did you like my benediction?" Rev. Wadsworth asked.

I looked up at him. "I thought it was powerful. You truly stated why we should be thankful today and why we should bless the United States." But I breathed in heavily, not knowing whether I should, or should not, continue—but I did. "However, I do not understand why you concluded your prayer at a non-denominational service in a Jewish synagogue with the words, "We pray in the name of Jesus Christ *our* Lord," and I emphasized and stressed the word *"OUR."* "You know that Jesus is not the Jewish Lord."

Once again Rev. Wadsworth smiled expansively. "Jack, it is true that this was to be a non-denominational service. But 'non-denominational' does *not* mean that you have to violate and transgress your own religious principles."

Rev. Wadsworth looked me straight in the eye. His smile had quickly been erased from his face. "Jack," he continued, "the New Testament, to *me,* is the holy word of God—and *I* follow it to the letter. It is *my* religious map, *my* religious radar screen. It tells *me* what to do and how to do it. And in the Book of Hebrews, Chapter 7, verse 25, the Bible says, 'Wherefore he is able also to save them to the uttermost *that come unto God by him,'*" and he emphasized the last phrase. "That verse is to the point. It does not have to be interpreted. When you want to 'come unto God,' it's got to be 'by him.' It's got to be through Jesus. It's got to be by invoking Jesus' name."

Then Rev. Wadsworth pointed his index finger at me and went on. "Jack, we believe without question or hesitation in Jesus' statement in John, chapter 14, verse 6: 'Jesus saith unto him, I am the way, the truth, and the life: no man cometh unto the Father but by me.'

"Jack," Rev. Wadsworth squared his jaw and gritted his teeth as if he was not sure whether he should continue—but he did. "Would you want me to violate my religious way of life merely to have people smile at me and pat me on the back? I wouldn't be able to face myself in the mirror to shave each morning if I did that."

Then he snapped his fingers and enthusiastically went on. "Jack, the New Testament is the foundation stone of my life. In Matthew, chapter 28, verses 19 and 20, Jesus says, 'Go ye therefore, and teach *ALL* nations'", and he extended and stressed the word *"ALL."* Without taking a breath, Rev. Wadsworth went on, "Jack, listen to the remainder of the sentence—'baptizing them in the name of the Father, and of the Son, and of the Holy Ghost: teaching them to observe all things whatsoever *I* have commanded you. . . .'"

Rev. Wadsworth went on, "Jack, you Jewish people have 613 Commandments in your Bible. You call them *mitzvot*. You wouldn't violate them if I asked you to transgress them. So, too, I have a *mitzvah* to preach Jesus whenever I can. I must admit that last night when I originally wrote my benediction I omitted the last line 'We pray in the name of Jesus Christ our Lord.' But when I came to that point in my prayer right here in the synagogue I felt as if Jesus Christ himself was talking to me and encouraging me to add that statement—and I did. I felt that I would be fulfilling *my mitzvah, my* commandment, and helping your Jewish membership see the truth."

I shook my head from right to left indicating my disagreement, but Rev. Wadsworth went on. "Allow me to go on, Jack. John [4:22] told us, 'Salvation is of the Jews.' Do you know what he meant?" He did not wait for me to respond. He merely continued on. "He meant that salvation came from someone who was a Jew—Jesus Christ, and that is important."

Again, Rev. Wadsworth did not give me a chance to utter a comment, a response, or a rebuttal. It was as if he was "on a roll" and he was not going to "give up the table" to anyone. "Jack, Paul described this so vividly when he said [*Galatians* 2:15-16], 'We who are Jews by nature [by birth] and not sinners of the Gentiles, knowing that a man is not justified by the works of the law, but by the faith of Jesus Christ, even we have believed in Jesus Christ, that we might be justified by the faith of Christ, and not the works of the law: for by the works of the law shall no flesh be justified.'"

Rev. Wadsworth's eyes were now squinting. It was as if he had totally forgotten the coffee and the cookies at the reception.

It sounded to me as if he was on a crusade. I still did not have a chance to interject a word. He was no longer pausing between sentences. It was like being in Galveston during the summer and watching one wave after the other roll in.

"Jack, if you saw a poor person who did not have a roof over his head or a morsel of bread to feed his family and you had a charitable foundation consisting of five million dollars, wouldn't you give him one thousand dollars to get an apartment, get some food for his family, and help him get a job? Well, that's the way we look at Jesus. He is our charitable foundation and there are loads of people in this world who are lacking sustenance. We are offering our help to assist those people to achieve eternal life—and there is only one way to accomplish that, and that is through Jesus."

The minister grabbed my hand and still did not take a deep breath. "Jack, to us, Jesus Christ is an insurance policy. We call it 'The Jesus Christ Eternal Life Insurance Policy' to help *you* achieve that eternal life. And, by the way, there is only one company that deals with that policy and it is the Christian Church. Jack, that's why I added the postscript to my prayer, to help all those who still did not know about that policy," and he grinned expansively.

For a moment, Rev. Wadsworth hesitated and it was then that I jumped in. "You are absolutely correct. There is only one company, the Christian Church, that carries 'The Jesus Christ Eternal Life Insurance Policy.' That is the policy that will get *you and your members* eternal life. But we Jews searched around and I must tell you that *we* found another company that deals with Eternal Life policies. It's called 'The Torah and *Mitzvot* Company' and it too sells an 'Eternal Life Policy' that fits *our* budget and *our* needs—and we are very satisfied with it."

I did not hesitate to take a breath because I felt that the Reverend would quickly monopolize the conversation again. "In the United States there is the New York Life Insurance Company and the Metropolitan Life Insurance Company. *Both* sell life insurance and each company has thousands of clients. Each one is a good company and it would be *chutzpah* and temerity on the behalf of one of those companies to say, 'We are the only company that truly sells life insurance.' Both have good policies. As a Jew I say to you, 'You should stick with your company but please allow us to stick with our company. We have been satisfied with it in the past and I am quite positive that we will continue to be satisfied with it in the future.'"

It was obvious that Rev. Wadsworth was about to jump in but again I did not stop to take a deep breath. I merely went on like the Mississippi River. "We Jews look upon Christianity as a good religion. It's like vanilla ice cream. However, we look upon Judaism as another good religion, chocolate ice cream. In fact, we look upon Islam as another good religion, strawberry ice cream. All we Jews ask is that we be permitted to eat our chocolate ice cream without being forced or coerced or pressured to eat vanilla or strawberry ice cream. We love the taste of chocolate. In fact, we are chocoholics. We *don't* want to change. We *don't* want to give up our favorite flavor. We *don't* want to modify our ice cream habit. All we ask of everyone is that we be allowed to enjoy life the way *we* want to enjoy it."

I could see Rev. Wadsworth's eyes rolling in despair. It was as if he had been filling with water what he thought was a jug but now he realized that it was only a sieve. Instead of retaining the water it was quickly leaking out.

But I felt obliged to add one more comment, a theological one. Rev. Wadsworth had been quoting verbatim so many statements from the New Testament that I felt it was necessary for me to interject at least one meaningful statement from our Jewish Holy Scriptures.

"But there is another reason why we Jews feel compelled to stick with what Christians call our *Old* Testament and not embrace the Christian *New* Testament with its new theological concepts. I can never forget the words of our prophet Jeremiah who stated in chapter 32 verse 40, *'V'cha-ra-tee la-hem brit olam,'* 'And I will make with them, with the Jews, an *everlasting* covenant.' God said to us that he would *never* change the covenant that he made with us during the time of Moses. That covenant is *'brit olam'*, an *everlasting* covenant, a *perpetual* covenant, an *eternal* covenant."

I looked straight into Rev. Wadsworth's eyes and softly continued, "We believe that God *always* tells the truth. If he told us more than twenty-five hundred years ago through his prophet Jeremiah that his bond with us will never be changed, then we believe that it will never be changed. We do not ask others to accept that premise. We merely ask others to allow *us* to accept that hypothesis."

It was obvious to me as I gazed at Rev. Wadsworth that I was getting nowhere. I wanted to quickly terminate the dialogue, so I asked him, "Rev. Wadsworth, might I ask you a question?"

"Yes."

"Next year the service is scheduled to be held in your church."

"Yes."

"You will be inviting clergymen to participate in the service. I have a friend that I would like you to invite to give the benediction."

Rev. Wadsworth smiled, "Of course, what's his name?"

I waited for a moment then replied, "Sami Farouk."

Instantly, Rev. Wadsworth's eyes blinked sharply. "Is he Catholic, Protestant, or Jewish? I never heard of him."

"Neither," I sheepishly replied. "He's a Moslem. He's a clergyman of the religion of Islam."

Rev. Wadsworth shook his shoulders and gritted his teeth. "I didn't think we were expanding our clerical invitations to invite other religions, but if that is your wish, Jack, that will be done. The Rev. Sami Farouk will deliver the benediction next year."

But before he could leave the pulpit to enjoy the reception I added one more question. "Do you know how he recites a benediction?"

Rev. Wadsworth squinted. "No, I've never attended a Moslem Service."

Again I smiled and continued. "Well, let me tell you because I *have* attended Moslem programs."

Doubt was written all over Rev. Wadsworth's face. "Well, tell me what he does or what he says."

"Well, they always end it with the words, 'We pray in the name of Allah—*Allah achbar,* May Allah be praised."

The minister contorted his face. "Exactly who is Allah?"

"That's the name of the Moslem God," I quickly responded.

"It's *not* Jesus. It's *not* what you call Yahweh or Jehovah. It's the Moslem God called Allah and they have a different concept of God. And they also add that Mohammed is their most important prophet."

Rev. Wadsworth vigorously shook his head indicating his disapproval of my suggestion. "Jack, you and I don't believe in Allah. I think it would be sacrilegious to inject a God into our Thanksgiving Service that would be in opposition to almost all in attendance. The members of my church would be infuriated. They would be incensed. My phone would be ringing off the hook as soon as I returned home—and rightfully so. Allah belongs in a mosque, not in a church or a synagogue."

Rev. Wadsworth once again energetically shook his head from right to left indicating his displeasure and disapprobation. "Jack, I'll OK any request you make but not one that runs counter to my religious beliefs. We don't want Allah in my church. I'll support your friend to worship his God in *his* house of worship but not in *my* church in the midst of *my* congregants. None of us would feel comfortable."

I breathed in heavily, expanded my chest, and then exhaled. "If that is so, why did *you* end *your* benediction in a Jewish synagogue the way *you* did? This was supposed to be a non-denominational service. Didn't you know that Jews attending the Service would feel uncomfortable with this denominational prayer? If a Jew voluntarily attends a service in a church, he knows what the center of attention will be—Jesus. But when he attends a non-denominational Thanksgiving Service in a synagogue he expects it to be non-denominational and not a Christian Service.

"I believe strongly in the proverb that says, 'What's good for the goose is good for the gander,' or what Rabbi Hillel said in the Talmud two thousand years ago [Shabbat 31a], 'That what you do not want your neighbor to do to *you, you* do not do to your neighbor.'"

Rev. Wadsworth continued shaking his head indicating his disagreement with my comment. "Jack" he quickly spewed forth as if indicating a strong desire to terminate the conversation. "I think the coffee at the reception is getting cold and I'll bet all the good cookies and cakes have already been consumed." A false smile enveloped Rev. Wadsworth's face as he added the final exclamation mark to our conversation. "Jack, I'll discuss the question of the Rev. Sami Farouk with some of my colleagues and I'll get back to you in a few weeks. We still have plenty of time to next Thanksgiving Day. I'm sure you'll agree."

He then took me by the arm, escorted me off the pulpit, and walked with me to the reception.

Three months later, in February, I received an unexpected letter from Rev. Wadsworth. It read:

> Dear Jack,
>
> Several months have already gone by since our Thanksgiving conversation. Your request that Sami Farouk deliver the benediction is a valid one. He obviously is a friend of yours. None of my colleagues, however, seem to know him or have ever heard of him. He is also not in the phone book. He either has an unlisted number, which is unlikely for a minister, or he probably lives out of town.
>
> Therefore, I am purposely writing to you before you extend an invitation to him because our committee met last night and it was decided that we are going to be obliged to terminate the non-denominational Thanksgiving Service. Many of my colleagues stated that their church members felt they were being ignored. They wanted to have their own Christian church services on Thanksgiving Day. It should be obvious that a storm is brewing and I have always believed in nipping the problem in the bud.
>
> Yes, I truly enjoyed the years we had our church-synagogue services. But, unfortunately, beginning this year the joint services will be ended because the churches will be conducting their own.
>
> I hope I will see you at other functions.
>
> God bless you.
>
> Sincerely,
> Dr. Don Wadsworth

I do not know why, but I had a strong feeling that my conversation with Rev. Wadsworth marked the beginning of the end of these services. The non-denominational Thanksgiving Service was the brainchild of one of the Houston rabbis. A Jew had conceived it and given birth to it, and rabbis had nurtured it throughout the years. I felt that my conversation with Rev. Wadsworth was, unfortunately, the *coup de grace* to terminate these well attended services.

However, I must admit that his letter got me "off the hook." I did not know a Rev. Sami Farouk. I never heard of a Rev. Sami Farouk. And Rev. Sami Farouk never existed. He was a figment of my imagination. I merely spontaneously "gave birth" to Rev. Sami Farouk on Thanksgiving Day because I was quite positive that Rev. Wadsworth would not be happy having a Moslem deliver the benediction in his church. I merely wanted him to realize how insensitive he was to Jewish congregants in a synagogue. However, had I been wrong, I would have had to search for a "Rev. Sami Farouk" or eat crow instead of turkey the next Thanksgiving Day.

• • • • •

1) "Politeness costs nothing, but gains everything."
—Lady Mary Wortley Montagu

2) Good manners may in Seven Words be found:
Forget Yourself and think of Those around.
—Arthur Guiterman

Chapter 12

Even An Enemy Should Not Be Punished In A "Cruel And Unusual" Manner

Even though Beth Yeshurun has always been a very large congregation and the daily rabbinic duties were manifold and numerous I never turned away any person who asked me to perform a Jewish function. I never asked anyone whether he, or she, was a member of my congregation. If a person needed aid or assistance I always answered in the affirmative. Even if I was extremely busy I always fit that individual into my daily activities.

I remember the call very well. It had been "pouring cats and dogs" for three days and it was still "coming down in buckets." The caller sounded young, as if he was in his early twenties. "Rabbi Segal," he softly stated with a sad intonation in his voice, "I hope you can help my family."

He spoke softly but deliberately. "I'm a Graduate Student at the University of Texas and my younger brother is a sophomore there. We were raised in Oak Hill*, about ten miles from Sealy, and my folks have lived there since they were married twenty-six years ago. My father developed a lucrative business there selling tractors and other farm equipment."

The young man breathed in heavily, hesitated for a moment, and with a quiver in his voice continued. "This morning my mother told me my father awoke as usual at 5:30 A.M. He walked over to her bedroom and told her that he was not feeling well." Again he hesitated for a moment and then continued. "I guess you're wondering why my mother and father did not share the same bedroom. Well, the reason is because they did not get along with each other. They're in the process of a divorce but neither of them wants to leave the house." He then sobbed, "And within thirty minutes he was dead. The doctor said it was a massive heart attack."

"I'm so very sorry," I instinctively and sympathetically commented.

"Rabbi," the young man went on, "my name is Barry Green* and my mother is Gwen*. You don't know us because we don't belong to your synagogue. However, the reason is simple—we're about sixty miles from Houston. It was always too far from us to join your synagogue.

"But we need a favor," he went on. "My father and my brother and I are Jewish and we want him to be buried according to the Jewish tradition. Could you do a favor for us and officiate at his funeral?"

"How is your mother doing?" I asked instinctively.

Once again there was a pause. It was as if Barry did not hear my question. So I asked it again, "How is your mother doing?"

Barry's reply was almost a whisper. It sounded as if he was ashamed to reveal a secret. "My mother," he finally mumbled, "doesn't want to get involved with his burial. It hurts me bitterly to say this but during the past two years she has developed a deep hatred and animosity for my father." Again Barry halted. But then it sounded as if he amassed sufficient energy to remove a ponderous burden that was weighing heavily on his conscience. "Two years ago," Barry blurted forth, "my mother unexpectedly went to my father's office late one evening to get some money. My father had told her that he was spending the evening in Houston with some business associates to clinch a big business deal. However, when she opened the door she discovered that my father was not in Houston but in his office, and he was not clinching a business deal with business associates but having an affair with his twenty-two year old secretary, a girl that *I* had dated in high school."

I could now hear anger in Barry's voice. "My mother," Barry professed, "refused to have anything to do with him since then. The only time she talks to him is through her lawyer, and the divorce is a very messy one. My father is very rich and my mother wants to get every penny possible from him. She feels as if she gave him her life and he betrayed her.

"My brother and I would like to bury him in the small Jewish cemetery in Oak Hill a day after tomorrow. We can come in to Houston tomorrow to speak to you about our father and make arrangements with the Funeral Home. My mother, of course, will not come in. She does not want to have anything to do with his burial even though legally she is still his wife and has the final say about everything."

Barry was now speaking in a quicker tempo. "My mother initially said that she wanted him cremated and his ashes spread over the Gulf of Mexico so that nothing of him remained. 'Let the fish have a good meal,' she said. But I told her that that was against Jewish tradition. Judaism was opposed to cremation and insisted that a person be buried in a Jewish cemetery.

"She then countered by insisting that my father be buried in your cemetery in Houston; however, my brother and I persisted by saying that he was our father—regardless of the terrible act he had committed—and we wanted him buried in Oak Hill. Previously we never argued with our mother but this time we were adamant and firm. My mother kept on repeating, 'How would *you* feel if when you're married for twenty-five years you'd find *your* wife in bed with a twenty-two year old stud?' However, we did not answer her question but merely continued to demand that dad be buried here—and she finally gave in."

Barry continued to speak to me for another five minutes and I told him that I would officiate at his father's funeral in Oak Hill.

That night I attempted to contact Barry's mother, Gwen, to talk to her about her husband, Alfred*. But she informed me, in no uncertain manner, that she did not want to speak to me about him. She told me that the two of them had been in the process of a divorce, an acrimonious and bitter divorce, when he died and the only information she would give me for the eulogy was that I was never to say that he loved her or he treated her well or he cared for her—or anything positive about their relationship. "Speak about the kids if you so desire," Gwen decreed, "but don't mention my name in conjunction with his. Otherwise, I'll walk out of the chapel—and I mean it." Gwen was very adamant and I knew that she was not joking. She was not issuing meaningless threats. So I told her that I would abide by her wishes.

Two days later, I drove to Oak Hill for a 3 P.M. funeral. It was still pouring. In fact, the rain was cascading down in torrents. We had not had a letup in five days. The creeks had become rivers and the rivers had been converted into oceans. I was so glad that the funeral ritual would be in the chapel and it would not be a graveside funeral.

But, then, a miracle occurred. At about 2:30 P.M. the rain began to subside and by 3 P.M. it stopped. However, the ground was still super-saturated. In fact, the undertaker told me, "Rabbi, we're going to have a problem with the burial. The grave is filled to the top with water. We'll never be able to inter the casket with Mr. Green."

I smiled and informed him that he should not worry. *I* would tell Gwen and the two sons about the flooded grave and *I* would suggest to them that we conduct the burial service in the chapel, as per schedule, and I would return the next day to Oak Hill for a private internment in the grave after the water had subsided.

The solution was immediately accepted by Alfred's two sons, but when Gwen heard this recommendation and proposal she bellowed and shrieked, "*One* funeral is even too much for him. *Two* funerals are definitely out of the question. I will *not* permit it."

I attempted to reason with her, placate her, and appease her but her reply was always the same, an emphatic and accentuated "NO!"

I shrugged my shoulders. How were we going to bury Alfred when the grave was full of water? But then I said to myself, "Instead of having a twenty minute service, I'll extend it to forty-five minutes by reading extra chapters from the book of Psalms and also reading some contemporary poems." It was my hope and my prayer that by 3:45 P.M. the water in the grave would subside and the burial would be able to proceed.

About one hundred and fifty people filled the chapel, and at 2:59 P.M. the family filed into the chapel for the service. They filled the first two rows of seats. Gwen sat between Barry and Ronnie* in the front row while Alfred's parents and sister and brother, and their spouses and children, sat in the second row. Gwen only spoke to Barry and Ronnie but did not even turn in the direction of Alfred's parents or siblings.

At 3:05 I asked the "mourners" to rise for the cutting of the ribbon. It is traditional at Jewish funerals for "mourners" to attach a small black ribbon to their jackets, shirts, sweaters, blouses, or dresses and to recite a blessing as the rabbi cuts the ribbon. This is done while the "mourners" are standing, and traditionally the "mourners" are the father, mother, brother, sister, husband, wife, son or daughter. However, when I approached Gwen she was still seated and she handed back to me the ribbon with the bland comment, "This is *not* for me."

This was not the time for a theological debate. It was obvious that Gwen did not want to share any outer expression of mourning for Alfred since she was not inwardly mourning for him. However, it seemed that all eyes were focused on her. All the "mourners" were standing and wearing a small black ribbon that I was cutting—all, that is, except Gwen.

During the eulogy I spoke elaborately and profusely about Alfred's relationship with his children—how he spent time galore with them as they were growing up. I related stories about their fishing trips, hunting escapades, the University of Texas football games that they would attend together, how he regularly barbecued hamburgers for them every Sunday when they attended grammar school and high school, and how he would fly kites with them when they were children.

I also spoke about Alfred's business ventures and how he began his entrepreneurial life strapped with a mountain of student loans, but he always seemed to be in the right place at the right time and zoomed like a comet in the business stratosphere with success after success.

Then I trudged through his charitable activities, attempting to relate anecdotes how he helped each one: Red Cross, Child Builders, Special Olympics, City of Hope, Meharry Medical College, M.D. Anderson Cancer Center, Jewish Federation, American Jewish Committee, Israel Bonds, Jewish Children's Regional Service, JINSA, and so many more.

However, I did not say a word about Gwen, as per her wishes. In fact, prior to the funeral service she once again emphatically reminded me that if I even merely mentioned her name she would walk out.

I also read Psalms 15, 23, 24, 91, 121, and 130, both in the Hebrew and English, and added three contemporary poems from A. L. Alexander's book *Poems That Touch The Heart*. This was topped off by the *Ale Malay Rachamim* memorial prayer both in the Hebrew and English. It was obvious to me that the congregation was getting a bit restless with all those Psalms and poems. However, it was now 3:50 P.M. and I felt that it would be safe to go to the cemetery.

Very few who were in the chapel followed the hearse on the five minute trip to the grave but as soon as we drove into the cemetery I knew that we were in for trouble. Yes, the rain had stopped a little more than an hour ago but the drainage at the cemetery was very poor and about a half inch of water still covered the ground.

We trudged around plots behind the casket and my heartbeat accelerated as we came within sight of Alfred's grave. It was filled with water. No hole was visible. No opening was apparent. It merely looked like a small swimming pool filled with murky water.

The undertaker looked at me with dilated eyes. "Rabbi,

what should we do? There is no way that we can bury him now. He's in a wooden casket and it's merely going to float. This land is filled with clay and it's going to take five to six hours before the water will go down." And once again he repeated, "Rabbi, what should we do?"

I quickly approached Gwen and repeated to her what the undertaker had stated. I attempted to temper her anger by telling her once again that I would be happy to return the next day to conclude the burial ritual; however, she once again responded with wrath and fury. "He is still *my* husband," she growled at me, "and I still have the legal right to dictate how he is going to be buried."

Gwen then abruptly turned away from me and clangorously shouted at the undertaker, "Jim*, put that casket down in the grave. Alfred is going to be buried today—right now."

The ten or so friends who had accompanied the casket to the grave were awe-struck by this boisterous statement, and Alfred's parents, brother, and sister quickly began arguing with Gwen. "Alfred's in a wooden casket. There's no way we can have a burial today. The casket is going to float in the grave."

There was bitterness in Gwen's eyes as she once again ordered Jim to place the casket on the water in the grave—and he complied. Alfred's family was correct—the casket was floating in the grave. It was like a cruise ship preparing to leave its Fort Lauderdale dock.

"I'm going to have a heart attack," Alfred's mother lamented, and her husband seated her on one of the damp chairs surrounding the grave.

"He's still legally *my* husband," Gwen wrathfully directed at Alfred's family, "and I have the legal right to decide how and when he is to be buried." Gwen then stared at Alfred's brother and sister. "I should have cremated him and spread his ashes over the Gulf of Mexico."

I attempted to tranquilize Alfred's family but that seemed impossible. I then went again to speak to Gwen but it was as if she had "turned off her hearing aid" from my words. The casket merely sat on top of the waters, and the waters refused to subside or abate.

"Just keep the two sides separate," I thought to myself, "and Gwen will quickly realize that a burial is impossible today. The casket will not descend into the grave." So I wandered from group to group hoping to sedate one and to inject common sense and decency in the other. Even Barry and Ronnie once again attempted to convince their mother to put off for the next day the burial, but their endeavors also came to naught.

After fifteen minutes, Alfred's friends left. Only family remained. We all felt that Gwen would soon capitulate and concede that her wish could not be fulfilled. However, she barked at the undertaker, "Jim, call Alfred's office and have one of the boys bring over a backhoe. We'll pile earth on top of the casket and that will force the casket down and the water out." Jim stared at Gwen but she brazenly ordered him again, "Jim, do it now."

The family erupted once again but Gwen continued to ignore their pleas.

A half-hour later, a backhoe entered the cemetery and approached the grave. Barry and Ronnie pleaded with their mother to desist from this insulting act but Gwen stared at Barry and quickly retaliated, "Your father didn't think of me when he went to bed with your high school girlfriend. He didn't care how he was insulting me. I'm honoring him now by *burying* him and not *cremating* him."

Gwen signaled the driver of the backhoe and he began dipping his scoop into the soaked earth and piling the supersaturated and waterlogged earth upon the casket. The driver did this over and over again as Alfred's father stared aimlessly at this activity and Alfred's mother sounded as if she was on the verge of collapse as she reiterated time and time again, *"Oi vey, oi vey. On oom-glick.* [Woe is me; woe is me. What a tragedy.]"

However, no matter how much earth was cascaded down upon the casket, the waters did not give in and the casket did not descend.

I sat down next to Gwen on one of the damp chairs, shook my head, and attempted to reason with her. "You'll have to put tons of earth on the casket before it will budge downwards and there is no place on the top of the casket to pile so much earth. It's a law of Physics. It's called Archimedes' Principle."

Gwen stared at me. "What are you talking about?" she barked at me. "What's this Archimedes' Principle that won't allow me to get Alfred in this flooded grave?"

I moved closer to her and I took her right hand in both of my hands and softly continued, "I don't want to be technical but Archimedes' Principle says 'A body surrounded by water is buoyed up by a force equal to the weight of the water it displaces.'"

Gwen momentarily looked at me with questioning eyes. "What are you talking about? What does that mean?" Her voice was now softer but it was still belligerent.

For a fleeting second I thought that she was retreating and was going to relent; however, Gwen quickly snapped her fingers, breathed in heavily, and exclaimed with a smile on her face as her eyes focused on Jim. "Jim, call the office and tell them to bring down a hand drill. We'll bore six or eight holes in the bottom of the casket. In that way the casket will sink to the bottom of the grave and we'll be able to conclude this burial right here and now."

Barry and Ronnie immediately shouted their protests. "You can't do this to Dad," while Alfred's mother cried forth another *"Oi vei,"* and his father's eyes rolled as if he was going to faint.

Jim left immediately for the drill. He did not even protest. It was obvious to me that he did not want to lose a "sale." However, I pleadingly asked Gwen to wait in the car until Jim returned. "It will take at least twenty minutes for him to return—maybe even more," I said to her. "Let's sit in the car. It will be more comfortable there. Please!"

I was surprised but Gwen relented. I had the feeling that it was because it began to drizzle slightly again. It was not because she wanted to hear my words.

"Gwen," I implored her, "just give me a few minutes to talk to you."

Surprisingly she did not protest. She merely coldly replied, "Go ahead."

"Gwen," I went on, "there's no question about it that Alfred treated you badly. He was dishonest and he was dishonorable. He was deceitful and he was immoral. He was fraudulent and he was a libertine. He was a Lothario." I kept adding adjective after adjective to my description of Alfred until I ran out of adjectives, and every time I would add another one I would notice a small smile expanding on Gwen's face. I felt as if we were beginning to be on the same frequency.

"He treated you wrong and he treated you dirty." I looked at her straight in the face. "You are a very beautiful woman. He was crazy not only from a moral point of view but also from an aesthetic point of view. He had gold in his house and he went out searching for bronze. He must have been dumb or stupid—or both."

A broad smile now appeared on Gwen's face, and in a calm voice she responded, "Thank you, Rabbi."

I felt that I was getting to her so I continued, "Gwen, we still have a few minutes before Jim returns. Let me tell you a brief story."

"O.K," she resolutely acknowledged my request.

The momentum, I felt, was now mine, so I quickly continued. "On the East Side of New York there was an elderly rabbi. He was about eighty years old. He had a small synagogue in his home which was over a small 'Pop and Mom' grocery store. The Rabbi, Rabbi Moscowitz, lived upstairs on the second floor in a room adjacent to the room where a handful of elderly men would come to pray every day.

"However, many younger people would seek the Rabbi's advice every day. The Rabbi was known in the community as a very wise and sensible individual. Visiting a psychiatrist or psychologist would take many weeks of consultation and be very expensive but visiting Rabbi Moscowitz was truly an experience. He would attempt to help people in one or, at most, two sessions, and Rabbi Moscowitz would always also serve cookies and coffee to those visiting. He had no wife to help him because he was a widower.

"Rabbi Moscowitz would meet these young people all over the East Side and when he saw that they had a problem he would always write his name and address on a piece of paper and give it to them. But when they would seek his advice and counsel and search for the synagogue at the address given to them all they would find would be a small grocery store. However, the grocer would always take them outside and point to a sign showing an arrow pointing upwards with the words "Rabbi Moscowitz Is Upstairs," and they would know that they had to walk up the stairs to receive his counsel."

I looked directly into Gwen's eyes. It was surprisingly obvious to me that she was deeply interested in my story. There was no longer anger or ire written all over her face. So I continued.

"However, one day Rabbi Moscowitz suffered a severe heart attack and he died. He had no children or relatives, and he had no money. So the elderly members of his congregation scraped together some money to pay for his funeral and burial. It was a major task for them but they accomplished it.

"But almost a year later another problem arose. It was time to set a monument on his grave to recognize that he was buried in that grave and to have a brief inscription on it to describe what kind of person he was. But there was no money for this project and even his elderly friends and congregants could not raise the money to pay for this memorial.

"They felt defeated and vanquished. They felt beaten and checkmated. There simply was no money for this project for Rabbi Moscowitz.

"But one of the old men, Mr. Dershowitz*, arose, closed one eye, and intoned to his elderly cronies, 'I've got an idea. I know how to get a monument for Rabbi Moscowitz—and it won't cost us anything. Just be at the cemetery, at his grave, this Sunday at 11 A.M.'

"They looked at him with puzzlement in their eyes and doubt on their lips but he merely smiled at them and once again commented, 'Be there Sunday at 11 A.M.'

"That Sunday, fourteen elderly men assembled at Rabbi Moscowitz's grave, and to their amazement and astonishment they saw a large sheet covering a three-foot projection from the ground that looked like a monument.

"'Mr. Dershowitz,' one of the old men called out when he saw him arrive, 'what kind of monument did you get and where did you get it?' And it was obvious from the faces of the other thirteen that they too wanted an answer to those questions.

"Mr. Dershowitz smiled at all of them, said nothing, walked over to the monument and quickly removed the sheet. There, before everyone's eyes was the 'monument.' It was the sign that had for years been outside of the small grocery store: 'Rabbi Moscowitz Is Upstairs,' and the arrow was pointing upwards.

"Mr. Dershowitz put down the sheet, pointed at the sign, shook his head as if affirming the message, and proclaimed, 'Doesn't that sign truly describe Rabbi Moscowitz? He spent his entire life helping others. He was never interested in himself, only in helping and assisting others. Every day of the year he fulfilled the *mitzvah* [good deed] of *'Pato'och tiftoch et yodcha lo',* 'Always open your hand to help and aid your neighbor' [Deuteronomy 15:8]. Rabbi Moscowitz is truly with God now. Rabbi Moscowitz is truly upstairs now.'"

I waited for a response from Gwen but all I could see were several tears trickling down from her eyes. That simple story had touched a nerve within her. That anecdote had obviously found her heart. So I quickly continued with softness in my voice and compassion in my heart. "Gwen, as I said, Alfred treated you badly. In fact, he treated you miserably, but two wrongs don't make a right. You've got to be bigger than him. The arrow on *his* tombstone will probably be pointing downwards now, but the arrow on *your* personality should be pointing upwards now."

It was obvious to me that the tears were now more than a trickle. They were constant. They were like a barometer informing me that she was being torn in two directions: show compassion or indicate anger and demand revenge.

I did not hesitate. "Gwen," I persisted, "you now have the opportunity to either derive much love from your children or make them feel great antipathy toward you. Yes, they know that their father betrayed you but they do not want him buried in an insulting manner. If you merely acquiesce to their wishes of burying their disloyal father with some aroma of dignity, by not publicly burying him in some outrageous manner of drilling holes in his casket and flooding it and basically drowning the dead, I feel that your sons will indicate their appreciation by showing you an outburst of love.

"Gwen," I went on as I squeezed her hand tightly, "what would you rather have, a personal moment of revenge against

Alfred or years and years of strong love from Barry and Ronnie? Postponing the funeral until tomorrow, until the waters go down, and not drilling holes in his casket, does not mean that you forgive Alfred. It simply means that *you* don't want to lower *yourself* to *his* standards."

Gwen took out a Kleenex and wiped the tears away from her eyes. "Rabbi," she sobbed as she attempted to adjust her damp mascara, "tell me what our Judaism, our Bible, our rabbis instruct us to do when you hate someone as I hate Alfred."

I stared at Gwen and now squeezed both her hands. "King Solomon told the Jews what to do when facing such a problem. He said [Proverbs 25:21], *'Im ra-ev son-ah-cha, ha-ah-chee-lay-hu la-chem; v'im tza-may, hosh-kay-hu mayim;* If your enemy is hungry, give him bread to eat; and if he is thirsty, give him water to drink.' "

I squeezed both her hands more tightly and continued. "Gwen, King Solomon did *not* say that you are to feed your enemy steak and lamb chops. He did *not* say that you are to give him expensive wines and champagne to drink. But he also did *not* say that we are to starve him to death and torture him through dehydration. King Solomon simply told us that we are not to forget that he is still a human being and must not be tortured or degraded. Yes, we do not treat an enemy as if he is staying at the Waldorf-Astoria, but we also do not treat him as if he is in Auschwitz Concentration Camp."

Tears were now cascading out of Gwen's eyes. "We were married twenty-five years," she lamented. "I thought he loved me. He'd always buy me expensive gifts but for two years he was having an affair with that young bimbo. How can I forgive him?"

I shook my head from right to left. "I'm not asking you to forgive him. He never asked for forgiveness and he never showed remorse, I was told. He was simply a Casanova and a Don Juan acting as a loving and loyal husband. He does not deserve forgiveness. But *you* should not lower yourself to his level of perfidy and dishonor. You're bigger than that. You've always been a respectable and honorable woman. Everyone has told me that. Don't change that description now."

Gwen sighed strenuously. "Rabbi, I want *you* to do a favor

for me. *I* can't do it. Go tell Jim to take Alfred's casket back to the Funeral Home; tell Barry and Ronnie, my in-laws, and Alfred's brother and sister that because of the bad weather and the poor condition of the cemetery we will do the internment tomorrow afternoon at 4 P.M.—if that's OK with you, Rabbi."

I smiled broadly and zealously and gave Gwen a quick kiss on her cheek. She held me tightly and muttered, "I hope I'm doing the right thing. I hope I didn't let you bamboozle me."

Immediately, I opened the car door and went to speak to the members of the family who were now the only ones present. I informed them of Gwen's decision as I saw Jim approaching with an oversized drill. "That won't be necessary any more," I informed him, and even Jim smiled and exhaled enthusiastically. "Thank God," was his only comment.

Gwen remained in the car but Alfred's parents and his sons approached the automobile to speak to Gwen. It was obvious that Gwen was not in a speaking mood but Alfred's mother grabbed Gwen's hands and with a flood of tears careening from her eyes whispered, "Alfred was my precious son. I always loved him—even when I discovered that he had had an affair with that young *floozy*. What mother can abandon her flesh and blood? I could even understand your hostility and hatred. I would probably feel the same way if *my* husband cheated on me. But I could not see Alfred degraded and insulted by flooding him in his casket."

Alfred's mother breathed in heavily, released Gwen's hands, blew her nose in an expensive handkerchief, then kissed Gwen on the cheek. "I respect you and love you very much. You are a mother and I know that you understand how I, a mother, appreciate your actions toward my son now that he is dead. May God's blessings always be upon you."

From outside of the car came a response from Alfred's father, a hearty "Amen!"

The next afternoon the sun shone brightly, there was not even a single cloud in the sky, a brisk wind cooled the cemetery, and there was not even a trace of dampness on the grass. In the presence of Gwen, Alfred's two sons, father, mother, brother, and sister—and with Jim supervising all the details—I officiated at Alfred's burial and *all* recited the Mourners' *Kaddish,* even Gwen..

I concluded the service by praying, "May Alfred's soul be bound up in the bond of eternal life. Amen!"

• • • • •

1) "The difficult is that which can be done immediately; the impossible takes a little longer."

—*George Santayana*

2) "Character is doing the right thing when no one is looking."

—*Congressman J.C. Watts (Republican, Oklahoma)*

3) "Heaven has no rage like love to hatred turned, Nor hell a fury like a woman scorned."

—*William Congreve,* The Mourning Bride,
[1697], Act III, 8

CHAPTER 13

To Pray Or Not To Pray, That Is The Question

I had been in Houston only a short time when a woman met with me in my office and exclaimed, "Rabbi, you're got to do something about it. You just simply *must* do something about it."

I did not have the foggiest idea about what she was talking so I merely shrugged my shoulders, smiled, and asked, "*What* is it I must do something about?"

The young woman, who was probably in her late thirties, crinkled her nose, focused her eyes on me in disbelief, and declared, "I'm talking about the Christmas tree they put up in the lobby of Bellaire High School. It doesn't belong there. The principal is openly violating the First Amendment to the American Constitution—Separation of Church and State. Religious articles don't belong in public schools."

She hesitated for a moment waiting for me to respond but continued on when she was met with mere silence on my behalf. "Don't you agree with me?" she questioned. "By putting up a Christmas tree in a public high school the principal is teaching our children that it is permissible to violate American law, to ignore the Constitution, and to make up one's own rules and regulations. This is un-American. Religion does not belong in our schools. It belongs in our homes, synagogues, and churches but not in our schools."

It was obvious to me that she was cemented in her views so I decided to merely express to her my feelings about this subject without going into great detail. "I agree with you, that the First Amendment *is* a foundation stone of our Constitution. That's why, I guess, it was stated as the first of all of our Amendments. But I personally don't think that our forefathers wanted to exclude *all* religious symbols from public areas. I think they merely did not want them to be used as missionary tools in public areas. Therefore, I personally feel that instead of bombarding the principal with *demands* to remove the Christmas tree, we *request* of him that he also include a Channukah Menorah in the lobby and play some Channukah tunes over the P.A. system in addition to the Christmas carols. That would give equal time to the different religions and I personally feel that that would be *kosher* according to the First Amendment."

The young woman's face blanched. It was as if her ears had heard a statement that was obscene and vulgar and her eyes had viewed a photo that was pornographic and lewd. "I am literally stunned by your words," she angrily growled. "I don't know a single rabbi in town who would agree with you. The principal is violating the First Amendment of our Constitution—Separation of Church and State."

We debated this issue for about ten minutes as her voice continually rose but neither side was willing to budge.

"Maybe we can continue this discussion tonight," I suggested in order to end this skirmish. "I've got another appointment in five minutes."

The young woman rose to leave. "I can't make it tonight," she irritably noted. "I'm taking my children downtown tonight."

"Oh," I commented merely to end our conversation on a pleasant note. "I guess it's a family shopping night."

"No," the young woman sheepishly stated as she opened the door, "my two younger children want to see the Christmas lights in the department store and sit on Santa's lap."

The door closed and she did not call for another appointment.

On another occasion there was almost a rebellion amongst the Jewish high school students at Bellaire High School.

The major high school programs are usually scheduled at least a year in advance, and on this particular year the annual graduation prom was reserved for a Friday evening.

It was just about a week before the prom and a delegation of about ten Jewish Bellaire High School students made an appointment to visit with me and discuss the subject. "They can't do this to us," one of the students stormed at me. "They can't ignore us and insult us this way. Friday night is Shabbat and that's our day of rest and the evening of our religious services. The principal is simply thumbing his nose at the Jewish students at Bellaire. We want the prom date changed to a non-Friday night."

All the other students vehemently agreed with their spokesman, and then he added, "Almost all the rabbis are in agreement with us and we've decided that if they refuse to change the date of the prom we're going to call upon all the Jewish students at Bellaire to demonstrate outside of the high school." Immediately, the other students acclaimed their agreement.

I listened attentively and I told the students that I would contact the principal the next day to see what could be done; however, I told them that only a little more than a week remained until the prom and I doubted that any changes would be made. But I promised them that I would attempt to discover *why* the prom was set for Friday evening, the Jewish Shabbat.

The next morning I called the principal. Mr. Graves* suggested that I meet with him at the high school that afternoon and I accepted his invitation.

After we went through the expected smiles, handshakes, greetings and salutations I directly asked Mr. Graves, "Sir, please tell me, *why* did you and the faculty and the school advisers schedule the prom for Friday night? Didn't anyone, if not everyone, in that group know that that was the Jewish Sabbath? Would anyone even suggest that a prom be held on Sunday morning when Christian church services are conducted? Don't you think that equal respect should be given to Jewish students and *their* religion as is given to Christian students and *their* religion?"

Mr. Graves seemed stunned by my question. "Rabbi Segal," he quickly replied, "no one ever gave a second thought to this question because so many of our basketball games and football games are held on Friday nights and almost all the Jewish kids are *always* present. Never once has a Jewish student said to me, or to anyone else on the faculty, 'I would like to play football, or basketball, for Bellaire but I can't because games are on Friday evenings and it is our Sabbath and I attend services then.'

"Rabbi Segal," Mr. Graves went on, "I attend many of the Bellaire games and I always see loads and loads of Jewish boys and girls there on Friday nights. We felt if it is not a problem for the football and basketball games to be held on Friday nights, why should it be a problem for the prom?

"Rabbi Segal," Mr. Graves continued, "we simply used plain logic. We did not see the difference between one and the other. If the Jewish kids could go to the basketball and football games on Friday night why couldn't they go to the prom on Friday night?

"But in addition to that," Mr. Graves proceeded, "we only have a little more than a week for the prom. There is no way we can change the date at the present time and there is no way we can get out of the contract with the hotel. We make commitments with hotels a year in advance. We *can* do something about next year so that it will be on a Saturday night rather than a Friday night but there is nothing we can do about it this year."

Mr. Graves and I spoke for about an hour and we agreed that in the future proms would not be held on Friday evenings. We shook hands, exchanged additional pleasantries, and then I left.

Late that afternoon, a committee of five Bellaire seniors came to my office to meet with me. Rabbi Schachtel, the Reform Rabbi of Temple Beth Israel, was already in my office. I had called almost all the other rabbis in Houston and he was the only one who agreed with me that it was too late this year to do anything about the prom. Mr. Graves had made a major concession to me—no Friday night proms in the future—and Rabbi Schachtel and I felt that that was a major victory.

"We have one Orthodox boy in our class who is graduating," the spokesman for the committee bellowed at me, "and we want him to be at the prom."

"Besides," another student growled at me, "eight o'clock on Friday night is the time that every synagogue and temple has Services. We consider it an insult to all Jews to schedule a school social event when Jews are at Services."

I squinted at the high school student. "Tell me," I pedagogically inquired of him, "do *you* usually go to Services on Friday nights?"

He hesitated for a moment then aggressively replied, "NO, but that's not the issue. Our friend goes to Services on Friday night."

For a moment I ignored his reply. "Tell me," I went on, "how many Jewish students who are seniors go to Services on Friday evenings?"

There was no reply from any of the five. So I continued. "You probably have more than a hundred Jewish students graduating. Do fifty attend Services on Friday nights?" However, I was met with blank stares.

"How about forty-five?" Again there was no response.

How about forty, or thirty?" But this time they merely gnashed and ground their teeth. It was obvious that anger was setting in.

So I accelerated my pace. "How about twenty or ten?" But again I was met with silence and obvious displeasure and wrath. I felt like Abraham bargaining with God when God pronounced that He was going to destroy Sodom and Gomorrah

Finally, one student rose from his seat, jutted out his jaw toward me, and with spleen bellowed, "Mr. Graves is trying to treat us in an un-American way. In our history class we were taught and quizzed about the First Amendment to the American Constitution: 'Congress shall make no law respecting an establishment of religion, or prohibiting the free exercise thereof.' Rabbi, that law states most emphatically that my public high school has no right to prevent me from worshipping my God, but that's exactly what Mr. Graves is trying to do. He's put us in a position where we have to make a serious and important choice—either we pray to God or we go to the dance. We can't do both and it's all because of Mr. Graves."

The other four quickly chimed in their acquiescence. The spokesman continued, "He's denying us our American rights; he's violating the Constitution; he's trying to start a religious war in school; he'll never keep his word for next year."

Rabbi Schachtel softly and delicately attempted to assuage their tempers and anger but his dramatic presentation also fell on deaf ears.

"We're getting no place here," one of the students frustratedly called out. "Let's go. Let's go see some of the other rabbis. I know they'll give us a sympathetic ear—especially my rabbi. I've already discussed this matter with him." And in unison all five arose from their seats, mumbled a cold "Good-bye," and left without shaking hands with Rabbi Schachtel or me.

Rabbi Schachtel turned toward me and in his thespian deportment and his peerless and unmatched manner pronounced, "I feel now just as General Robert E. Lee must have felt when he met General Ulysses S. Grant at Appomattox Court House on April 9, 1865. He gave his maximum—but he lost."

Throughout my incumbency at Beth Yeshurun I have been approached by numerous Jews of all ages who have espoused the principle of *total* Separation of Church and State. Some vehemently spoke to me espousing the belief that nuns should not be permitted to teach in public high schools while wearing their clerical vestments; others even went as far as to preach to me that Jewish teachers in public schools should not be permitted to outwardly wear *Magen Davids* (Star of David) over their dresses; still others made appointments with me to emphasize that post office lawns should not be allowed to display crèches during the Christmas seasons; many called me to influence me to write to the President, my Congressman, and the Texas Senators to inform them that my congregants and I opposed placing the Ten Commandments in courtrooms or public parks; and time after time I would receive e-mails or letters or phone calls from members of my synagogue and other Jews in Houston asking me to forcefully and energetically speak out from my pulpit against prayer in public schools or even a moment of silence beginning the public school day—and I often spoke on these subjects from my pulpit but I did not always satisfy the requests and parameters of many of my congregants and friends.

Recently, I preached another sermon on the subject of Separation of Church and State at Brith Shalom Congregation in Houston. I did this because many in Texas were up in arms in regard to a local problem pertaining to this subject that had come before the Supreme Court of the United States. I entitled my sermon, "To Pray Or Not To Pray, That Is The Question."

> The people in Santa Fe, Texas love their Friday evening football games, and before each game at this public high school a prayer is recited and someone leads the spectators in prayer.
>
> However, two families, one Catholic and one Mormon, opposed this practice. They said this was a violation of the First Amendment of our Constitution, a violation of the principle of Separation of Church and State.
>
> Local residents were offended by that declaration and they cried out, "No one is going to stop us from praying. If you don't like what we do here, don't come to the games." Or, they cried out, "If you don't like the prayers that we recite just before the games begin, come after the kickoff. It's *our* right. It's *our* tradition."
>
> But when the school leaders were told that *they* could not be involved in these prayers, that it was against the law, they turned the prayer program over to one of the students, Marian Ward, the daughter of a Christian minister and a student at the school. Every week she would lead the spectators at the games in a Christian prayer and the people at the games seemed satisfied because the vast majority of the people in Santa Fe were Christian.

The people said, "We have circumvented the prohibition. The *school* is not involved in this project. A *student* arranged for the prayer, and a *student* led it. The country guarantees all of us freedom of religion and we are simply exercising that freedom."

Eventually this question came before the Supreme Court of the United States: Are these *student-led* prayers at public high school football games *kosher or traife?* Are they permitted or are they prohibited?

Justice John Paul Stevens, speaking for the majority of six justices, wrote the decision for the Supreme Court—this tradition was *traife,* not permitted. He said, "The delivery of a pre-game prayer has the improper effect of *coercing* those present to participate in an act of religious worship." He also added: "[You've got to stop it.]" Justice Stevens stated, "[The Santa Fe policy] allows only one student for the entire season to give the invocation." The Supreme Court Justice wrote in the majority decision that it recognized "the important role that public worship plays in many communities [but] such religious activity in public schools, as elsewhere, must comport with the First Amendment."

I feel that this was a brave and courageous step on the behalf of those six of the nine members of the Supreme Court, and the reason should be obvious. Recent polls have indicated that eighty-three percent of Americans favor what Santa Fe was doing. For every six people in our country, five said, "We like what you are doing." However the majority of the Supreme Court went against the national grain and said: "You've got to stop it."

Friends, I feel that what I'm going to tell you now will probably irk and rub the wrong way seventy-five percent of those present in the synagogue this evening. Maybe twenty-five percent will agree with me. However, I merely ask you to listen to me.

On several occasions when I have gone to football

games, I want you to know, I have prayed. The same has been true when I have gone to a handful of basketball games or hockey games—I have prayed.

If it was late in the afternoon and the sun was setting, I walked over to a corner of the stadium and *davenned Minchah.* If it was even later, I walked over to a corner and *davenned Ma'ariv.* Therefore I must admit to you that on occasion I have prayed at public sports events. But I did not take out *Tallit* and *Tephillin,* or *Etrog* and *Lulov,* or *Shofar* and state to everyone near me: "Please bow your heads and join me in prayer." I did it *privately* and *inconspicuously,* as an individual.

And I am quite positive that God heard my prayers even as everyone was shouting: "Throw the ball"—and no one was offended and no one felt uncomfortable.

My friends, I am *not* opposed to prayer. I *daven* every single day. I also do not feel that our government is, or has ever been, opposed to us praying. I also believe that the majority of our founding fathers believed in prayer.

In the Declaration of Independence, I am sure everyone remembers the statement:

We hold these Truths to be self-evident that all Men are created equal, that they are endowed by their CREATOR [that means 'God'] with certain unalienable Rights, that among these are Life, Liberty, and the Pursuit of Happiness.

There is also reference in the Declaration of Independence to "NATURE'S GOD."

There is also a statement in the Declaration of Independence "appealing to the SUPREME JUDGE of the world," (meaning "God").

We also find in the Declaration of Independence the phrase: "With a firm reliance on the protection of DIVINE PROVIDENCE," (again meaning "God").

Does that sound as if the Founding Fathers of our nation opposed religion in regard to our nation? Does that sound as if the Founding Fathers of our nation wanted to eliminate *every* aroma of religion in public life? Of course not.

Are you familiar with the American Constitution and how it ends?

Article VII concludes with the statement:

Done in convention by the unanimous consent of the States present the Seventeenth day of September in the YEAR OF OUR LORD one thousand seven hundred and eighty seven. . . .

Tell me, do *you* write that way? I surely don't. Tell me, does that sound as if our government was opposed to every iota of religion in public life? Of course not.

Also, look at our coins. What is inscribed on them? "In GOD we trust"—and that statement has survived many law suits.

What about the Pledge of Allegiance? Don't we say: "One nation, UNDER GOD, indivisible, with liberty and justice for all"?

Also, the Senate and Congress begin their days with a prayer by a Chaplain who is paid with our tax dollars.

Similarly, do you remember Lincoln's words in his *Gettysburg Address:* ". . . that this nation UNDER GOD shall have a birth of freedom—and that government of the people, by the people, for the people shall not perish from the earth"?

Do you know that the Ten Commandments are inscribed on the marble of the United States Supreme Court?

Do you know that there is a beautiful stained glass window in the United States Capitol depicting President George Washington kneeling in prayer?

Do you know that at the top of the Washington Monument there is a plaque which boldly proclaims in Latin: "Praise be unto GOD"?

Have you ever seen Arizona's motto: "GOD enriches"?

How about South Dakota's motto: "Under GOD people rule"?

How about Colorado's motto: "Nothing without the DEITY"?

So, if we see so much religion in our state governments and federal governments, what is wrong with that high school girl leading invocations at the team's football games?

However, the answer is really simple. She was doing more than *PRAYING*. She was actually *PREACHING*—and there is a difference between praying and preaching. It is not *PRAYING* that is prohibited. It is *PREACHING* that is prohibited.

That girl was the only one permitted to lead the invocation and she always articulated her thoughts with a *Christian* prayer.

I think the Supreme Court decision would have been totally different if the students would have assembled together and written on different cards:

Catholic
Protestant
Jewish
Buddhist
Shintoist
Moslem
Atheist
Humanist
And several others

And each week a different card would have been drawn from a bag and one of the students would have said: "It's now your turn to lead the pre-football prayer or statement." Each week, a student of a *different* religion would have led those in the stands who wanted to join him, or her, in the different ethnic devotions or in a patriotic statement. I am quite positive that even the atheists would have been able to present a patriotic pronouncement and I believe that the Supreme Court would have been satisfied with such an arrangement.

I cannot forget the words of the Prophet Isaiah who twenty-seven hundred years ago said (56:7): *"Kee vay-tee bet tephillah yee-ka-ray le-chol ha-ah-mim* [My house should be a house of prayer for *all* people]"—not merely for one group, the majority.

However, I have a feeling that this suggestion would have created much anger and irritation, dissension and outbursts in Santa Fe because almost the entire town would have cried out, "We Christians are the majority. We want *Christian* prayers at our football games. We don't have Buddhists or Shintoists and we only have a handful of Jews. The old statement 'Majority Rules' should apply to the high school football games in Santa Fe."

Therefore, I would like to suggest another solution if the card choosing solution, giving everyone a chance, is not satisfactory.

Just before the football games, why don't those people going to the games gather in small groups *outside* of the stadium and each group recite its own individual prayers that is meaningful to its members?

Or, before the games, why can't groups gather for dinner or coffee at Denny's or McDonald's or Burger King or Pizza Hut and recite a prayer there? The same prayer that can be recited in the stands of the football stadium can be recited quietly and peacefully and privately just before, or after, dinner.

Or, why can't a prayer be recited at home before the game? Why can't all the members of the family hold hands for thirty seconds and recite a brief prayer together?

Or, why can't the local churches of Santa Fe be open one hour before game time when those who desire to recite prayers will go to their individual churches and recite their prayers together with their ministers or their priests—or by themselves?

Or, why can't a student simply stand before the spectators at the football games and say: "Can we please have thirty seconds of silence" and everyone will do as he or she desires? Some will pray; some will read a newspaper; some will do nothing; some will close their eyes; some will do their homework; however, there will be respect and honor and silence during those thirty seconds—but no one will be preached to or coerced to do something that will make that individual uncomfortable.

My friends, prayer *is* important, and so is penicillin important. But if you give the wrong dose of penicillin or if you give it for the wrong ailment it can be dangerous and injurious—and the same is true for prayer, if it makes one uncomfortable.

Prayer should *unify* people, not *divide* them.

Public high school football games should not be places for religious *preaching*. That should be done in churches, synagogues, or in our homes. Or it should be done outside of the stadiums, or it should be done at Denny's before or after the games.

King David, three thousand years ago, said (Psalm 133:1), *"Hee-nay mah tov oo-mah na'im sheh-vet ah-chim gom ya-chad;* How good it is when brothers can live together in harmony."

That is one of the purposes of prayer. Prayer was never made to divide us and separate us. It was made to unite us and embrace us.

I pray that the people of Santa Fe and the United States will learn the true lesson of prayer—to unite us—and that they will *pray* whenever and wherever they desire, but they will not *preach* to others of different religions who have gone to see a football game.

AMEN!

It has always been my belief that this country was not established to be a monolithic nation. It was established so that people could espouse different beliefs and not be hounded down because of them. It has always been my hope that the people of this nation would learn to respect the feelings of other individuals rather than foist their beliefs on the minority. No one should ask anyone to do things or believe concepts that are antagonistic to them. Therefore in our *public* prayers I would hope that those leading the prayers would be sensitive to minority groups in their midst and respect their beliefs.

• • • • •

1) "Now, there's even a 'dial-a-prayer' for atheists.
You call a number and nobody answers."

—Author Unknown

2) "The fool hath said in his heart, 'There is no God.' "

—Psalm 14:1

CHAPTER 14

Violence In The Synagogue

Our synagogue, in recent years, has become one of the largest in the United States. Every day, every corner of the congregation is occupied by some activity.

This requires a large staff, not only of clergy, cantor, and teachers but also of workers to move equipment, to see to it that the synagogue is always clean, that the electricity and plumbing are always functioning properly, that food is cooked, meals are served, trash is emptied, the public address system is working efficiently, pianos are moved where needed, and prayer books are replaced in the pews. These duties, and many more, always required a large and a loyal staff—and that is what we always had.

However, in the late sixties and early seventies our support staff was entirely Black while the foreman was White. His name was Ernest Walter Hilliard*, and we called him Ernie, for short.

Ernie always had a smile on his face but on rare occasions he would come forth with a joke about Blacks that was derogatory and disparaging, insulting and offensive. I would tell him that I did not appreciate such pejorative comments because

"We are all children of God. God created all of us." But Ernie would slap his backside, smile, and apologetically state, "You've got to excuse me, Rabbi. I was raised in a small town in Alabama and that's the way we always talked. However, I'm slowly learning the new ways of life." Ernie would then smile and add, "We've got to treat everyone as equals—even the Blacks. As you said Rabbi, even they were created by God." And then he would always inject a postscript, something like, "Rabbi, I'm like an old water hose that's been taped over ten times. Every so often it begins to leak again, but you tape it up again and it's all fixed up."

I would not know whether he was mocking me and mimicking me or whether he was slowly but surely changing his ingrained way of thinking. He always seemed to get along well with the Black workers so I would always give him the benefit of the doubt. Was that not the American way of life—a man is innocent until *proven* guilty? It surely was the Jewish belief. Twenty-one hundred years ago, Rabbi Joshua ben Perahyah said (*Avot* 1:6), "Always give everyone the benefit of the doubt. [Always judge people favorably when there is no proof that the person is guilty.]"

However, one day as I was walking from the Sanctuary to my office I heard shouting—and I do mean thunderous and ear-splitting screaming—coming forth from the Executive Director's office. It sounded as if someone was being beaten up, someone was being terrorized. Three voices were quite audible. One voice was filled with anger and fury: "I'll kill you;" "I'll murder you;" "I'm going to break you in half." The second voice was replete with pain and fear: "You're hurting me;" "You're breaking my neck;" "Get offah me, you Black (expletive)." The third voice was that of our Executive Director, Barry Kaplan*, and it sounded as if he was anticipating a cataclysm or a human convulsion. He was pleading and imploring the other two to listen to him and settle their differences in peace: "Please stop this;" "Let's sit down and discuss your differences;" "Nothing good will come out of this violence;" "Please stop this and let's talk."

The volume of the shouting kept increasing and increasing;

the threats continually became more and more taunting; but the appeals for peace and consideration seemed to be decreasing and diminishing as the seconds ticked by. It truly sounded to me as if someone was being killed in Barry's office.

I therefore grabbed the knob of his door expecting to turn it and gain entrance to his office but I immediately discovered that the door was locked. "Barry, what's going on in your office?" I shouted. "I can't get in."

The shouting of the antagonists continued but I heard Barry's voice over their voices: "He's killing him. He's killing him. We've got to stop this immediately."

I banged on the door once again and shouted, "Let me in; let me in." But the only response that I could hear over the din of the shouting was Barry's voice: "I can't get to the door to open it. They're fighting near the door. Call the police."

I really do not know why I did not immediately call 911. Maybe it was because I felt that act was futile. It would have taken a minimum of at least ten minutes for the police to come and I kept hearing a voice screaming, "You're killing me. You're killing me."

Again I banged on the door but no one opened it. I therefore raised my right foot and forcefully and violently smashed it against the door paneling just below the doorknob and the door burst open. I had obviously broken the flimsy lock, and part of the wood from the door had splintered.

I pushed the door wide open even though the two struggling men were leaning against it. There before my eyes was Barry standing behind his desk while two men, Booker* and Ernie, were fighting. It was not simply an oral disagreement. Booker's right arm was wrapped around Ernie's neck and he was squeezing it with Herculean strength while Ernie was merely shouting and screaming entreaties to let go or shrieking expletives denigrating and sullying Booker's racial origins.

Barry began shouting, "Rabbi, Rabbi, separate them, separate them." However, Booker cast a threatening and menacing eye toward me. "Rabbi, I like you," he quickly screamed at me. "Stay out of this fight. He's done this once too often. I told him many times that I'd kill him if he did it again but all he does is laugh."

Meanwhile, Ernie was shouting, "Rabbi, get him offah me. Get him offah me. He's crazy. He's crazy. He wants to kill me."

Ernie's face was as red as a beet. His eyes were bulging. He was now gasping for breath. It seemed as if Ernie was correct in his analysis of the situation—Booker wanted to kill him and he was well on the road to achieving his goal.

"Booker, Booker," I shouted at him as I stared straight into his eyes, "let go of him. You're hurting him."

But a big smile came over Booker's face. "That's exactly what I'm trying to do—and what I'm going to do," and he applied even more pressure to Ernie's neck.

I therefore acted instinctively and moved in front of the two of them, grabbing Booker's right hand that was the source of the pressure. I was pulling with both of my hands, but with no success. Therefore, I began pulling on Booker's left arm with my right hand and with my left hand on Booker's right arm hoping that the combined forces would relieve the pressure around Ernie's neck. I continued this tactic for a full fifteen seconds that felt like an eternity. I was grunting and groaning while Ernie continued shouting, "He's killing me" and Booker was counter-shouting, "Rabbi, he deserves it; he deserves it."

Finally, Booker turned his head toward me, stared me in the eye, and snorted, "I don't want to hurt *you,* Rabbi. I like you. You've been good to me and my people. I'll let go of him only because *you're* asking—but don't let him get out of the office or this time I'll really cripple him. I want to settle this matter once and for all." With those words, Booker released the pressure on Ernie's neck and Ernie fell exhausted and coughing to the floor.

"He's broke my neck," Ernie began screaming and screeching.

I bent down on my knees close to Ernie. The red color had now totally escaped from his face. He was now ashen and pallid. "I'll call an ambulance," I whispered in Ernie's ear. "They'll take you to the hospital."

However, Ernie quickly indicated his opposition to my suggestion. He merely continued shouting, "I don't need an ambulance. I just want the police to come and lock up this Black (expletive)."

I grimaced as he continued with his racial insults and slurs. "Stop using that profanity; stop using that vulgarity," I salvoed at Ernie. I knew that Booker was going to strenuously retaliate for those comments so I quickly jumped up and grabbed Booker around the waist and attempted to restrain him but it was a Sisyphusian frustration—for every foot I dragged him backwards he advanced two feet.

"Booker," I pleaded with this mass of man who was now like an active volcano, "please give me a chance. Nothing good will come out of you hitting him. Let me try to settle this matter."

To my utter surprise, Booker stepped back. "Rabbi, it's only because I like you that I'm going to let him live—even though he doesn't deserve it. Every time he sees any of the Black help here, men or women, he always calls us (expletive), or (expletive), or (expletive). We've taken enough crap from him. But when the Black girls who work here in the kitchen told me that he always follows them upstairs into the Boy Scout Room where they store much of the kitchen paperware and he puts his hands all over them—and they don't say anything because they don't want to cause any trouble because they think they may lose their jobs—I decided that enough was enough. I told him a dozen times to stop but he always says, 'Mind your own business, you Black (expletive).'"

I intentionally stood between Ernie and Booker because Booker was fuming and steaming and I thought that at any moment he would catapult forward and choke Ernie again. However, after five minutes I was able to tranquilize Booker while Ernie cowered in fear on the floor sporadically shouting, "He's a murderer. He's a murderer." Finally, I shouted at Ernie, "Shut up; shut up; enough's enough"—and he was quiet.

Barry and I then met individually with the two opponents, first with Ernie and then with Booker. First, we sent Ernie home for the day. About ten minutes later we sent Booker home. We purposely staggered their release from their synagogue duties that day because we did not want them meeting in the parking lot. We felt that if that occurred Booker would have obliterated

Ernie because I was not able to defuse his anger and wrath even when he finally left.

Later, several leaders of the synagogue came to the congregation and questioned the Black help. Every one of them, both male and female, without exception and without knowing what had transpired, stated that Ernie habitually addressed them with racial slurs, and the women added that he regularly followed them into the storeroom where he always attempted to put his hands on them.

However, they added that they had never previously complained to the synagogue authorities because they needed their jobs and they feared that "when push came to shove, the White man would be kept and the Black women would be fired because they were troublemakers." So, they merely grinned and bore their pain. They simply confided in Booker but he too, they felt, could do nothing because he was Black.

My heart growled with anguish as I was informed of the report. Here were people right under my nose who were silently suffering simply because they felt that "the White man would fire them" and therefore they had to be quiet. They needed their jobs in order to have bread on their families' tables and roofs over their heads.

I wondered how all this animosity could have been simmering all around me and I was totally oblivious of it. I had always had an excellent relationship with the Black workers in the synagogue and the same was true for my association with Ernie. In fact, on many occasions, Ernie would bring his son, Ernie Jr., to the synagogue, and Ernie Jr. would always ask me, "Where's your son, Jeffrey? I'd like to play with him." But I would always reply, "Jeffrey's in school. It's a school day. Aren't you supposed to be in school now?" But Ernie Jr. would simply smile at me and walk away.

Several times I even rhetorically asked Toby, "Do you think I should invite Ernie Jr. over to the house after school hours to play with Jeffrey?" But I would always immediately answer my own question, "I don't think that's a good idea. He's at least five years older than Jeffrey. He should have his own friends who are his own age." I felt sorry for Ernie Jr., not being in class on school days and not having friends of his own age. But Ernie Sr. had never asked me to solve his problem and therefore I thought it would be presumptuous on my behalf to discuss this subject with Ernie Sr.

But the scuffle between Booker and Ernie was a serious matter and had to be solved, and the synagogue leadership did solve it—and quickly. The next day they met individually with Booker and Ernie and it was decided that we could not tolerate racial hatred, racial animosity, and racial strife—and it was obvious that Ernie had precipitated it. The synagogue decided to give Ernie four weeks severance pay and terminate his relationship with the congregation.

I felt that this was fair and just. We could not tolerate bigotry, prejudice, intolerance, discrimination, and bias under our roof. The Bible tells us (Leviticus 19:23-24), "[If a stranger lives near you, don't make life miserable for him. . . . You should love him just as you love yourself because you, too, were a stranger in Egypt. . . .]" Just because someone is different from you is not an excuse to taunt him, deride him, or ridicule him. King Solomon, three thousand years ago, in the book of Proverbs (3:18), said, "The Bible is a tree of life for those who embrace it." It is not merely a good piece of literature. It is God's roadway of life, teaching us how to conduct ourselves, and that means that prejudice and bigotry are not to be tolerated.

The only thing that bothered me was Ernie Jr. With his father's dismissal we would not be seeing him anymore and no longer would I hear his repetitious requests to play with Jeffrey.

Ernie was dismissed and as time went by his name faded from my consciousness. However, several years later I was truly startled. There, on my television screen was Ernie Jr. He had not won a 4H award; he had not been granted a scholarship to a prestigious university; he had not excelled in basketball and been granted a multi-million dollar contract. Ernie was on television because he was being booked on suspicion of murder.

I could not believe what my eyes were seeing on the television screen. This was the same Ernie Jr., just older, who would always ask me, "Can I come over to your house to play with your son?" He had always seemed so placid and tranquil, so well behaved and so courteous. "How about this afternoon, Rabbi Segal, can I play with Jeffrey?" And the only reason I had always answered negatively was because Jeffrey was either in school or being carpooled to an athletic game in which he was to play. True, I was not exuberant about the fact that Ernie was about five years older than Jeffrey, but that never really became an actual problem since Jeffrey was always away when Ernie Jr. wanted to come to my home. And when I would ask him, "How come you can come to play so early, at 1 P.M.?" he would always smile and reply, "We have early dismissal on certain days."

But days ran into weeks, and weeks ran into months, and Ernie Jr. was put on trial and convicted of being involved in the murder of twenty-seven young people. It was unbelievable; it was incomprehensible; it was implausible. The young boy who always had a smile on his face and a good word on his lips was not only convicted of being involved in the murder of twenty-seven youths but also involved in torturing them. It was truly mind-boggling.

The crimes were indeed heinous and vicious acts, and that is the way the jury, the court, and the judge saw them. Every evening on the TV news, and every day in our newspapers there were more revelations about these violent crimes—the discovery of more bodies, the admission that specific youngsters had been murdered but their bodies could not be found because Ernie and his accomplices had forgotten where they had disposed of the corpses, statements concerning tortures they had inflicted upon their prey, and every day the newspapers carried pictures of the young people who had been killed.

I just could not extirpate that story from my mind. All the victims were young—loads and loads of teenagers. I could not eliminate from my psyche the old statement: "There but for the grace of God go I." Time after time Ernie Jr. had requested an invitation to come to my home, but something always was going on that prevented Jeffrey from privately meeting with Ernie Jr.

Eventually, the judge came forth with his decision—Ernie Jr. was sentenced to five hundred and ninety-four years in prison. I do not know how the judge calculated the five hundred and ninety-four years, but however he did it *I* believe he was a good mathematician. Murder is murder and we dare not be flaccid and flabby when we impose a punishment upon a heartless, cruelhearted, cold-blooded, and insensitive person who terminates the life of a human being with less thought about it than one who squashes a roach.

On the day that Ernie Jr. was sentenced I waited until all were out of the chapel, then I entered the chapel and switched on one center light. Everyone was gone from the synagogue except two porters who were vacuuming the rugs in the main sanctuary. I ascended the pulpit and pulled on the drawstring. The curtain covering the ark opened exposing eight Torahs (the first five books of Moses written on parchment) to my sight. I had seen those Torahs every day since I arrived in Houston in 1965, but on this particular day they seemed extra holy to me and extra large to me. It was as if I was having a private audience with God Himself. Slowly I put my hand on one of the Torahs, retracted it, kissed my hand, and recited the traditional words, *"Baruch ata Adonai, elohaynu melech ha'olam, hagomel l'chayavim tovot, sheh-gemalani kol tov selah,* [Blessed are Thou, O Lord our God, King of the universe, who does good to average people, and has done good unto me and my beloved ones.]"

I felt driven to state that prayer because Jews have always recited it when they found themselves in a dangerous situation and were safeguarded from any evil consequence. If one was ill but eventually was cured, if one had been in an accident but was not severely hurt, if one had been in the military and had returned from battle unscathed or not severely hurt, if a woman was told by her physician that she could not have children and eventually had a child—all these people would recite the *gomel* prayer. "Thank you God that I have overcome my problem." At that moment, I too felt a strong need to recite that prayer—"O thank you, God. I have overcome my problem."

Several years after Ernie Jr. was sentenced I received a letter from him from the Huntsville jail.

Dear Rabbi Segal,

I have been reading my Bible since I was sentenced to

jail and I've decided that I want to be Jewish. I would like you to convert me to Judaism.

Ernest Hilliard Jr.

As the years had gone by, Ernie's name and criminal acts had evaporated from my mind but this letter quickly resurrected them. A week later I sent the following letter to him.

Ernie,

I was glad to hear that you were reading the Bible and that God's words were leaving an impression on you. However, I cannot convert you to Judaism because conversion requires a one to one relationship between the one requesting conversion and the religious guide for the conversion (me). I cannot visit you in jail. (You are in Huntsville.) And you cannot visit me in Houston.

I would therefore suggest that if you are interested in conversion that you meet with Rabbi Bernard Margareten* who is the Jewish chaplain for the Texas Department of Corrections. He will advise you.

Rabbi Jack Segal

On many occasions I have met with Rabbi Margareten at my synagogue, at rabbinical meetings, and at social events. But he told me that he had never heard from Ernie Jr.

• • • • •

1) "If you are kind to the cruel, you will eventually become cruel to the kind."

—*Midrash*

2) "The fault, dear Brutus, is not in our stars, but in ourselves."

—*"Julius Caesar," I. ii. 134; William Shakespeare*

Part Two

The Thing That Costs The Least But Does The Most Is A Pleasant Smile

Chapter 15

Tragedy In The Middle Of The Night

The call came in to my home at 11:45 P.M. on a Saturday evening. Toby and I had returned a half-hour earlier from a Bar Mitzvah reception and I had undressed and was unwinding by watching the television news.

"I'm sorry to bother you so late," the voice seriously stated, "but my name is Charles Slater* of Oxfordsville*, forty miles southwest of Houston. I'm calling to inform you that two members of your synagogue were in a bad accident in our town."

I crinkled my eyes and pursed my lips anticipating additional bad news—and it came. Ralph Ellenbogen* and his son Joseph*, Charles continued, "were driving through out town when they were hit by a pickup—and killed."

"Oh, no, no," I whispered to myself as my heartbeat began to accelerate. Joey had been my student in Confirmation class just a year earlier. He was only seventeen. Ralph used to regularly attend our TNT (*Tallit 'n Tephillin*) Sunday morning service with Joey and Brian*, Joey's brother who was five years older than Joey, and also with Susie, their seven year old sister.

"What happened? What happened?" I quickly interrogated my caller.

The response was slow but deliberate. "It seems that Ralph and Joseph were returning to Houston about nine o'clock when they had a flat. It was late and all the filling stations in our town were closed. So the two of them decided to change the flat themselves. They pulled over to the side of the road and removed the flat tire. Joseph was changing the tire and Ralph was standing at his side. But as Joseph was putting on the spare tire, along came a sixteen-year-old local boy in his pickup. Unfortunately, he had obviously been drinking. His girlfriend was at his side and he said that he turned to give her a kiss."

Charles hesitated for a moment, then continued on. His voice was now hushed, as if he was embarrassed to make his next comment. "He said he didn't see Ralph or Joseph. He merely heard a big thud and thought he had hit a road marker sign. He stopped to see what damage he had done to his fender. He and his girlfriend got out of his pickup and he began shouting that his father was going to kick his butt because of what he had done to his fender. But he turned around and he saw Ralph and Joseph lying on the side of the road."

There was a pause, but Charles went on again. "The Chief of Police was immediately called and he called me because I'm the only undertaker in Oxfordsville. Both Ralph and Joseph were killed instantly because the boy was driving pretty fast. The Chief got Ralph's name and address from his license but Ralph also had your card in his pocket. We assumed that you were his minister."

I still had not absorbed the severity and reality of this tragedy. Then I recalled that two weeks earlier I had given Ralph my card and asked him to call to help me with the Sunday morning TNT breakfasts. He was to cut the bagels and serve the coffee.

"Rabbi," Charles went on, "we live quite a distance from Houston and we didn't want Ralph's wife to get this news from a cold telephone call from an undertaker in Oxfordsville whom she didn't know. We felt that it would be a bit easier if *you* broke the news to her. She knows you and you are her minister."

I felt a big lump in my throat. It was obvious that this was going to be an extremely difficult task. Death is always difficult; an unexpected death is an impossibility; and double unexpected deaths are an insurmountable obstacle. However, Charles was correct. Someone who knew Betty*, Ralph's wife, had to break the news to her. Of course it would still be a painful horror but this was not the time to begin quibbling as to which relative would be best to inform her. Firstly, the only relative who lived nearby in Houston was her seven-year-old daughter Susie* who lived with her. Her son Brian* was a student at the University of Houston and he did not live at home. . Secondly, I was quite positive that the story would be on the early morning TV news. I did not want her to first hear of this calamity from a news broadcaster.

After concluding our talk and hanging up, I called Information to get Brian's phone number. I did not know his specific address or with what friends he lived. I hoped that I could reach him first and the two of us would go together to break the news to his mother. But the operator informed me that his number was unlisted and she could not divulge any information about it.

Quickly I dressed and drove to Betty's home, which was about fifteen minutes from my home. It was now 12:45 A.M. and the streets were quiet. They were almost totally deserted.

I parked in front of Betty's home, hesitated before leaving the car, and breathed in heavily. "There's no sense sitting in the car any longer," I said to myself. "If I'm going to do it I better do it now." I opened the door, stepped out into the cool evening breeze, and closed the car door. It sounded to me as if I had smashed a hammer on the car's door because the entire neighborhood was totally quiet.

Slowly I ascended the three steps to Betty's home. The entire house was dark, as were almost all the other houses on the block. I quickly pushed the doorbell with my index finger. A few seconds later I saw a light go on in a room upstairs. About a minute later I could see the rustling of one of the downstairs drapes as if Betty was peeking out to see who it was. Ten seconds later I saw Betty's face through the front door window. Her face was ashen and tense.

Immediately, the door was rapidly opened. I could see that Betty was breathing heavily and quickly. "Why are you here so late at night?" she asked with fright in her eyes, terror in her voice, and panic in the movement of her hands. "Did something happen to Brian or was it Joey and Ralph?" She did not give me a chance to reply. "Tell me. Tell me. Tell me quickly. Tell me quickly," she continued as her body began to visibly quiver and shake.

I stretched forth my arms and palmed her two hands. Softly, and with tears in my eyes, I replied, "Ralph and Joey have been in a bad accident about forty miles from Houston."

Before I could say another word, Betty turned around, stepped back into her home, and cried out, "Were they badly hurt? When can I see them? I must see them now."

I followed her in, closed the door, and held both of her hands and softly said, "They were hit by a pickup truck. They both died." Those last three words stuck in my throat but I felt that this was the best way to convey bad news—quickly, directly, and abruptly. Bad news is always painful and agonizing. There is no good way to relate hurtful news. Why drag it out over several lengthy and ambiguous sentences? They only give false hopes that are quickly smashed down.

"Oh no, no, no," she began to shout and I put my arms around her to attempt to help her in this most difficult and traumatic moment. Betty put her head down on my shoulder as she wept and whimpered uncontrollably, "I can't believe it. I can't believe it. We were all going to a Bar Mitzvah in Miami next weekend. How could this happen? How could this happen?"

For a moment Betty was silent. Then she looked into my eyes. Her eyes were now red and wet. Tears were coursing out of her eyes onto her face. "Rabbi, tell me I'm having a bad dream. That's all it is."

Again I breathed in heavily. "I wish I could do that, Betty," I responded.

But then I heard the living room door open. Susie was standing over the threshold and rubbing her eyes. "Mommy, Mommy, why are you crying?"

Betty stepped back from me, stretched forth her arms toward Susie, and wept, "Come to me, my baby. Come to me."

Susie quickly rushed over to her mother. Fear was now written all over her face as Betty embraced her.

Betty held Susie tightly as tears ran down both of their faces. She then held Susie's face in her two hands and motherly and lovingly stated, "The rabbi came to tell us that Daddy and Joey were in a bad accident out of town." She hesitated momentarily as she pressed Susie even closer to her body and added, "and they were both killed. They're dead." Once again she began sobbing and weeping violently.

Betty moved her hands from Susie's face and put them up to her own face as she attempted to wipe some of the tears away from her face; however, the innocent and pathetic expression on Susie's face was quickly erased and she turned toward me and began shouting and screaming, "It's a lie, a lie. The rabbi is a liar." And she began kicking me and scratching the arm of my jacket. Betty quickly picked Susie up and attempted to tranquilize her, but it was not an easy chore.

After Betty finally subdued Susie's shouting and screaming, we sat down for a few minutes as I listened to Betty bewail her fate: she was a child during World War II living in London when the Nazis bombarded that city; and Ralph was a survivor of The Holocaust who saw all his relatives murdered by the Nazis.

"Fate is so terrible," Betty lamented. "Ralph was the only one of his family to escape the Nazis, the death camps, and the crematoria. His life was saved—only to be killed by a drunk teenager in America. I guess Hitler's hand was still sticking out of the ground to get Ralph. He got his whole family. He only needed one more—and now he's got him."

What could I say to her? I held her hands as she spoke and I embraced her when she was sobbing.

After a while I told her that we should call Brian and tell him. It was necessary for him to be with her and her daughter. Then we called several close friends who came over immediately.

I remained with Betty until 5:30 A.M. and helped her make arrangements to have Ralph's body and Joey's body returned to

Houston after the mandatory autopsies were performed. I also contacted our local Jewish undertaker and we made arrangements for Tuesday afternoon funerals at our synagogue cemetery.

As I left, I told Betty that I would return at noon. She was still weeping. "It is impossible for me to believe it. This morning he smiled at me when he left and he said, 'I'll see you late tonight,' but I'll never see him again and I'll never see Joey again." Betty stared at me and added as a postscript, "I'm a dead woman now. I've got nothing."

But I embraced her and cradled her again and stated, "Yes, you've lost a major part of your life, Ralph and Joey. But as the days go by you will begin, once again, to concentrate on Brian and Susie. They need you now so very much. We'll help brace your shoulders. We'll help you stand up tall again. We'll help you help your children."

Betty sighed heavily, "From your mouth to God's ears—but I don't think it will be possible again."

She opened the door for me, I left, and some friends escorted her to a chair.

Life was not easy for Betty after losing her son and husband but she did not give in and she did not give up. She refused to concentrate on what she had lost but focused on what she still had left.

Later on, she became the "Cookie Manager" for Susie's Girl Scout troop. In fact, Brian married a girl he had met in college and the two of them also became active in Susie's Girl Scout troop and the family was awarded "The Outstanding Family Award for Girl Scouts."

Betty also did volunteer work in Susie's Elementary School: tutoring children who had problems and also tutoring children in mathematics, reading, and English.

In addition to that, she would often knit Afghans and sweaters for friends and members of her family, and when friends or family members were ill she would always prepare for them pots of chicken soup and refer to them as her "Jewish Penicillin."

However, Betty really regained her second wind when both Brian and Susie were married and each had a child. Her grandchildren were now her wealth and her opulence. They were her present and her future. They were her strength and her energy. They gave her a yearning to look forward to smiles in the future rather than concentrate on the tears of the past.

Betty passed away several years ago at the age of sixty-six. Life was not easy for her but during her last few years she would always smile at me and say, "Tomorrow will definitely be a better day."

• • • • •

I realized my new limitations,
    only to find new strengths.
I lost my quickness and agility,
    only to discover patience.
I lost my short-term memory,
    only to find ways to become more efficient.
I lost my ability to think quickly,
    so that I could give up trying to control.
I lost my job,
    only to discover what I labored for out of love.
I lost my driver's license,
    only to appreciate my true dependence on other people.
I lost my stamina and energy,
    only to re-prioritize the importance of things in my life.
For each of my losses,
    I discovered a strength.
I am still becoming stronger.

A Journey of Discovery
Dr. Jane Summers

Chapter 16

"A Slip Of The Lip Can Sink A Ship"

A) The Russians Are Coming

There is an old statement in the rabbinic literature that says (*Avot* 1:11), "Wise men, watch your words because one mistaken word can cause you a monumental amount of damage." In fact, during World War II, I remember an omnipresent statement that was plastered on walls throughout our country: "A slip of the lip can sink a ship," and next to that phrase was a picture of an allied cargo ship that had just been torpedoed by a Nazi submarine.

I rarely gave thought to that rabbinic comment or to that Madison Avenue advertisement. It did not apply to *me,* I thought. I had no military information needed by an American foe, and I did not think that any of my comments could be the cause of "a monumental amount of damage." However, I must admit that on at least two occasions, my thoughtless comments were eventually deeply regretted by me because they resulted in action and attitudes by others that I never initially envisioned.

Our Friday evening services at Beth Yeshurun Congregation were always well attended. Almost every weekend we had a Bar Mitzvah, a Bat Mitzvah, or a combination of both. Hundreds of people—friends and congregatnts—would come to the synagogue to join the celebrants or simply to participate in the Shabbat Prayer Service.

It was always my contention that the prophet Isaiah was correct when he said (Isaiah 55:13) *"Ve-ka-ra-ta la-Shabbat oneg,"* "Thou shall proclaim the Sabbath a delight." The Sabbath should never be a morbid day, a depressing day or a dispirited day. It should always be a day of happiness and joy, of singing and dancing, of smiling and laughing. Therefore I would always attempt to inject humor into my sermons, lively music into the Service, contemporary poetry into the readings—and my ears were always open to any innovations that would be brought to my attention by congregants to enliven our Services.

Marriages and anniversaries are always moments of smiles and happiness. Therefore I would always write a personal letter to all the members of the congregation inviting them to attend Services at the synagogue on the Friday evening prior to their anniversaries at which time I would call out the names of the celebrants, ask them to rise, invoke upon them a blessing, and present each celebrant with a one-fifth of a pound Hershey chocolate bar stating that just as the Hershey chocolate was sweet, so, too, their next year of marriage should be one of sweetness and happiness and joy.

And if a couple was celebrating a twenty-fifth or fiftieth anniversary, I would call them to the pulpit to stand before me and not only would I bless them but I would also present them with a full pound Hershey chocolate bar.

But there was one more group that I would call to the pulpit—couples who were going to be married during the following week. In addition to my personal blessing I would present them with my "Marriage Kit" that contained two candlesticks and some candles for the bride to light each Friday evening to usher in the Sabbath, a pamphlet containing all the prayers normally recited on Friday evening as one sat down to his/her Sabbath meal, a cassette recording of all the tunes usually chanted at the Friday night meal, a cookbook containing recipes for Jewish delicacies, and I would also present the young couple with *two* pounds of Hershey chocolates—one for the groom and one for the bride—so that they might commence their married life on "an avenue of sweetness and joy."

Everyone would usually applaud the young couple as they would descend from the pulpit amidst cries of "Congratulations!" and *"Mazal Tov"* from those in the synagogue, especially relatives and personal friends who had come to view the blessing.

I will never forget one young couple as they descended from the pulpit. He was twenty-seven, quite muscular and handsome, and she was twenty-four, quite attractive and shapely. As the groom left the pulpit he held on tightly to his bride with his left hand, and with his right hand he raised high his Hershey bar and waved it about as if it were a trophy that he had just won at a tennis match. Everyone was laughing or smiling, and many were still applauding them.

And as they walked off the pulpit I too was caught up in the joy of the moment and I announced, as I usually did, the place, date, and time of the wedding *chuppah* (ritual). I happily stated, "The wedding will take place tomorrow night, 7:30 P.M., at the Omni Hotel."

However, everyone seemed to be in a super-joyous frame of mind, and something that I cannot explain obviously got into me. I added a few more words to my usual declaration of date, time, and place of the wedding. I stated, "The families are very happy about the forthcoming wedding. Therefore, anyone who would like to attend the wedding just be at the Omni Hotel tomorrow night at 7:30 P.M."

Everyone present laughed hilariously at this unexpected comment, and even I laughed heartily. Everyone knew that I was joking and joshing but the comment was totally unanticipated—and therefore the responsive laughter was quite strong and voluminous.

The next evening, Saturday evening, I entered the hotel at 7 P.M. I usually arrived a half hour before the Service so that the marriage papers (*Ketubah*) might be properly signed, a special blessing invoked upon the bride and groom prior to the ceremony, and the groom be given the opportunity to place the bride's veil over her face, as is the Jewish tradition prior to the commencement of the ceremony.

However, as I entered the room adjacent to the Grand Ballroom to pick up the card indicating at what table Toby and I would be seated for dinner, prior to inquiring about the whereabouts of the bride and groom for their pre-wedding blessing, I noticed six people standing before the card table attempting to talk to a man and woman. But it was quite obvious that the man and the woman did not comprehend what was being said to them.

Immediately, the bride's brother approached me. "Rabbi," he said in an excited manner, "do you speak Russian or Yiddish? We have two people here who obviously speak only Russian or Yiddish. But none of us here speaks Russian or Yiddish. *We* don't know what they are saying and *they* don't understand what *we* are saying."

I quickly pacified the bride's brother by informing him that even though I did not speak Russian, I did speak and understand Yiddish.

The young brother led me over to the man and woman and said to me in an exasperated manner, "This man and woman seem to be saying that they were invited to the wedding, but my parents don't know them and didn't invite them and David's* parents [the parents of the groom] don't know them either and surely did not invite them. And so, too, David and Sue* [bride] say that they don't know them and didn't invite them—but they seem to be insisting that they were invited to Sue and David's wedding."

The bride's brother breathed heavily and then whispered in my ear, "My parents are thinking of calling Security to toss them out or have them arrested for trespassing. They may be dangerous people."

I smiled at the bride's brother and told him to "hold off" for a few minutes until I spoke to the man and woman.

Briskly I walked over to the couple and addressed them in Yiddish, "*Voss iz di tzorres?* [What is the problem?]"

The man's outer expression quickly changed from tension and trepidation to calmness and composure. A smile expanded across his face like a wave behind a surfer in Hawaii. *"Baruch Hashem,"* he cried out in delight. *"Aymitzah iz da voss ken redden tzu mir in Yiddish, un ich ken far-shtayin voss err zogt.* [Thank God someone is here who can speak to me in Yiddish and I can understand what he is saying.]"

The man obviously did not speak English and his wife looked terribly embarrassed and about to faint. Then the man stared at me and continued in Yiddish, "[*You* are the rabbi of Beth Yeshurun Congregation where I *davened* [prayed] last night. *You* are the rabbi who stood on the pulpit and invited us to the wedding tonight.]" He looked directly into my eyes and pathetically continued, "[Don't you remember your words? You said, 'Whoever would like to come to the wedding, please join us at the Omni Hotel tomorrow night at 7:30 P.M.']"

The man spoke Yiddish with a thick Russian accent, and when I did not say anything in the next five seconds he added, "[We just arrived from Moscow two weeks ago. Everyone has been so gracious and generous toward us. The Jewish community has given us an apartment in which to live, money to start our lives in Houston, food for several weeks, and it even helped me find a job as a petroleum engineer. We are blessed to be part of the Jewish community of Houston.]

"[Last night, one of our Jewish sponsors in Houston invited us to go with him and his wife to *Shul* [synagogue]. Previously, I had been in a *shul* only twice in my lifetime, years and years ago. Please remember that I was born and raised in a Communist country where religion is a detriment to one's life—especially if you are Jewish.]"

The Russian breathed heavily and continued, "[And now, last night, I heard my fellow Jews extending another hand of welcome to my family—to attend a Jewish wedding. Never before had I been to a Jewish wedding. We were married by a judge in a courtroom. I was afraid to have a Jewish wedding because I thought I would lose my job. All my bosses were Communists and atheists.]

"[In fact]," he continued with enthusiasm and a smile written all over his face, "[my wife and I were going to bring along our eighteen year old daughter and our fifteen year old son. We thought that our daughter might meet a young Jewish man at the wedding who would become interested in her. She is *very* pretty]," and again he smiled broadly. "[Remember, *you* invited them, too. You said, '*Anyone* who wants to attend the wedding is invited. Just be at the hotel at 7:30 P.M.']"

I winced at his words and attempted to interject an explanation; however, he was now all wound up and even his wife had a joyous and rapturous smile on her face from ear to ear. It was as if she believed that I held their invitation in my pocket.

Once again, he continued, "[The only reason we didn't bring our children was because Jewish Family Service arranged for a group of young boys and girls to take them to a party—where there would be many American teenagers.]"

I sighed heavily as the bride's brother impatiently said to me, as he jabbed me in the side with his finger, "Have you already told them that it's all a mistake? They were never invited to the wedding."

He looked down at his watch and continued, "Rabbi, there's only fifteen minutes until the ceremony and my mother is upset. In fact, she's taking it out on my father who is totally innocent. He doesn't know anything about this matter or where these people came from. He told me, 'Get the rabbi and have him explain to the people that they made a mistake.'"

I breathed heavily again, turned to the two Russians who continued to smile happily, and I asked the husband in Yiddish, "[What are your names?]"

The husband proudly proclaimed, "[Vladimir Pushkin*, just like the famous author's last name. But I must admit to you that when I was born my name was Vladimir Pressburger . But when I was applying for a job as an engineer in Moscow I knew that I would not get it if my name was Pressburger. It was Jewish. So I had it changed to Pushkin—and I got my job.]" And he quickly added, "[My wife's name is Rosa Pressburger*—Dr. Rosa Pressburger. She's a Pediatrician but she doesn't have a license yet to practice in Houston.]" Once again a big, bright, and proud smile exploded over his face. "[But she'll have that license soon. She graduated number one in her medical class.]"

"[Wait one moment,] I said to the Russian couple in Yiddish as the members of the wedding families around us continually looked at their watches and breathed heavily as if time was quickly running out on a solution to this problem.

Once again I turned to the bride's brother. "Go quickly to your mother and bring her here. I want to tell her something and quickly solve the problem."

The young brother shook his head as if he knew that his mother definitely did not want to see the Russians; however, I dogmatically ordered him, "Go now, there's no time to waste if I'm going to start the wedding on time. I don't want to have to tell your mother that *you* were the reason why we had to start late."

The brother quickly scampered off toward the Bride's Room and returned with his mother and father three minutes later.

The bride's mother was aflame. I could see fire in her eyes and hear anger in her voice. "Rabbi, did you tell them yet that no one invited them to the wedding? The wedding is supposed to begin in ten minutes *and I don't want it delayed.*"

There was deep apology in my voice and heavy breathing as I addressed the bride's mother. "Sophie*, it's all *my* fault. Last night at the Services, I saw how happy everyone was and I simply wanted to add a little more joy to your children's wedding—so—as a joke—nothing more than that, just as a joke, I said, 'Whoever would like to attend the wedding, please be at the Omni Hotel at 7:30 P.M.'"

I waited for five seconds to see her response but none was forthcoming. Her face remained fiery and anger-filled, so I continued. "I *knew* everyone would laugh, and they did. I *knew* no one would take that invitation seriously. It was just a joke after the blessing of your daughter and son-in-law. In fact," I added as if to prove my argument, "I looked toward *you,* Sophie, and *you, too,* were laughing.

"But these two people—Vladimir, a petroleum engineer, and his wife, Rosa, a physician, a Pediatrician—had just arrived from Russia a few days ago. They did *not* know I was joking. To them, a synagogue is a holy place from the minute they enter to the moment they leave. They have never heard jokes in a synagogue—because this is only the third time they've been in a synagogue.

"They were therefore so happy and elated that strangers, who didn't even know them, had invited them to their children's *chuppah* [marriage ceremony] and dinner."

I looked pathetically into Sophie's eyes, and I went on as I grasped her right hand in both of my hands. "Sophie, *I* goofed. *I* made a mistake. *I* fouled it up. Why blame *them* and embarrass *them?* He's wearing the only suit he owns. The Jewish Family Service probably got it for him this week at J.C. Penney. His wife is wearing her best dress. The Jewish Family service also probably got it for her this week at J.C. Penney. Why blame *them* for *my* mistake?" I felt comfortable speaking so frankly to Sophie about the plight of the Russians because I knew that they spoke no English and did not understand any English.

I looked into Sophie's eyes. I could see that the fire was no longer as intense as it had previously been. "Sophie," I pleaded, "Let them stay. *I'll* pay for the two dinners."

I was speaking slowly and softly and Sophie could see that contrition and remorse were written all over my face.

"Rabbi," Sophie replied as she breathed heavily and deeply, "I noticed that nine couples who stated that they were coming did not pick up their place cards. Probably six of those couples will be no-shows. Tell the Russians that they are guests of my husband and me. Tell them that Americans are extremely compassionate people. Inform them that we welcome them to the United States and realize how they suffered under Communism."

But then Sophie looked me straight in the eyes as if laser beams were coming forth from her eyes, totally piercing mine. However, now she had a big and effluent smile all over her face. It was obvious that she wanted the Russians to think that she was truly delighted and elated by their presence. But to me she softly, but decisively, enunciated very distinctly, "Rabbi, we have five minutes left before the wedding is to begin—and I want it to begin on time. Let them enjoy themselves here, but promise me that you'll never do again what you did Friday night." Now, her voice was rising in volume and pitch but the smile was still plastered like a mask on her face. It was as if she wanted *me* to know that I was being officially chastised but she wanted the *Russians* to feel that she truly felt honored that they were going to be at the ceremony and the dinner. "What if a *hundred* newcomers from Russia had been present? If you want to be a comedian, do it at Laugh Stop Show Place, but not at my wedding."

Sophie hesitated for a moment, continued to look through me with her laser beam look, and added as a postscript, "I must, however, admit that Friday night I thought your comment was stupendous."

She then kissed me on the cheek and proclaimed, "On with the wedding."

Everyone present around the Russians sighed deep sighs of satisfaction and relief, especially Vladimir and Rosa.

• • • • •

B) One Wrong Word Can Result In Exile

While I was in the active rabbinate I led four different congregations. The second one was in McKeesport, Pennsylvania, a city about seven miles southwest of Pittsburgh. It was a relatively small congregation with about one hundred and twenty-five families as members; however, I was quite active in inter-religious activities in McKeesport.

One day, I was asked by the minister of the largest Protestant church in town if I would speak to a combination of his adult education groups on the subject "What Is Judaism?" and I told him that I would be happy to do that.

On the designated date, I arrived at the church and was quite pleasantly surprised to note about three hundred and fifty men and women in attendance for this adult education program. The minister told me that his congregants knew very little about Judaism and were extremely thirsty to learn more of the religion that had given birth to their Christianity. "Jesus was a Jew before he was a Christian," the minister proclaimed to me. "That's why my people are like a sponge. They want to absorb anything and everything you can tell them about their Savior's original religion of his youth."

I told him that I would do my best and I spent the next hour explaining to the church members the primary beliefs of Judaism and also how Judaism differed from Christianity. You could hear a pin drop during my lecture.

I began by quoting for them the ancient Talmudic statement made by Hillel (*Shabbat* 31a) who was asked by a non-Jew to teach him all about Judaism while he stood on one leg (in a very short period of time—one to two minutes). I told them that Hillel did not become angry or exasperated by that request even though it was obvious that the questioner wanted to irritate and annoy Hillel. Hillel merely said to him, with a smile on his face, "That which is annoying to *you,* do not do to your friend. That is the primary and most fundamental principle of Judaism. The remainder is merely an explanation."

It was obvious to me that this topic was very important to those present. They wanted to know the basic principles of Judaism and how they differed from those of Christianity, and the reason for this profound interest in my religious beliefs quickly became evident as soon as the program was opened for questions.

"Rabbi," the first questioner queried, "don't you know what John said in the *New Testament?* He said [John 3:16-18], 'For God so loved the world, that He gave His only begotten Son, that whosoever believeth in Him should not perish, but have everlasting life. . . . He that believeth on Him is not condemned; but he that believeth not is condemned already, because he hath not believed in the name of the only begotten Son of God?'

"Rabbi," he continued, "don't you want to gain everlasting life? Don't you want to go to heaven when you die?"

As he concluded his question, many in the audience indicated their agreement with the questioner by audibly interjecting, "He's right," or "That's a good question," or "Why would one want to sacrifice his eternal life with God?"

I did not get a chance to reply to the first man before a

young woman, about thirty years of age, rose and in a sweet and delicate voice asked, "Rabbi, aren't you familiar with Jesus' words [John 14:6], 'I am the way, the truth, and the life: No man cometh unto the Father, but by me'? Don't you want to be with God, with Jesus, after you die?"

The group was an extremely enthusiastic one. Hands were shooting up from all sides of the auditorium. However, they were not even waiting for my reply to the previous question. They simply injected additional questions, one after the other, but all of them echoed the same theme: "It is difficult to believe you do not accept Jesus as your Savior; we are all sinners and we all must be saved—and better sooner than later."

After five questions, all of them dealing with what would happen to me after I died, the minister arose, held up his arms, and called out, "Let's give the rabbi an opportunity to answer one question at a time. You're flooding him with questions. We all know *our* beliefs. We came here to hear the rabbi speak about Judaism, *his* religion, not Christianity, *our* religion."

The minister smiled at me, sat down again, and authoritatively stated, "The floor is yours," while pointing to me.

I thanked him and spoke to the audience about Judaism not accepting the principle of "Original Sin," that Adam had sinned in the Garden of Eden, and *we,* his descendants, had inherited his sin and *we* had to search for forgiveness from a Savior.

I even attempted to solidify this statement by adding, "In fact, every morning a traditional Jew recites in his prayers the words, *'Elohai, neshamah shenatata be, tehorah he . . .'* 'O God, the soul that you gave me is a *pure* one.' It is *not* a soul born with sin. It is a soul born milky white."

It was quickly obvious to me that many of those present strongly objected to my thesis because they were vigorously shaking their heads from right to left indicating "No!"

I continued by informing them that Judaism did *not* believe in "Vicarious Atonement," that the only way a person could achieve forgiveness was by accepting the fact that *Jesus* was put to death on the cross so that we could be pardoned and absolved for *our* transgressions. I emphasized to them that in our Jewish beliefs we preached that everyone was responsible for his own actions. If *I* broke a window, *I* had to pay for it. I could not hold Jesus responsible for that act and obligate him to pay for my damages. If *I* murdered a person, *I* was to be tried in court—and if *I* was found guilty, *I,* and *not Jesus,* was to be put to death. Each person was responsible for his own trespasses and wrongdoings.

In fact, I even added, "Don't you remember what God said in the book of Deuteronomy [24:16], 'The fathers shall not be put to death for the children, neither shall the children be put to death for the fathers; *every man shall be put to death for his own sins.'* Therefore how can Jesus' death bring *me* forgiveness for *my* sins. I have to achieve that all by myself."

However, once again I saw the heads shaking from right to left, but many more were now shaking their heads than before, indicating their total disagreement with me. In fact, many were smiling as they were shaking their heads as if to say they knew a secret that I did not know.

It was obvious that many wanted to vocally dispute with me and indicate the veracity of their Christian beliefs. But the minister arose several times saying, "Let's wait until the rabbi has completed his comments before we add ours."

Then I appended as an emphatic postscript, "Judaism also does not ascribe to the Christian concept of 'Grace,' that we cannot achieve forgiveness through our own actions, through our good works, by performing *mitzvot* [good deeds]. We do not accept the Christian belief that you quoted before from the *New Testament* [Ephesians 2:8-9], 'For by Grace are ye saved through *faith;* and that not of yourselves: it is the gift of God: *not of works,* lest any man should boast.'

"On the contrary," I stated most emphatically as I held aloft the *Tenach* (the Jewish *Bible*). "Christianity believes that everyone has to be *saved* because they are now lost souls. But *we* believe that we were never lost and therefore do not have to be saved by a second party. If we do something wrong we correct it by repentance and by doing good deeds, *mitzvot.*"

A cacophony of voices immediately broke forth: "You are wrong;" "That is totally incorrect;" "Don't you believe in God?"

But the minister once again arose and with a grand and

broad grin on his face spoke into the microphone and softly pleaded, "Please give the rabbi an opportunity to conclude his Jewish beliefs."

I briefly thanked the minister and continued, "Judaism believes that religion is like the New York subway system." Many laughed at my analogy and simile.

But I raised my hand, smiled, and went on. "I say that because New York is made up of five boroughs. In the north, you have the Bronx. In the south, you have Brooklyn. But in the middle you have Manhattan. If you want to go from Brooklyn to the Bronx, or from the Bronx to Brooklyn you must go through Manhattan. However, there are three ways you can go from Utica Avenue in Brooklyn to reach Burnside Avenue in the Bronx." And as I spoke I drew a diagram on the blackboard so that my audience could see with their eyes a vivid picture of what I was attempting to stress.

"You can take the 4th Avenue train at Utica Avenue and traverse the *East Side* of Manhattan and finally arrive at Burnside.

"Or you can take the 6th Avenue train at Utica Avenue and go through the *center* of Manhattan and eventually arrive at Burnside Avenue.

"Or you can take the 7th Avenue subway at Utica Avenue and pass through the *west* side of Manhattan and eventually arrive at your destination at Burnside Avenue."

Many people were now smiling very heartily and one even called out, "Rabbi, I'm not traveling to New York. I'm going to heaven with Jesus," and many indicated their agreement by applauding.

But again the minister arose and politely requested, "Ladies and gentlemen, in just a few moments we'll be able to ask more questions and make comments. Please wait a few more minutes," and surprisingly, it quickly became quiet once again.

I hesitated for a moment and began again. "Well, Judaism is like that subway system. *We* say that the 4th Avenue train is the Catholic religion. They want to achieve their religious goals by going through the eastern part of Manhattan with Jesus and the Pope—great. That is their choice.

"The 6th Avenue train is like the Protestant religion, *we* say.

They want to achieve their religious goals by going through the center of Manhattan with Jesus and the *New Testament*—great. That is their choice.

"However, Jews want to travel from Utica Avenue to Burnside Avenue on the 7th Avenue train through the western part of Manhattan with Moses and the *Torah*. That should be *our* choice and everyone should respect our choice. Why should we be forced to take the 4th Avenue or 6th Avenue trains to get from Utica to Burnside? This is the United States of America. Freedom of religion is guaranteed to me and to all by the First Amendment to the Constitution."

I waited for a moment to see if there would be a response but all I noticed was a plethora of eyes staring at me, so I continued. "Utica Avenue and Burnside Avenue, to *me*, symbolically represent two very important aspects of all three religions—ethics and morality, how we treat our fellow human beings who are like us or who differ from us. We all have different ways of achieving those goals—but achieve them we must. We must treat our neighbors with honor and respect, with dignity and courtesy, with adoration and esteem. And if we do that, I tell you we'll have a better world in which to live."

I hesitated again for a moment, smiled, spread forth my arms, and softly added, "That's it."

Immediately, at least twenty-five arms shot upwards indicating that there were an abundance of questions awaiting me.

The first one was direct but simple. "Rabbi, aren't you worried? What will happen to you when you pass away?"

However, no matter how I answered that question and similar questions, all the questions dealt with the hereafter, what will happen to me when I passed away. And no matter how strongly I emphasized that Judaism stressed *this* world rather than the *next* world, the questions always reverted to Heaven and Hell, the hereafter, life after death, and where will *I* be spending my eternity.

But then one elderly gentleman arose and stated in a plodding and drudging presentation, "Rabbi, I've known quite a number of Jews through my business dealings. They are very good business people. There is no question about that.

"However," he stated as he looked about the audience, "please tell me why it is that when Jews bury their dead they don't bury them as we do by lying them in the ground horizontally on their backs? The Jews bury their dead vertically, standing up. They simply dig their graves deeper."

I looked about the audience and I could see stares galore, as if the audience was astounded by this revelation. It seemed as if the gospel truth had been stated by their friend and they, too, wanted to know the answer.

I thought the man was joking and joshing just to break the tension of the moment. So, I decided to add to the humor of the moment by stating, "Your statement is *almost* correct." I then looked at the questioner with a straight face and added, "Not only do we bury our dead vertically in the ground but we bury them with their heads downward and their feet upward. However, the reason is quite simple. In this way, you can get three caskets in one grave. You buy one cemetery plot but you can bury three members of your family in the grave. It's economical. It's good finance. Its terrific money saving."

Everyone merely stared at me, but then one man laughed and quickly it was like a flood, a barrage—everyone was laughing, and even I was laughing. I thought that I had defused the pressure and tension of the meeting. Smiles were now over everyone's face. Even the minister was howling with laughter. I felt good because I thought that my silly comment was a good exclamation mark for the conclusion of the study session.

The minister ended the meeting with a meaningful prayer. He asked everyone to hold hands and he prayed, "O God, we are so thankful for this meaningful talk by our esteemed friend and rabbi. He has opened our eyes to the Jewish faith, to the original faith of our Savior, Jesus Christ. We pray that relationships between Jews and Christians will always improve so that we will both be able to preach the word of God."

The minister hesitated for a moment, looked at me, and then with a warm smile on his face intoned the words of the Prophet Micah (6:8) who preached to his people 2700 years ago, "What does God really require of you—only to do justice, to love kindness, and to walk modestly with God."

The minister paused for about ten seconds and lowered his eyes toward the ground as those present continued to hold hands. I felt very good. This was true ecumenism. The minister realized that I was Jewish and therefore concluded his prayer with a statement from a *Jewish* Prophet, Micah. I truly wanted to congratulate him for being so courteous, respectful, warm-hearted, and polite; however, he then raised his head heavenwards and in a soft and mellow voice punctuated his prayer with the words, "We utter these words in the name of our Lord, Jesus Christ, Amen!"

"I guess I came to my conclusion too quickly," I said to myself immediately after the minister's "Amen", even before the woman to my left and the man to my right disengaged hands with me.

We lingered on in the church auditorium for about fifteen more minutes as members of the Study Group and the minister offered kind comments to me, and then I went home.

Two days later, the minister and I crossed paths again in front of the McKeesport Daily News building.

We shook hands, smiled at each other, and exchanged pleasantries. Then the minister shook his head from right to left and a truly broad smile captivated his face. "Rabbi, you Jews are not smart. You're not wise."

For a moment I thought he was going to spout forth with a harangue of anti-Semitic vitriol—and I did not know why. I thought that a very comfortable relationship existed between us. But then he continued, "Rabbi, my phone has been ringing constantly since you gave your speech at my church. Everyone agrees that you Jews are *BRILLIANT,*" and he emphasized that word. "There are no people like you Jewish people when it comes to common sense and good economics and making money."

I stared at him as if I did not know what precipitated that comment, and he continued, "Rabbi, who in the entire world could think of burying the dead vertically so that you could get three dead in one grave—bury three for the price of one—and that's exactly what it is. We gentiles should have thought of it, but we didn't. But you and your *Jewish* ancestors beat us to the punch. You are truly *BRILLIANT,*" and once again he emphasized that last word.

"However, one thing no one can truly understand," he went on as he sighed heavily, "Why do you have to bury your dead with their heads down. But my people said," and his smile now almost circumscribed his entire head, "if the *Jews* do it, it must be good. Now many of my church members want to do the same thing—buy one grave and bury three in it vertically, but their choice is to bury the dead with heads up. It's good economics."

I could not believe what he was saying. That comment at the church was made as a joke, not as a serious statement. "Reverend," I sighed heavily as beads of perspiration quickly appeared on my forehead and as my armpits rapidly became damp. "I did not mean that statement to be taken seriously. There was great tension in the room and I simply wanted to break it." Again I sighed heavily, and I slowly added in a very soft but delicate manner, "I was only joking."

The Minister's smile quickly evaporated and disappeared from his face as if he had been electrified by a cattle prod and a scowl replaced the smile. "Rabbi, this was a religious study group, not a comedy workshop. We came to hear the *Jewish* word of God as the Jews understand it, not a Milton Berle comedy routine."

I felt as if I was sinking into the ground. I felt like Korach must have felt when he opposed Moses, and God smote him by having "the earth open up its mouth and swallow him and his cohorts" (Numbers 16:32).

"I apologize; I apologize," I meekly and shamefacedly confessed to the minister. "I made a mistake; I goofed; I should have known where I was speaking. I should have answered serious questions in a serious manner. Please accept my apology," I added in an obsequious and servile manner.

The minister's eyes were piercing my body. Anger was written all over his face. But in a flash of a second he began heartily laughing. "Jack," he said in between laughs, "your comment was exactly what we needed at that meeting. The one who asked that question was pretty dumb to ask that question. Where did he hear that stupid comment that the Jews bury their dead vertically—at a KKK meeting? It's stupid—and a stupid question deserves a stupid answer."

The minister hesitated momentarily and while still laughing added, "Jack, you must admit that your comment was pretty stupid—'We bury our dead heads down, three to a grave.' I've heard dumb ones before, but that one is at the very top of the list."

Quickly, the minister grabbed my arm, smiled reassuringly, and enthusiastically proclaimed, "Let's go for lunch. You look as if you're about to collapse. Lunch is on me."

I exhaled heartily and then quickly inhaled vigorously as if I had been submerged in the depths of the seas and had finally come to the surface, and with a smile blossoming forth all over my face proclaimed, "Hallelujah! The Messiah must be coming. This is true ecumenism."

"Why?" the minister quizzingly asked. "Is it because *I* have forgiven you and I'll try to explain your humor to my church?"

"No." I meekly responded. "It's because you're paying for the lunch."

The minister looked up toward the heavens, shook his head, and loudly called out—right in the middle of the street—"God, he's doing it all over again."

• • • • •

A newspaperman once asked Sam Rayburn: "Mr. Speaker, you see probably a hundred people a day. You tell each one 'Yes,' or 'No,' or 'Maybe.' You never seem to make notes on what you have told them, but I never heard of you forgetting anything you have promised them. What is your secret?"

Rayburn's hot brown eyes flashed: "If you tell the truth the first time, you don't have to remember."

—D. B. Hardeman

CHAPTER 17

A "Miracle" On The Caribbean

Beth Yeshurun Congregation in Houston, Texas is a very large congregation—over two thousand families. There are close to six thousand individuals associated with the Synagogue. It required me to be "on call" seven days a week, twenty-four hours a day—and that went on for thirty-one and a half years. It was strength-consuming and emotion-sapping.

The "religious year" would begin in August, before Roth Hashanah and Yom Kippur, and when July would come along I usually had had it for the year and was ready for an extended vacation.

In 1985, Toby discovered "cruising" as a form of vacationing. A friend had told her that it was "a stupendous way to relax, vacation, and enjoy yourself."

Initially I opposed this novel approach to vacationing. I told Toby that it would be restraining and suppressing, harnessing and muzzling. "You're stuck on a ship in the middle of the sea," I said. "You can't get off, except for a short period of time."

However, Toby persisted—and I eventually gave in. I capitulated. But now as I look back at that decision, I must admit that that was one of the most pleasant decisions I made.

Everything is aboard ship: swimming and dining, entertainment and exercising, sunning one's self and dancing, playing shuffleboard and getting books from the library. It's all-inclusive.

Our first ship was the Song of America of the Royal Caribbean Cruise Line. It was a beautiful and modern ship and I was told that on Friday evening Jewish Services were conducted aboard ship. Generally, a rabbi was not present. The Cruise Company did not contract with a rabbi to be aboard ship each week. However, a special room was always set aside for the Jewish Service: candles were on a table to usher in the Sabbath, a cup with "Kosher wine" was also on a table for the traditional Kiddush blessing, and yarmulkes (skull caps) and abbreviated prayer books (consisting of several photostated pages) were also provided.

Usually a knowledgeable lay person would volunteer to lead the service, and then refreshments (gefilte fish and matzah ball soup) would be served buffet-style to all those present.

About a day into the trip I met the Cruise Director and told him that I was a rabbi and I would be happy to lead the Friday evening service. However, I had one request—on Thursday afternoon at about 5 P.M. I wanted a five second announcement to be made over the ship's public address system: "Rabbi Jack Segal of Houston will lead the Friday evening Jewish Service at 5:30 P.M. on Friday evening."

Initially, the "Cruise Director" was reluctant: "We usually don't do that. We don't get too many people to the Jewish Services. Last week we only had twelve at the Service."

I shook my head and said: "This ship left from Miami. There must be loads of Jews aboard. They probably either did not know of the Service or did not give it any thought. You always need a reminder."

He looked at me with skepticism and said: "Don't all Jews know that Friday night is the eve for Services? Why do you have to advertise?"

But I smiled and commented: "Look at Sears Roebuck and J. C. Penney—don't they always advertise? They are gigantic companies but still they advertise. Everyone knows that they exist. Everyone knows that they have everything—but still they advertise. They want to keep their names and their products on the tips of the tongues of the people in the community.

"So, too, Kroger and Randall's also advertise. They are enormous supermarkets—but they want their names repeated and repeated. And the result is that they do more and more business each year."

I guess I must have worn him down with my brief "speech" and he replied: "O.K., we'll make the announcement, but only once and only for five seconds."

I smiled and added: "Thanks. That's enough."

That Friday afternoon about thirty minutes before the Service I went to the area where the Service was to be conducted. I saw a young woman, about twenty-five years of age checking the microphone and the "prayer sheets." I introduced myself to her and told her that I would be conducting the Service that evening.

The young woman smiled: "Good, the Cruise Director already told me."

She then introduced herself and said: "I usually lead the Jewish Services when no Jew volunteers to lead them." However, when she told me her name, it sounded Italian to me, not Jewish—Nina Garibaldi.*

I therefore said: "You must be a Sefardic Jew [those originating in Spain who were expelled in 1492 and emigrated to other nations on the Mediterranean Sea]."

She grinned: "No, I'm not a Sefardic Jew. I'm a Roman Catholic—and a devout one. My grandparents came from a small town near Naples. However, everyone aboard ship has to do many things. We all have to wear many caps and one of my caps is leading the Jewish Services on Friday evenings."

I was momentarily taken aback. "Where did you learn Hebrew? Who taught you the melodies of the Service?"

Once again she grinned and said: "It was easy. I'm the singer for the band on the ship and we had an Israeli who worked as a waiter in the dining room. He liked my voice—and me, too—and he suggested that I conduct the Jewish Services. He told me that he would get me the music from a friend of his who was a cantor and he would also get me a transliteration of the Service. He would get someone to write in English the sounds of the Hebrew words. I started doing this about a year ago and I've become very proficient at it. My Israeli friend, who eventually was transferred to another ship, told me that I sounded 'schmaltzy'. I took that as a compliment.

"However, I'm glad that you, a rabbi, will conduct the Service tonight. But I must tell you that every week after my first prayer I always get a burst of applause, and often I get a standing ovation. I never knew that Jews applauded after the singing of a prayer. And I must also admit that after the last prayer I could make a fortune if I had the Kleenex concession. Everyone—and I do mean everyone, especially the elderly people—is crying. This happens every week when I conduct the Service."

For a moment I was baffled and befuddled. I assumed she began the abbreviated Friday evening Service with the prayer L'chu ne-ra-ne-na or the prayer L'cha do-dee. I have heard countless cantors chant those tunes but never has anyone arisen to applaud the cantor—not even a solitary individual. People always enjoy and appreciate those prayers about welcoming the Sabbath; however, I have never heard them applaud.

Every single week I have also listened to our magnificent cantor at Beth Yeshurun sing the concluding song of the Friday evening Service, Adone O'lam, but again, I have never seen congregants, young ones or old ones, weeping or crying. On the contrary, usually they are smiling or grinning, beaming or smirking, or clapping their hands—because the tune is usually a lively and peppy one.

I therefore asked her the obvious question: "What do you do to get this unique response? I heard you sing with the band and you are excellent but you must also possess a special religious charisma to bring forth that reaction during the Service—applause and tears."

Nina smiled once again: "I followed the instructions of my 'Israeli master'. Rabbi, look at the prayer sheets we use aboard ship that he prepared for me.

"We always begin with *Kol Nidray* [the opening prayer that

is sung on Yom Kippur eve, the holiest day of the Jewish year. *Kol Nidray* is not part of the regular Friday evening Service.] He told me that the congregation would quickly forget that I am Italian-Catholic as soon as I sang that song—because I always introduce myself before the Service begins and tell the people a little bit about my background. And I must admit, every single time I've sung that song there has been applause from the entire congregation, and often, when we have a large congregation, the applause is ear-splitting—with many even shouting, 'Bravo! Bravo!'

"And when I conclude the Service about a half hour later, my Israeli friend told me to always finish by singing 'My Yiddishe Mama' ['My Jewish Mother'—a song from the 1920's when the Yiddish Theater was very popular in New York. That song was very nostalgic and spoke about the small and elderly Jewish mother who had sacrificed so much for her children so that they could get a good education, become professionals, or begin good businesses. It would always bring forth feelings of guilt and remorse. It, too, is not part of the Friday evening Service.] You could hear a pin drop. It seemed as if everyone had his or her handkerchief out of his pocket or her pocketbook, with all of them dabbing their eyes.

"And when I sounded the last notes and words, there usually would be total silence for about five seconds and then you'd hear everyone saying: 'Goot Shabbes! Goot Shabbes!' And smiles would be regenerated on their faces, and so many of them, especially the older ones, would come over to me and embrace me and hug me, and some would even say to me: *'A gezunt oif dein keppele'* ['May there always be good health on your head']. Some would even say to me: 'I've got a young grandson. He's handsome and single and he's a doctor or a lawyer or an accountant. You'll like him. Give me your address.' And they would always add after telling me about their grandsons: 'Did you ever consider converting to Judaism?' "

Then, a broad smile blossomed forth on Nina's face: "Rabbi, are you also going to begin the Service with *Kol Nidray* and end it with My Yiddishe Mama?"

I commended her for everything she had done in the past

and would be doing in the future for the Jewish passengers but I told her that I was going to revert to the traditional Service—if it was OK with her.

Again there was that beaming smile: "Of course, rabbi." However, she added: "The drummer in the band is Jewish and he usually chants the *Kiddush* for us every Friday evening over the wine. He loves wine. Do you think he could do it again this week?" I shook my head in approbation and replied: "I'd love to have him sing the *Kiddush*. I always invite participation—and I'll give him an extra-large cup of wine."

I then put my hands on her head and invoked upon her a personal blessing—and she gave me a big kiss before she left.

"Miracles" truly can happen on the Caribbean.

• • • • •

Faith is more than praying
    In humble solemn tone,
It is more than trusting
    When weary and alone.

Faith is more than believing
    In a well-adorned life;
It is more than victory
    Over sin and strife.

Faith is more than planting
    Seed beneath the sod,
Faith is daily walking
    Hand in hand with God.

—James Edmon Knowles

CHAPTER 18

Modern "Rituals" Add Spice To Ancient Jewish Traditions

I was young, only twenty-five, when I came to my first congregation in Homestead, Pa., The Homestead Rodef Shalom (Pursuers of Peace). That is why I often received invitations from youth groups and youth organizations to participate in their programs or speak about the subject: "How to Keep Our Jewish Youth Within Judaism." I was not much older than the members of those groups.

While taking care of my small congregation in Homestead, I was also quite active at the Y.M.H.A (Young Men's Hebrew Association) in the Oakland section of Pittsburgh near the University of Pittsburgh. I was simultaneously enrolled at the University, taking Mathematics and Chemistry courses, and I would go to the "Y" after classes to lift weights, to "pump iron." After three months at the "Y" I was already able to "Bench-Press" 186 pounds. People knew me and I knew many of the teenagers and young adults at the "Y".

One day, toward the end of 1954, I received a call from one of the officials at the "Y". "Rabbi, we all know that within the four months that you have been in the Pittsburgh area you have done much to get to know the Jewish youth and for them to get to know you. You have been a great asset to our Jewish community—and especially to our Jewish leadership. You're athletic and bright. You're part of the University community. You haven't hidden in a theological cocoon. The Jewish kids in Pittsburgh know you—and like you."

I felt very good because of his laudatory and flattering comments; however, I knew that those words were stated because he wanted something from me.

"We need your help," the "Y" official continued. "We're going to sponsor a Saturday evening *Havdallah* Service in two weeks. [This is a brief service at sundown, Saturday evening, in order to officially end the Sabbath. Three symbols are used. A blessing is recited over the wine because the Bible says (Psalm 104:15): 'Wine makes a person's heart happy.' Sunday was always a work day in the Holy Land and therefore people would be depressed on Saturday night because they knew that the Sabbath was over and Sunday was a work day; however, a little wine always elevated their spirits. A blessing was also recited over a box of spices because smelling the aroma of spices also improved the spirits of those who felt depressed and dejected. It had the same effect on people as perfume. It smelled good and it made the people feel better. So, too, a third blessing was recited before a braided candle with many wicks to indicate that the future was going to be bright, not dark. Do not feel downpressed and disheartened. The Sabbath is only six days away. Before you turn around, it will be back.]

"The Service will be at the 'Y', not in a synagogue, and we hope to have at least 250 teenagers there. We would like you to chant the Service and lead the Service. We will provide the candles, the spices, and the wine. It will be a big youth activity—and one of a religious nature. We want to kindle a big spark of Judaism in our youth and we all know that you can help us immensely. Everyone has told me that the Jewish youth of Pittsburgh *love* you—not *like* you, but *love* you. Will you participate with us in that Service?"

As I said, I was quite young then and his plaudits overwhelmed me and swelled my head. I immediately replied, "Yes." I did not even wait one second to answer him.

That Saturday evening, when I arrived at the "Y" I asked the security guard: "Where is the youth function?"

The guard pointed toward the gymnasium and said: "At the pool," and I immediately went in that direction. I did know why they chose the pool area for the Service but I surmised that they had a good reason.

Upon opening the door to the gym I noticed that scores of teenage boys and girls were leaving the gym and going to the pool area. However, the boys were wearing bathing suits and the girls were also wearing bathing suits—most of the girls' suits were two piece and quite revealing. I thought I was in the wrong place. Maybe I had mixed up the date for the *Havdallah* Service. Maybe it was for *next* Saturday night. This was supposed to be a *Havdallah* Service, a religious service, not a Swim Party.

But the coordinator of the program saw me and quickly smiled at me. "Rabbi," he exuberantly cried out over the youthful chatter, "you're just in time. We've been waiting for you. Come up to the diving board. The microphone is there. You will chant the *Havdallah* Service from the diving board."

I did not know what to say. I was taken by total surprise. The "Y" coordinator was holding me by the arm and directing me toward the diving board. "Where are the candles?" I tepidly asked. "Where are the spices? Where is the wine?"

But the coordinator merely smiled: "Don't worry," he replied, "that has been taken care of. They will be here in a minute."

Before I could even say another word to him, the lights dimmed and four girls, about sixteen years of age, dressed in skimpy bathing suits entered the pool area from the girls' locker room and moved toward the four corners of the pool. Each girl was immediately given a tall, braided *Havdallah* candle and all four candles were lit. The light from the candles seemed to undulate over the surface of the water of the darkened pool.

Then, two male teen-agers, also about sixteen years old, entered the pool area from the men's locker room area. One was holding a spice box and the other was holding a tall cup of wine. Both of these teen-agers were wearing bathing suits just like everyone else and they immediately stood beside me on the diving board, which was quite cramped and crowded.

I was glad that I knew the brief *Havdallah* Service by heart because the only light we had in the pool area came from the four flickering candles and from a handful of bulbs on the walls of the pool area.

But then, as the two boys stationed themselves next to me on the diving board a bright light was spawned from a spotlight at the rear of the pool area and focused on me. The beam of light struck me by surprise.

The coordinator of the program quickly signaled to me in a loud whisper: "Go ahead, Rabbi, that's your cue."

I did not know what to do. I had never previously officiated at a "Bathing Suit *Havdallah* Service"—so I instinctively began chanting the Service. There was nothing else I could do. Two young teenagers were standing behind me on the diving board and ahead of me was only the water of the pool and about three hundred teenagers all dressed in bathing suits and waiting for the festivities that would commence after the completion and conclusion of the "religious service."

When I concluded the Service, the four scantily clad girls holding the four flickering candles immediately dove into the pool, quickly extinguishing the light from the four candles, while the teenage boy holding the large cup of wine consumed the entire contents in one long swig and gulp—to shouts of the teenagers. All the teenagers then made several circles around the pool, held onto each others' shoulders, and began singing *"Eliyahu Hanavee"* (a song about the Prophet Elijah that is usually sung at the termination of the *Havdallah Service*), while shaking, rolling, and reeling from right to left, oscillating and swaying like an electric wire that had just been activated.

As the last words of the *"Eliyahu Hanavee"* tune were concluded a blusterous and riotous roar came forth from the almost three hundred bathing suit clad teenagers as the boy on the diving board just behind me, who was holding the now empty tall cup that had been previously filled with wine, dove into the pool still holding the cup, and the boy holding the spice box did likewise.

The coordinator of the *Havdallah* Service then shouted over the P.A. System: "Let's dance and let's swim." Then he turned to me and quickly shouted over the teenagers' roar: "Thanks, Rabbi. That's it. I guess you won't want to stay any longer. You didn't bring a suit. I should have told you to bring your bathing suit. You can leave now if you so desire."

He then turned to one of his assistants to talk about the punch and potato chip refreshments.

I guess I should have remained and mingled with the teenagers but most of them were jumping into the pool or talking to friends. I guess my *Yeshivah* (Theological Seminary) had not prepared me for this unique and modern *Havdallah* "Service"—but I learned quickly how to adjust to the new, the "modern", and the contemporary.

• • • • •

"One must be absolutely modern."
—Arthur Rimbaud from
"Une Saison en Enfer. Adieu"
("One Season in Hell. Goodbye"), 1873

• • • • •

"Life can only be understood backwards;
but it must be lived forwards."
—From "Life" by Soren Kierkegaard

Chapter 19

"Conversion" At Denny's

It was late on a Sunday night and Toby and I were returning from Austin where we had been visiting two of our children who were then students at the University of Texas.

It had truly been a long day. We had started for Austin at 1 P.M. after I had concluded my duties at the synagogue and had arrived at our children's apartment a little after four. We talked for a while about everything and anything and then at 6 P.M. we went for dinner at a small restaurant near the University. We spent about an hour and a half at the restaurant eating and talking and then we left our children at about 8 P.M. in order to make the three hour drive home.

However, as we were driving on I-10 about a half-hour from our home I said to Toby, "Let's stop at that Denny's up ahead and have a cup of coffee and a piece of apple pie. It's been a long day and I've got to unwind. I've got *shpilkes* [pins and needles] in my pants. I can't sit any longer. We'll be able to stretch our legs and get a second breath."

Toby normally does all the driving when she goes with me and she was doing the driving that night. She always claimed that my driving made her nervous. Therefore, I would sit on the passenger side and read the mail or a good book as she would escort me from place to place. In that way I would feel that I was killing two birds with one stone—getting to my destination and completing my reading. In fact, I would even often read when we were traveling at night. I would take along a flashlight and use that for my illumination.

We pulled into the Denny's parking lot and noticed that even though it was already 10:30, the parking spaces were almost all taken. We entered the restaurant and could not find an empty table. An elderly waitress asked us to wait "a few moments" and about five minutes later said, "Follow me," as she dragged her legs while escorting us to a table adjacent to the kitchen. "I'll be with you in a few minutes," she automatically stated in a robot-like manner. However, within one minute she was back with two cups and two pots of steaming coffee. "What would you like, regular or decaff?"

We told her our preferences and she quickly took our orders: apple pie for me and cherry pie for Toby.

However, while the waitress went to get our order, I noticed that there were two tables in front of ours. One was occupied by a man about seventy years of age wearing a ten-gallon hat, dungarees, cowboy boots, and a tasseled jacket. He looked as if he was well over six feet tall and weighed over 225 pounds. He was eating a thick steak, corn, beans, and a baked potato—and he was washing all that down with steaming black coffee. Sitting with him at his table was a woman at least twenty-five years his junior who was eating a house salad and drinking a cup of black coffee. They were not talking, merely eating.

About ten feet away from his table was a circular table with five young men and five young women. They were seated in a staggered manner—young man, young woman; young man, young woman; etc. They were all, it seemed to me, between the ages of eighteen and twenty-two, with the young men being slightly older than the young women. And it seemed to me that they were boyfriends and girlfriends. Otherwise, I rationalized, the young men probably would have been sitting in close proximity to each other, and the same would have been true for the young women. And I noticed that in addition to the thick sandwiches, milk, and coffee that they had before them, they also had Bibles on the table, ten in all, one for each person—and they were talking about the Bible. It was very easy for me to overhear their conversation.

They were discussing "salvation," believing in a "savior," and being "saved." Their discussion and conversation was most interesting.

"The Jews," one young blond girl intoned, "don't believe in salvation as we Christians understand it. To them, salvation is merely a term that describes being saved in battle from an enemy." She opened her Bible and instructed those with her: "Look at Judges 13:3-5 in the Old Testament. There, God is talking to Mano'ach's wife who was barren and could not have children but yearned to have them. The angel said to her, 'Behold, you are barren; you have not given birth to a child; but I promise you that you *will* conceive and bear a son; however, a razor shall not shave his head because he will be a Nazarite of God, and he shall save Israel from the hands of the Philistines.' Eventually she gives birth to a boy and they name him Samson. They considered him a 'savior' because he saved them from the enemy, from the Philistines."

Smiles sprouted forth over all the faces of the others around the table. In fact two of the young men even applauded.

But, then, another young woman, sitting on the opposite side of the table, interrupted the applause. "Unfortunately," she proclaimed as she raised her voice so that all could hear her, "the Jews have misinterpreted the meaning of salvation, of being saved, and it's our duty to teach them the true meaning of that concept."

All eyes were now glued on this equally attractive young woman. "We have to teach them that salvation is a work of God's mercy, not of man's activity. It is a product of God's grace."

She then began turning pages in her Bible and directed the others to do likewise. "Turn to Titus 3:5-6," and everyone followed suit. "Look what it says there. 'Not by works of righteousness which we have done, but according to His mercy, He *saved* us . . . by renewing of the Holy Ghost: Which He shed on us abundantly through Jesus Christ Our Saviour.'"

Everyone around the table shook his or her head in affirmation. "However," the young woman continued, "it is our duty and obligation to teach them the true path to salvation. Jesus said [John 14:6], 'I am the way, the truth, and the life: *no man cometh unto the Father but by me.*' There is only *one* way to get to God, and only one way to fulfill God's wishes, only *one* way to please God—and that is by accepting Jesus as our savior."

I was deeply interested in their conversation and wanted to tell them that Judaism preaches (Maimonides, *Laws of Repentance* 3:15), *"Cha-see-day oo-mot ha-olam yesh la-hem chay-lek la-olam ha-ba,* The righteous of *all* people have a share in the world to come." To Judaism, belief in a specific deity *is* important but it is not the primary commandment of God. To God, doing good deeds is primary. Hence, if a non-Jew performs good deeds for his fellow human beings, for God's children, he has fulfilled God's major goal. To a Jew, *deeds* are more important than *creed.* Belief may be important, but not as important as one's actions. To a Jew, action speaks louder than words.

I asked Toby if she thought I should introduce myself to the group and add a Jewish dimension to the conversation; however, a scowl quickly enveloped Toby's face and three words immediately came forth from her lips: "Are you crazy?" So I dug into my apple pie that the waitress had brought and, I must admit, continued to eavesdrop on the theological conversation of the young group at the next table.

However, the elderly "cowboy" at the other table seemed to be having an argument with his lady friend. (She was *not* wearing a wedding ring.) And every few minutes he would turn around toward the table with the young men and women and look toward them with a deep frown upon his face as if he was upset by their seeming joy and happiness and their animated conversation. The younger woman at his table was not participating in the argument. She was merely staring at her salad and eating one piece of lettuce at a time. The "cowboy" was, however, getting more and more agitated but I could not comprehend the source of his problem. Many people at other tables, however, were casting quick glances of irritation and annoyance in his direction.

Then, one of the young men who had been discussing the question of salvation interrupted the others. "It's 11:15 and I've got an early class tomorrow morning. I think it's time to call it quits."

Several at that table looked at their watches to confirm the time, others took out their wallets to pay for their meals, but all simultaneously interlocked hands. All heads turned toward the young woman who had spoken about only *one* direction toward God and several said to her, "Go ahead, lead us in prayer." Without further ado they all lowered their heads and in a low voice I could hear her say, "O God, this was a splendid evening. We enjoyed a warm companionship this evening, shared the spirit of Your holy words, and participated in a delicious, delectable late dinner. We are thankful that You heap so many blessings upon us and have given us directions as to the proper way to fulfill Your wishes. May we help bring others to Your service and to a profound belief in You. We pray in the name of Jesus Christ our Lord." Everyone, as in a chorus, replied, "Amen".

The conversation of the "cowboy" became more animated and a grating sound came forth from his table. He was getting up, and the chair merely rasped across the floor as he rose. However, he did not search for his wallet or for a menu. He merely walked briskly toward the table where the ten young men and women were still sitting and talking. It was obvious that anger was written all over his face.

"What the heck were all of you doing holding hands a minute ago," he shouted at the group. "Are you a bunch of 'pansies'—gays and lesbians?"

His face was marked with wrath and fury. It was evident that he was searching for an argument or even a fight. However, the ten young men and women did not take the bait. The young man who had stated that it was late merely smiled at the "cowboy" and tranquilly responded, "No, we are not gays and lesbians. In fact, everyone here is with his girlfriend or her boyfriend. We're all engaged to be married."

The young man momentarily hesitated as the "cowboy"

continued to snort and fume. Many in the restaurant were now looking at the "cowboy." "Well, if you're not 'pansies' why were you holding hands?" the "cowboy" sardonically brayed.

The young man looked up at the "cowboy", smiled, and softly replied, "We all belong to a Couples' Club at our church and we held hands to show how much we care for each other as we recited a final prayer before leaving the restaurant. We had all been to church this evening to hear a lecture about Salvation and we all wanted to thank God for being believers and for being saved."

The "cowboy" was taken aback. He was just itching for a fight but his opponents turned out to be churchgoing believers.

The "cowboy" seemed to shrink a bit, get a little shorter, but once again he barked a question. "What's that paper on the table?"

The young man picked up the piece of paper, perused it quickly, and replied, "It's our bill. We were just about to pay it."

The young men at that table were staring at the "cowboy" but fear seemed to be etched all over the young women's faces as the "cowboy" continued to howl his questions—and I noticed the same expression of fear on Toby's face.

However, from the other side of the restaurant I could see the young manager and a young male waiter approach our section. The "cowboy" walked closer to the table of the young men and women and quickly stretched forth his right arm. For a moment I thought that he was going to strike someone at that table, and several of the young women gasped in fear. But the "cowboy" merely grabbed the bill from the young man's hand and bellowed, "The bill's on me. I didn't know you were churchgoing people. I didn't know you were praising God. I didn't know you wanted to get married. I didn't know Jesus was so important to you."

Tears actually appeared in his eyes as his lady-friend approached the table and in a low voice apologetically stated, "You'll have to excuse Bill*. He had a few too many drinks tonight at the club. I normally just ignore him, but seeing all of you hold hands just set him off tonight. He can't stand 'fags'."

The spokesman of the young people arose, put his arm around Bill's shoulder, and sympathetically stated, "Bill, two thousand years ago, Our Lord, Jesus, stated [Luke 6:27, 35], 'Love your enemies ... and your reward will be great.' Even if you don't like someone, learn to change your ways. Learn love, not hatred; learn compassion, not anger; learn friendship, not disgust."

Again he hesitated for a moment and then softly suggested, "Bill, how would you like to meet with me during the week? Maybe I can take you out for a cup of coffee."

Quickly, a broad smile came over Bill's face and he once again growled, "Make it a bottle of beer and it's a date."

"A bottle of beer it is," the young man joyfully replied, and everyone at the young people's table shouted, with smiles on their faces, "A bottle of beer it is."

Bill and the young man exchanged telephone numbers. Bill pulled up a chair and joined the young people at their table, ordered them not to leave yet but remain for another fifteen minutes, and he gruffly shouted at the waiter, "Bring us twelve chocolate sundaes—for my young religious friends, my girlfriend, and me."

All eyes in the restaurant were focused on the young people's table. Toby and I were smiling. There was peace, not disturbance at the table, and all began singing, "For he's a jolly good fellow."

I turned to Toby and remarked with a smile on my face, "These young people just performed an extremely meaningful *mitzvah* [good deed]. I think they're really going to help that grouchy man. I think they've found their vehicle to get them their salvation—DOING a *mitzvah.* And I also feel that they are going to help Bill find *his* vehicle to achieve *his* salvation—a solution to *his* problem of prejudice and bigotry, intolerance and narrow-mindedness."

• • • • •

> "A man's true character may be determined by three things: his drinking habits, his generosity in giving charity, and his tendency to 'fly off the handle.'"
>
> —*Talmud,* Eruvin 65b

Chapter 20

One Kind Act Or Word Can Soothe Many A Depressed Heart

Since the days of my youth I have always enjoyed exercising. As a high school student I would work out on the chinning bar, parallel bars, play football and basketball, and I loved to swim.

But as I matured and grew older, my athletic interests changed and settled down to visiting a gymnasium and walking on the tread mill and working out with the weights, and I would attempt to do this three times a week.

However, when summer would arrive and the days were warmer and I would return from the synagogue on Saturdays at about 2:30 P.M., and I did not have to return to the congregation until about 7:30 P.M. for the evening service, I would often put on my shorts and sneakers and go for a 4.2 mile walk. It would begin at my home on Falkirk, turn right on Academy, then left on Bellaire, left at West Loop South, left on Beechnut, left on Academy, and then right on Falkirk, and back to my home. I would usually return hot and sweaty because the temperature during July and August in Houston usually hovers around one hundred degrees.

One Saturday afternoon was especially warm. In fact it was

hot. The temperature was one hundred and one degrees and the humidity was high. But I told Toby that I had to go for a walk. I wanted to "unwind." So I put on my shorts, sneakers, and T-shirt and called out as I closed the door, "I'll be back in about an hour and a quarter."

This time I decided to walk down Stella Link to Bellaire because it was a main street. I wanted to see some motion—walking people, moving cars—and I knew that no one would be walking on Academy because it is extremely rare to see anyone walking on Academy. But as I made a left turn from Falkirk to Stella Link, it quickly became obvious to me that I would be doing much perspiring before I returned home. This day seemed much hotter and much more humid than the other days that I had made this trek. But I was determined, so I continued on.

However, as I turned left from Stella Link onto Bellaire Blvd. after completing my first mile, it quickly became obvious to me that I was sweating profusely. My shirt was soaked, my mouth was dry, and I felt a great urge to wet my tongue. "I'm lucky," I thought to myself. "Right off Stella Link and Bellaire there is a Meat-King* fast food restaurant. I'll go there and ask them to give me a glass of water."

It was mid-afternoon and the restaurant was sparsely occupied. I walked up to the counter, exhaled heavily, and softy stated, "Could I please have a glass of water? It's hot outside and I'm just about burning up."

I waited for the attendant to bring me the water but he simply hesitated, and after noticing that I said nothing else, he looked at me in a puzzled manner and said, "What else?"

I looked back at him as the perspiration slowly dripped down my face and armpits. "I don't need anything else," I said to him in a friendly and courteous tone. "I merely need some water to continue my walk. I don't want to get dehydrated. It's very hot outside. I would be deeply appreciative if you would give me a glass of water."

The attendant, who was about thirty years old and who wore a name plate saying "Ass't Mgr" drew a glass of cold water, put it on the counter that separated us, and routinely remarked, "That will be ten cents, please."

I looked at him with wide opened eyes. "There's a charge for just a glass of water?" I asked in an embarrassed manner.

"Of course" was the reply. "Otherwise we'd have every Tom, Dick, and Harry coming in and saying, 'Can I have a glass of water?' Then they'd sit down and eat all the leftovers from people who didn't finish every scrap of their meals. We don't want that. That's why we charge ten cents for water, if nothing else is ordered."

I was embarrassed and felt uncomfortable. "I'd be willing to pay you the ten cents—but I don't have any money with me," and with these words I put my hands in the two pockets of the shorts, pulled them inside out and showed that I had absolutely nothing in my pockets. "I'm merely very thirsty, very hot, and very sweaty."

I took two deep breaths, inched up closer to the counter, and in a soft voice attempted to explain to him why I did not have any money in my pockets. "Today is *Shabbat* [the Sabbath] and I don't carry money on the Sabbath."

The counterman quizzically stared at me. "What are you, a Seventh Day Adventist?"

"No," I apologetically replied. "I'm Jewish and I don't carry money or do business on the Sabbath. I'm merely thirsty and thought I could get a glass of water here to quench my thirst and cool me off a bit."

The Assistant Manager merely shook his head. "Business is business. This is not the Salvation Army or the Star of Hope Mission. This is a money-making corporation. We're here to help you—but we also have to make a profit for our stockholders. For a dime, this water is yours. For no dime, it goes down the drain. Sorry, but that's our rule when nothing else is ordered."

The five minutes in the fast food restaurant was at least refreshing. The air conditioning felt good and it resurrected my desire to conclude the remaining 3.2 miles of my walk, so I left the fast food restaurant and lumbered on westward, along Bellaire Blvd.

Then I turned south on West Loop South. It was quite obvious to me that the temperature was now one hundred and two or one hundred and three degrees. It was super hot and exceedingly humid. But as I turned east on Beechnut Blvd., there, before me on the northeast corner, was a Texaco Station and on the southeast corner was a McDonald's fast food restaurant. I decided to try to get some water at both places.

I strode first into the repair shop of the Texaco Station, and there was only one mechanic working there. "Is it possible for me to get some water here? It's pretty hot today and I'm soaked with perspiration."

The mechanic did not even look up from repairing the flat tire he was working on. "There's a water fountain to the right of the oil cans," he shouted at me as the music from his radio blared forth a Rock and Roll tune. "Drink as much as you want. It's hot as hell today."

"Thanks," I called out to him as I went to the area where the oil cans were stacked one upon the other. I drank like a camel that had been marching for seven days with a heavy load in the Sahara Desert and had finally reached an oasis.

When I could no longer drink, I returned to the mechanic. "I don't have a car here and I didn't buy anything here," I said to him, "yet you allowed me to drink from your fountain. You didn't even charge me for the drink."

The mechanic raised his head, put down his hammer, and shouted over the din of the Rock and Roll music. "What do you think I am, a Nazi or a Communist? You *looked* hot and you said you *were* hot. That's why we have a fountain here—for thirsty people." The mechanic took a step toward me and went on, "My minister recently said to us, 'Do a good deed for someone and you will see that eventually you will be repaid for that deed. Smile at someone and very often you'll notice that it's contagious, that person will smile at someone else."

The mechanic was about to return to fixing the flat when he again turned toward me, this time with a smile on his face. "Let me tell you the story our minister told us in church last week. He told us that he once read how a man going to work left his taxi and said to the driver, 'I hope you'll have a good day.' The driver, that morning, had left his house angry at his wife. He was angry because she had burned his toast. But he now felt good because someone had taken the time to say a good word to him in addition to paying him his fare and adding a handsome tip.

"The taxi driver came home that night and gave his teenage son a big hug and a damp kiss and loudly stated, so that even his wife could hear, 'I love both of you so very much. You are the center of my life. Life would be meaningless without the two of you.' And to the boy he added, 'Bob, unfortunately, in past years I've ignored you, but something hit me today that made me realize how very important you are to me,' and he hugged him again. 'Bob, *with* you and your mother, life is meaningful. *Without* the two of you, life is meaningless.' The cab driver lowered his head and apologetically stated, 'Please excuse me for ignoring my greatest assets.'

"My minister then added, 'The boy broke away from his father and ran up to his room. The father merely stared at his wife in puzzlement. 'What did I do wrong?' So he followed his son up to the boy's room, opened the door, and saw his son sitting on his bed, with tears in his eyes, and holding an envelope.'

"My minister then told us what happened. The boy looked at his father and with tears running down his face tremblingly whispered, 'Dad, I was going to leave this envelope on the kitchen table tonight after you and mom went to bed.' The boy stretched forth the envelope to his father and softly said, 'Please read it.'

"The father was confused and bewildered. What had brought about this flood of tears, this running away to his bedroom, the writing of this letter? But the father opened the envelope and read:

> Dear Dad,
>
> I am now 18 years old and a senior in high school. I feel lucky that I have been able to get so far in school since I am not a good student. It seems that I have always been on the borderline, almost failing. However, I have learned to live with that.
>
> But I have not been able to learn to live with your coldness toward me. Since I've been a baby you've never taken

me anyplace, never played ball with me, never joked with me, never gone to my Little League games, never held me, never hugged me, and never kissed me. I could go on and on but I guess you get my point.

Therefore I made a decision. I'm going to end my life tonight. I don't want to be a hindrance to you anymore. I don't want to be a disappointment to you anymore. You will be much happier without me.

Good-bye. I've always loved you and I still do.

With all my love,
Bob

That was the letter he read."

The mechanic breathed in heavily and actually wiped a tear from his right eye with his greasy rag and it left a small smudge right below his eye.

"Can you imagine that?" he went on as he temporarily forgot the flat tire. A single sentence to a taxi driver—'I hope you'll have a good day'—had a ripple effect. It defused his anger and he spread his happiness and joy to his home. He wanted to share that spirit with his family when he returned home that night, and it caused his son to give up his thoughts of suicide because it indicated to the boy that his father really did love him."

The mechanic turned toward the flat tire, smiled jocularly, and boisterously called out, "If I continue with my minister's stories I'll never get home tonight." But he pointed at me in a pedantic manner and disseminated a moral lesson: "Be nice to your neighbors and eventually they'll be nice to you. A good act will always lead to another good act."

And as he walked back toward the flat tire, the mechanic called out to me, "I only gave you a little water but I'll bet dimes to doughnuts that you will be back here to buy some gasoline and maybe even have me change your oil. You look like a nice fellow, a moral person. I can read it in your eyes—you don't want anything for nothing."

The mechanic once again began fixing the flat but continued talking to me. "I could go on and on telling you my minister's stories," the mechanic began again, "but it's my wife's birthday tonight and I'm taking her out for dinner." Once again he began hitting the tire with the hammer to separate the rubber from the rim. I said a hearty "Thanks, good-bye" and I left.

However, as I said, across the street was a McDonald's fast food restaurant and something within me said, "Jack, go across the street and see if they will give you some water." Without hesitation I quickly crossed the street and entered the restaurant. It was quite busy and children galore were running around on the playground and in the restaurant.

I waited my turn because there were three people before me. Then I spoke to the counterman. He, too, had a small nameplate on his lapel that read "Ass't. Mgr."

"What else would you like?" he mechanically asked as he rang up "water" on his register.

"I really don't want anything else," I apologetically replied. "I'm doing my regular four mile walk and it's hot as heck outside and I'm soaked to the bone."

I thought he was setting me up for a proclamation: "That will be twenty-five cents." However, he picked up a tray, put a straw on it, drew a tall glass of water with ice, pointed to an empty table, and pleasantly added, "Enjoy yourself. It really is hot outside." However, he added as an aside, "Don't drink it too quickly. It'll get you sick. I'm a jogger and I tell all those who jog with me, 'Drink slowly and it will be more effective.'"

But I did not immediately turn toward the unoccupied table. "I have no money for the water," I wearily responded to his comment.

The Assistant Manager smiled at me. "We don't charge for water, only for food and prepared beverages. Enjoy your water and have a good walk." With that, he quickly turned toward the next customer and asked, "What can I get for you?"

I quickly looked at the name on his nametag and noticed that it was Hector Ramirez*. I filed it in my mental filing system, sat down at the unoccupied table, slowly drank my water, and left McDonald's to go home. As I left I called out a hearty "Good-bye and thanks" to Hector who immediately acknowledged my salutation.

That night, after the Sabbath was concluded I wrote four letters. The first one was to the local headquarters in Houston of Meat-King restaurants informing them of what had occurred and asking whether this was a local store policy or a city policy to charge a dime for a glass of water when no food was ordered with it. My second letter was to the state headquarters asking if it was a local store policy, a city policy, or a state policy. My third letter went to the national headquarters of Meat-King asking whether this was a local policy of an individual store to charge ten cents for a glass of water, a city policy, a state policy, or a national policy.

I then wrote a letter to the national headquarters of McDonald's telling them how I had been denied a glass of water at Meat-King unless I paid ten cents for it, while a smiling Assistant Manager, Hector Ramirez, had given me not only the cold water but also a kind comment.

For two months I waited for a response from Meat-King; however, none of the three offices to which I had written thought it important enough to respond. I was simply ignored. If one office had not responded but two had, or if even two had not responded but one had, I would have said that the letters had probably been lost in the mail. That was the reason for not hearing from them. However, three out of three no responses obviously indicated that they considered me a *nudnick* (a pest) and intentionally decided to turn their collective backs on me.

However, four weeks after writing to McDonalds I received a reply. It was from one of the executives. He wrote:

> Dear Rabbi Segal:
>
> Thank you for your kind letter about Hector Ramirez. Your letter of recommendation has been entered into his file and he has been informed of this. Hector simply put into practice what we preach to all those who work for McDonald's: Be kind to the customers. A kind word and a gentle act will travel long distances.
>
> Again, we appreciate your thoughtfulness and your letter.
>
> Please accept the enclosed as a token of our appreciation for your letter.

Enclosed in the letter were two complimentary tickets: once for a piece of pie and one for a cheeseburger (which I gave to my next door neighbor because it is not kosher).

In the early part of my walk I felt that people were generally cold to strangers; however, I am so thankful that I met the mechanic and the Assistant Manager. They taught me what the Bible tells us, that there are loads of people "who were created in God's image" (Genesis 1:27).

• • • • •

> "In making our decisions, we must use the brains that God has given us. But we must also use our hearts which He also gave us."
>
> —*Fulton Oursler*

Chapter 21

It Just Takes Twenty Seconds

One Sunday, while visiting my in-laws in Miami, I told my wife that I was going to attend a church service in Fort Lauderdale. I had seen the minister of this megachurch a number of times on television and I had enjoyed his preaching, the subjects he discussed, and his demeanor on the pulpit. Every Sunday, approximately three thousand congregants drank thirstily from the words of his sermons and I wanted to see why he attracted so many to his church every week of the year while synagogues could do that only on Rosh Hashanah and Yom Kippur (the Jewish High Holy Days) and, to a lesser degree, on days when they had Bar and Bat Mitzvahs.

I parked my car in the extensive and commodious parking lot and followed the crowd into the church. As soon as I entered the lobby I noticed about twenty men and women greeting many who were arriving. It was not possible to shake everyone's hand and say "hello" to all but they were doing their best to greet as many as possible. The flow of people was just too great and too quick to achieve their hoped-for goal. However, it seemed to me that these ushers were pinpointing and zeroing in on those who did not look familiar to them—the guests, the strangers, the vacationers—and they were warmly greeting them with smiles on their faces and also welcoming them with affable and amicable handshakes—and they were also handing them cards.

When I approached the ushers one of them said to me, "It's good to have you worship with us." He pumped my hand as if it was a manual water well that he had to pump hard to extract water from, and he handed me a card which I put into my pocket.

Upon being seated, and as the soloist was singing, I took out the card to read it. It merely asked for my name, permanent address, and my local address and phone number. I simply returned the card to my pocket and continued to be a spectator at the service, and I must admit that I enjoyed the minister's sermon, "Why I Disagree With Darwin's Theory of Evolution."

However, as I left amidst the flood of worshipers who were streaming through the magnificent and grandiose church doors, one of the ushers approached me and asked, "May I please have the card you were given when you entered the church?"

"I didn't fill it out," I apologetically stated to him with a weak grin on my face. "I was too engrossed in the service," I fibbed to him.

The usher sheepishly smiled at me and whispered, "The minister will raise Cain with me if I don't return all the cards filled out. Just take a moment to complete it. Here's a pen. It will only take you a minute or less to fill it out."

I did not want to insult him or offend him, so I took his pen, completed all the information requested, returned it to him, and left the church as he called out, "Thank you, thank you, Mr. S'gall."

That evening, I discussed the service with Toby and told her that I enjoyed the fact that I had been greeted in the lobby by an usher and welcomed to the church. I also thought it was a good idea to give strangers a card to complete; however, I hypothesized, "They probably wanted my address and telephone number to get a donation."

Tuesday morning, at about 8:30 A.M., the phone in my motel room rang. I put down the morning newspaper and answered the call.

"Mr. S'gall," the caller said, "this is Jerry* of the church you worshiped in this past Sunday. I'm one of the ushers who welcomed the arriving worshipers and gave you a card that you completed."

I grinned to myself, "These fellows don't wait long. They contact you while you're still warm. They want your donation while the iron is still hot."

"Just give me your address," I quickly replied. "I'll send you a check this morning."

However, to my utter surprise and astonishment, Jerry responded, "I don't want a donation from you. One of the other ushers and I want to take you out for brunch today and tell you what our church offers our congregants. We want to tell you about our Bible Study programs, our Good Deeds projects, and our Overseas Missions. We've got loads of programs that will be of interest to you. We don't want you to only visit us once. We want you to become part of our church family. We want to introduce you to one of our Service Corps people who will always keep in touch with you and invite you to his home, and we also want to introduce you to others from our church so that you will be able to quickly make friends and enjoy living in our community."

Jerry went on for close to five minutes telling me of the assets I would enjoy if I would become part of the church, and once again he extended an invitation to join him and a friend for brunch.

But when he momentarily hesitated to take a deep breath I quickly interjected, "I would love to join you and your friend, Jerry; however, my plane leaves for Texas at 2 P.M. today"—which was the truth—"and I do not have the time." I thanked him profusely for his interest in me and I added as a postscript, "I'll send the church a check today"—which I did.

I was truly flabbergasted and astonished. This was not a rural church in a tiny hamlet. This was a church of monumental size but still its members took the time and made the effort to extend themselves in an outreach program to befriend strangers and attempt to make them feel at home in the church. "They are to be commended for this," I told Toby.

Several months later, I was informed that a young woman who was a medical student, whom I had known for many years and who had been married about two years earlier, had committed suicide. It was almost impossible for me to believe. Whenever I had seen her, she always had a smile on her face. Whenever I had spoken to her, there was always humor in her conversation. Physically, she was a beautiful young woman, and intellectually she was extremely bright. In less than a year she was supposed to receive her M.D. degree.

Her death was contrary to reason. She had everything to live for. There was nothing about her life, that I knew, that helped me to understand why she had terminated her life. Her husband was young and handsome. He was already a physician. Whenever I saw them together they were always smiling and holding hands. Love seemed to be the current that united them and connected them.

On several occasions after her death, her husband visited with me and told me how much he missed her, how full of pain he was, how he anguished about his loss. "I feel like a balloon that has just been pierced by a sharp pin," he once confided in me. I listened to him as he shed tears and divulged to me how he had gone "from heaven with his beloved wife to hell without her."

"All I do now," he informed me, "is come home from the hospital every night, have a few beers, eat a cold dinner, and go to sleep."

The cycle of gloom, I felt, had to be broken. It was now three months after she had died and he was going from bad to worse. "After work, on Friday nights," I suggested to him, "why don't you come to the synagogue service. You'll be able to recite the *Kaddish,* [mourners' prayer] and talk to people. It'll help get you back into the mainstream of life."

At first, Joe* was not happy with my suggestion but after several visits and hearing me repeat my advice each time he capitulated and conceded with a smile on his face. "It can't be worse than what I'm experiencing now."

That Friday night, I saw Joe at our Shabbat Service, and after the *Alaynu* prayer at the end of the service he rose with the other mourners to recite the *Kaddish.*

As usual, the congregants at the end of the Service would all migrate to our auditorium for cookies, cake, punch, coffee, and tea, but I lingered for a few minutes to speak to Joe and then invite him to join the others in the auditorium.

This "ritual" went on for about three months. Then I noticed that Joe did not appear for three consecutive Friday evening services. I thought he was ill or possibly had moved to another city or perhaps was now frequenting another synagogue. Our friendship, I thought, was strong so I called his home one evening and, to my surprise, he was in. "I missed you at services, Joe," I told him like a father speaking to a son. However, he said he did not want to discuss it over the phone. He would rather speak to me personally in my office.

The next evening, at about 9 P.M., Joe met me in my office. I attempted to make some minor conversation at first but Joe wanted to immediately discuss the reason for our meeting. "Rabbi," Joe seriously blurted out, "I want you to know that I like *you* very much, and Susan* similarly liked you. She told me that she felt close to you when you were her teacher in Religious School and when you officiated at her Confirmation and graduation from Hillel High School. She also told me that she immensely enjoyed your relationship with the synagogue college students—sending all of them a college letter every two weeks on an important subject of religion, politics, personal life, or something like that."

Joe now looked directly in my eyes with what seemed like anger. His eyes were squinting. "However, Rabbi, I want you to know that *never once* on all those Friday nights that I was attending services at your synagogue saying *Kaddish* did anyone come up to me, introduce himself, and say, 'Don't sit by yourself. Join me,' or 'Join my family.' I entered all by myself and I exited all by myself. And when I went into the auditorium for refreshments after the service, the only time anyone ever spoke to me was when a young woman said to me, 'Could you please pass the coffee pot,' which I did. Yes, there was loads of conversation there. But it was between family members or friends, but not directed toward strangers."

Joe inhaled heavily. "Rabbi, I love *you* very much. But I need a warm synagogue, not a cold one. I need a congregation where people walk up to strangers, not turn their backs on them. I need a place to worship where you feel you're perspiring from the heat of friendship, not freezing from the frost of being ignored.

"Rabbi, that is why I left your synagogue. I hope you understand."

I attempted to give excuses but they all fell on deaf ears. I tried to rationalize but it was obvious that my words failed to leave an impression on Joe. After about thirty minutes of cross-conversation Joe rose, gave me a strong hug, kissed me on the cheek, and left.

I was devastated, smashed, and pulverized. I had always attempted to make my congregation a warm and welcoming synagogue, but, obviously, I could not see beyond the tip of my nose.

However, I attempted to rationalize this incident by telling myself that Joe was still in the midst of deep grief and he probably ignored or spurned the advances of friendship extended to him by others in our congregation.

But as the days blended into weeks and then into months, the memory of our meeting faded and I returned to believing that I had one of the warmest and affable, gregarious and sociable congregations in the state.

About six months after my last meeting with Joe, I was teaching the Adult Bar/Bat Mitzvah Class, a class for those who had not received a Jewish education as youngsters but now, in adult life, wanted to catch up on their Jewish education and formalize that period of study with the ritual of Bar/Bat Mitzvah.

The subject for that evening was "Abraham The Patriarch." I was attempting to show the class how kind and loving, warmhearted and friendly Abraham was—and I even added, "The same was true for God."

I instructed the class to open their Bibles to chapter 18 of the book of Genesis and I read for them the opening verses: "And God appeared unto him [Abraham] . . . [as] he sat in the entrance of the tent in the heat of the day." And I told the class of Rashi's comment (a French biblical commentator who lived from 1040 to 1105). He stated, "God went to visit Abraham because Abraham had just been circumcised at the age of ninety-nine and God went to comfort him." God could see his pain and hurt, his aches and his suffering. God was compassionate and understanding and attempted to aid and assist Abraham in his moment of anguish and agony.

And then I added, "Abraham was cut of the same cloth. He, too, attempted to aid his fellow human beings to the maximum of his abilities." And I went on to tell them the famous *Midrash* (legendary story) that relates how while living in the desert Abraham fashioned for himself a tent that had four openings, four doors—one in the west, one in the east, one in the north, and one in the south. He did this because he wanted everyone to know that all were welcome in his abode. No one had to search far to find the entrance to his tent. There was one in every direction. Abraham encouraged people to come in out of the hot desert sun, to enjoy a cool glass of water with him, to share with him his food, and even to cool off with a shower. His hand was always outstretched to convert strangers into friends and outsiders into brethren.

So, too, I added, the Jewish Bible tells us (Deuteronomy 10:19), "*Va-ahav-tem et ha-ger* ... [You should love the stranger because you were strangers in the land of Egypt]." I even added that during the festival of Passover when we read the *Haggadah* (holiday booklet recounting the exodus from Egypt and our liberation from Egyptian slavery more than three thousand years ago) we state, "*Kol dich-fin yay-tay v'yo-chal,* [Whoever is hungry, let him enter our house and eat with us the holiday meal]." I stated that Judaism teaches us to be warm-hearted and kind-hearted, affable and amiable.

I even went on to tell them the *Midrash* (*Avot de Rabbi Nathan* 7) that states that when Abraham met a stranger he would immediately bring him to his home. "And to the person who was not accustomed to eat wheat bread, he would serve wheat bread; to the individual who was not accustomed to eat meat, he would serve meat; to the one who was not accustomed to drink wine, he would give wine. He would treat everyone like royalty, not only that, but he also built spacious mansions along the highways, and stocked them with food and drink, so that whoever entered ate, drank, and thanked God. . . . Abraham derived unusual satisfaction in that whatever any person requested was to be found in his houses and mansions."

I was going to relate to my students one more tale of warm hospitality found in our Jewish literature; however, a woman in my class, about fifty years of age, raised her hand. "Rabbi," she chafed, "those stories are wonderful stories about Jewish warmth and friendship to strangers three thousand years ago. But I want you to know that when I enter the sanctuary of *your* synagogue I put on four sweaters. It's cold and freezing, chilly and occasionally even icy."

For a moment I did not comprehend why she had raised the subject but I grinned at her and authoritatively replied, "Dorothy*, I'll instruct our synagogue engineer to raise the thermostat in the sanctuary."

Dorothy audibly huffed and puffed as she rose from her seat. "Rabbi, I'm not talking about the thermostat on the sanctuary wall. I'm talking about the thermostat in your congregants' hearts."

I stared at Dorothy with a puzzled and confused expression. "What are you talking about?"

The eyes of the other thirty students were all focused on Dorothy. "Rabbi, I've been coming to your Friday night services for the past six months—since I moved from Cleveland—and I enjoy the services. However, not once, before or after the service, has anyone said to me, 'What's your name?' 'Where are you from?' 'Do you have family in town?' 'Would you like to have lunch with me?' I feel like a shadow in your synagogue, no one sees me. I feel as if I'm in Siberia—in mid-January."

Dorothy stared directly at me, crinkled her nose, squinted her eyes, raised her voice, and growled, "Rabbi, whenever I go to your synagogue I put on four sweaters. I don't want to freeze. Previously, my feeling was that if I wanted to go to Antarctica I'd make the arrangements through a travel agent. That is why I moved to Houston, to keep warm, not to be refrigerated. But when I go to *your* synagogue I feel as if I'm already in Antarctica."

I was startled by her words, not knowing how to respond. So I merely shook my head in confusion and meekly replied, "I'll definitely do something to correct that situation," to which Dorothy retorted by heavily sitting down and griping, "That's what they all say."

Dorothy's words refused to leave me: "Whenever I go to *your* synagogue I put on four sweaters. I don't want to freeze." They actually haunted me. I could not forget the church in Fort Lauderdale that Dorothy *probably* would have described as being on the Equator while my synagogue she already *definitely* labeled as being "in Siberia." For the next week I would awaken at 4 A.M., restless and perspiring. I had to do something about this problem. If it bothered Dorothy and Joe, it probably troubled others, too. The others were merely silent about the subject.

Therefore, at the next Friday evening service, just before the concluding benediction, I asked the congregation to rise and do something that had previously never been done at our synagogue. With a big smile on my face I instructed them: "Take twenty seconds; turn to your right and to your left; turn to those who are in front of you and in back of you; shake their hands with feeling and emotion; introduce yourselves to them; say to them '*Goot Shabbes* [happy Sabbath]'; say to them '*Shabbat Shalom* [May you have a peaceful Sabbath]'; introduce yourself to *at least* one stranger; and make this a warm *Shabbes,* a spiritual *Shabbes,* and a meaningful *Shabbes* for one and for all"—and I walked over to all those sitting on my side of the pulpit and shook their hands and wished them a *"Goot Shabbes."*

I quickly peered out of the side of my eye and saw that initially almost no one was moving. But then, a few began shaking their neighbors' hands, and some were even embracing each other, smiles were sprouting forth all over the sanctuary, and everyone was talking. I quickly pronounced an accelerated benediction in the midst of all the noise and said to myself, "I think the temperature in the sanctuary just went up ten degrees."

About a year later, two members of my synagogue scheduled an appointment with me. Irving and Rose Saperstein* entered my office with happiness and joy written all over their faces. They stated that they wanted to schedule a date for their daughter's wedding.

Irving was ebullient with delight as he spoke. "Rabbi, in a sense, *you* were the *shodchun* [matchmaker] for this wedding."

"Me?" I questioned in surprise. "I know your daughter but I don't know the boy. I don't even know his name. I never told a boy to take out your daughter. I never fixed her up with anyone."

Rose interrupted her husband. "Let me tell the rabbi what happened," and she began to relate how the two had met.

"About a year ago, my husband had *yahrtzeit* for his father. [It was the anniversary of the death of Irving's father at which time family members recite the *Kaddish* prayer.] So, Irving and I, my two sons and their wives went to the synagogue to the 6P.M. E.S.P. [Early Shabbat Prayers]. But my daughter, Leslie*, remained at home. She didn't want to go with us. She was then a senior at the University of Texas and said she was tired from the trip home that day."

Rose sat up tall in her seat when she mentioned her daughter's name, and she added, "Leslie is *very* pretty."

"Go on, go on. Don't editorialize," Irving uncomfortably prodded his wife.

"Well, as we came to the end of the service, you asked us to rise and shake hands and introduce ourselves to those in front of us and in back of us and on both sides of us. We all did as you asked to the members of our family. But Irving tapped the fellow in front of us on the shoulder and introduced himself and said, '*Goot Shabbes,*' and then said to him, 'I've never seen you here before. What's your name?' "

Irving had a big grin on his face. "Rose, let me finish it. It's my story." He gave her a pathetic look and she grimaced. "OK, go on."

"Well," Irving interjected, "I looked at him and he was about six foot, two inches tall and about twenty-five years old. He was quite handsome and he looked like Robert Redford. I also noticed that he was not wearing a ring on his third finger, left hand, and when I asked him what his name was, he replied, 'Stan Finkelstein*'.

"I asked him where he was from and he said that he was from North Miami Beach in Florida.

"I was inquisitive so I asked him what he was doing in Houston and he told me that he was a student.

"I then asked him where he went to school and he told me that he was a senior law student at South Texas College of Law.

"My family was *schmoozing* [talking] with each other but I continued on with Stan. I asked him if he had already had his *Shabbes* dinner and he told me, with a big grin on his face, 'I'm going to have it right after the service at McDonald's, a block away from the synagogue.'

"However, I grabbed his hand and held it tightly and told him, 'Oh no you're not. You're coming home with us to have a good *Shabbes* dinner. This is Texas, the land of hospitality. If my son was in *shul* [synagogue] in Miami on Friday night and your parents would see him there, I'm sure they'd invite him to their home. Come home with us. We live less than two miles from here and you'll have gefilte fish, hot soup with matzah balls, roast chicken, and chocolate cake. You'll have a Jewish meal, not a *farshtunkeneh* [ordinary] cold sandwich with an even colder Coke. Come home with us."

Irving quickly turned toward his wife and continued without even taking a moment for a deep breath. "Rose had overheard the last part of my conversation with Stan and now *she* began to invite him. He was lost even before he started to protest, especially after my daughters-in-law also chimed in with *their* invitations. In fact, one daughter-in-law whispered to me, 'He's going to like Leslie but I better call her to tell her we're bringing someone over. Otherwise she'll kill us. I'm sure she won't be happy about this but I know she'll want to put on some lipstick.'"

Rose was sitting on *shpilkess* (pins and needles). She no longer could control herself. "Irving, that's enough," she rapidly interrupted her husband. "Let me finish it."

"We told Stan how to get to our house and I told him that we expected to see him there in ten minutes. He was still protesting as we left him: 'I have so much homework to go over tonight;' 'I have an exam on Monday;' 'I haven't had much sleep lately;' 'I'm not really that hungry.' However, I held his hand and said, 'Stan, I wouldn't be able to sleep if I let you go to

McDonald's tonight.' Right then and there he gave in. He capitulated. He took the instructions to get to our house as my family left. I called out to him again, 'Ten minutes is a maximum it should take you to get to our house.'"

Rose then sighed ponderously as she raised her eyes toward the ceiling. "But when we came home I was greeted by my daughter. She was standing in the doorway—no lipstick, wearing a pair of shorts and an old shirt and old sneakers. Her hair was in a pony tail."

Rose continued to sigh heavily. "'Leslie,' I asked her, and shook my head in confusion, 'didn't Barbara* call you and tell you that we had invited a nice young man for *Shabbes* dinner tonight? We met him in shul.' But sparks were shooting forth from Leslie's eyes. She was angry, very angry.

"'Mom,' she strongly whispered to me as my sons and daughters-in-law began to arrive and approach the house, 'I told you never to play these tricks on me. Don't try to fix me up. I can fix myself up.' She then turned away from me and walked toward my other children. She gave them a big smile, and said, 'Mom's at it again,' and everyone laughed heartily."

Rose turned slowly toward Irving. "But I believe in the old adage," Rose quipped, "He laughs best who laughs last."

"And then, Stan arrived. We all warmly welcomed him into our home, all that is, except Leslie. She had gone into the kitchen for a glass of water, she said. It was obvious that Stan still felt awkward.

"We made petty chatter until Leslie entered the dining room—eating a sour pickle. It was obvious to all that Leslie did *not* share our spirit of joviality. But, Rabbi, once I undertake a mission I never give up. Even if Leslie did not want to meet Stan, I am a Jewish mother. Stan was in a strange city on Shabbes and I felt that he should be able to share our Shabbes family spirit with us. But, I also felt," Rose continued on as a broad smile blossomed forth on her face, "that Leslie would like meeting Stan." And again Rose added, "You know the old adage, Rabbi, 'Nothing ventured, nothing gained.'"

Rose went on, "I quickly grabbed Stan by the arm and escorted him over to Leslie and introduced them. Stan stretched forth his hand to shake her hand but Leslie responded with her hand still wet with pickle juice. 'I love sour pickles,' Stan commented to Leslie as he smiled and shook her hand, and then he even extended his left hand to hold her pickle hand with both of his hands.

"They spoke for a few seconds and I invited everyone to be seated at the table. I seated Stan at Irving's right side but I quickly noticed that Leslie sat down at the end of the other side of the table. But, as I told you, Rabbi, I don't give up that easily. So I quickly walked down to Leslie, held onto her arm, and smilingly brought her over to a seat next to Stan.

"Stan was speaking to Irving. So he did not notice what was transpiring. And even though I could *feel* Leslie's protests I knew that she did not want to make a public issue of this matter.

"Irving then made *Kiddush* [the prayer over the wine], recited the *ha-motzee* [prayer over the *challah*], and we began to eat and talk, eat and talk, eat and talk."

Rose took a LifeSaver candy from her pocketbook and put it in her mouth. "Rabbi," she went on, "we sat at the table for about an hour and a half and in the beginning it was only Stan talking to Leslie. She was only giving him one word or one phrase replies to his questions, but when he told her that he was a law student she became interested. She told him that she was a pre-law student hoping to get into the University of Texas School of Law.

"Then he told her that he enjoyed parachuting once a month and I heard her tell him how she had done this once at a small airport near Austin—and I almost died as I heard her reveal that secret.

"Then he related to her that as an undergraduate he had worked as a lifeguard at camps during the summer and he regularly worked out at a local gym. Athletics is very important to Leslie and she now seemed to be listening more attentively to Stan's words."

Rose put another LifeSaver into her mouth and preemptively squashed an attempt by Irving to continue the story. "But when we finished our coffee and marble cake, Stan arose and apologetically stated, 'I really must go. I have to study for my exam.'

"We all said good-bye to Stan and then Leslie softly stated, as I arose, '*I'll* show Stan to the door, Mom.' Quickly I sat down and inwardly I smiled.

"Yes, I was quite a distance from the door, but even over the talk and chatter coming from the family at the table I could distinctly see Stan's lips—and I could read his words: 'Would you mind if I called you this week? Good! I'd like to talk to you some more about Law School and parachuting.'"

Once again Rose put another LifeSaver into her mouth. It seemed to me that she was no longer sucking them but rather eating them or even devouring them.

"I kept staring at Leslie and Stan standing at the door," Rose resumed, "and as Leslie stretched forth her hand to say good-bye I noticed that Stan stretched forth both his hands to clasp hers, and I was quite surprised when I noticed that Leslie reacted by stretching forth her left hand to embrace both of his hands. It was two hands upon two hands and I smiled both outwardly and inwardly—and Stan left."

Rose turned toward Irving who looked like Man-O-War chomping at the bit as the horses waited for the gun to go off to start the Kentucky Derby.

Irving smiled radiantly. "I'll merely start where Rose left off. As Leslie came back to the table there was a big smile on her face and everyone was joking with her: 'We told you he was a handsome young man;' 'We told you we had met a Jewish student at Shul who didn't know anyone there;' 'We told you that it was a Jewish thing to invite a stranger to your home for *Shabbes* dinner.' Everyone was laughing and joking with Leslie, and Barbara even commented, 'I'll bet you he calls this week to ask you out for a date.' But Leslie merely shrugged off her statement stating, 'I'm going to bed,' and she went to her room."

Irving's smile was growing by leaps and bounds. "But thirty minutes later the phone rang. Rose answered it and I could see her face exploding with a smile like Mt. Vesuvius, and she called out so that everyone could hear, 'Leslie, it's for you,' and she hesitated for a moment and then continued, 'It's Stan—the young man who had dinner with us this evening.'"

Both Irving and Rose began laughing heartily. "Rabbi, that

was a year ago," Irving added. "Since then, Stan graduated from Law School and got a good job with a prestigious law firm in Houston. Leslie graduated from the University of Texas and decided to go to Law School at the University of Houston. And since that Shabbat eve Leslie and Stan have been a twosome—and now they want to be married."

Rose again interrupted Irving. "Rabbi, we came here for two reasons. Firstly, to get a date for their wedding. But even more important, to thank you for making the *shul* a warm *shul,* a friendly *shul,* a compassionate *shul,* and an understanding *shul.* We've attended services in many *shuls* but never at the end of the service has the rabbi suggested to the congregants to turn to all four sides and shake hands and introduce themselves to those nearby—especially to strangers. Had you not given those instructions to the congregants, Leslie would not have met Stan and Stan would not have met Leslie, there would not be a wedding for the two of them, and Stan would have merely had a cold sandwich that Shabbat eve at McDonald's. For this we want to thank you, for making our synagogue a warm and understanding congregation."

With that comment, Rose walked over to my chair and gave me a big hug and Irving emotionally shook my hand with both of his.

Six months later I officiated at the wedding of Stan and Leslie in the Sanctuary of our congregation—and it all started with a warm handshake on a *Shabbes* eve in the Sanctuary of our synagogue between a long-time member of the synagogue and a lonely law student.

• • • • •

> "Cast thy bread upon the face of the waters; for after many days you will find it again."
>
> —*Ecclesiastes 11:1*

CHAPTER 22

We Are All "Children Of God"

Part I

It was late 1965 and I had been in Houston as the Associate Rabbi of the synagogue only about six months. Benny Katz, the Executive Director of my congregation, saw me at Services Saturday morning. I could see sorrow and sadness written all over his face. "Jack," he whispered to me, "Don*, one of our workers, is very sick. He's in the hospital. I think he would appreciate a visit from you."

I knew Don fairly well. He was one of the workers who did everything all over the synagogue. He worked in the kitchen and in the school, in the office and the sanctuary and chapel. He was one of the general handymen who worked for the congregation. His educational background was minimal but he always had a smile on his face and a good word on his lips. Don was about sixty years of age and he was Black.

I told Benny that Toby and I had a Bar Mitzvah reception that evening but both of us would first go to see Don in the hospital and then go to the reception.

As we entered Don's room I noticed that several other people were also present: his wife, a son and two daughters. They gave us chairs upon which to sit and I held Don's hand as I spoke to him. He was very weak and very thin. I had seen him a week earlier at the synagogue but I had not noticed any signs of illness. But, now, it was obvious that he was quite ill.

"We all miss you at the synagogue," I enthusiastically told him. "Everyone sends his and her regards." Don was so appreciative. And he smiled at Toby as she spoke to him. "I truly feel like a member of the family of Beth Yeshurun," he confided in us in a weak voice.

Toby and I spent about thirty minutes with him and his family as I told Don about God's words to Joshua when he was about to enter the Holy Land (Joshua 1:6): "Chazok Veh-eh-motz, Be strong and have courage." I told Don that God had said that to Joshua, and eventually Joshua was victorious. I attempted to instill in him a spirit of optimism, a spirit of hopefulness, and before we left I held both of his hands and prayed that his tomorrows would be better than his todays, and his days after tomorrow would be better than his tomorrows.

Don kissed my hands before I disengaged and we left, and it was obvious to me that he truly appreciated our visit and my prayers.

Sunday night I again visited Don for about fifteen minutes. It was obvious to me that he was getting weaker and weaker because his eyes kept shutting as I spoke to him. But once again, as I concluded with a prayer for him, he kissed my hands and weakly mumbled, "May God's blessings be upon you and your family."

I told Don that I would see him again later the next day, Monday. However, Monday at noon, I received a call from Benny: "Don died early this morning." I instinctively recited the traditional Jewish prayer recited upon receiving bad news or news of the death of a beloved one or a friend: "Baruch dayan ha-emet. Blessed may God be, and may Don now be with God. Rest in Peace."

Later that week, Benny informed me that there was going to be a Service for Don in his church in the Fifth Ward and it would be a good idea if both of us would attend. So, Benny and I made arrangements to attend it together.

The church was in an area that required major repairs; however, the church itself was simple and well kept. The Service was scheduled to begin at 7 P.M. but when we arrived at 6:55 P.M. it was already in progress.

As we entered, I noticed that at least two hundred or more people were in attendance—standing room only. Benny and I were the only White people in the church. However, people galore greeted us as we were escorted to seats in the second row of the church.

The church was relatively bare and Don's casket was at the foot of the pulpit. He was dressed in a tuxedo and the funeral director, through the use of cosmetics, had made him look hale and hearty.

The minister of the church was reading quite loudly from his pulpit Bible because the church did not have a public address system. But as soon as the minister looked up and saw Benny and me he smiled radiantly and exclaimed toward the congregants, "Don's Rabbi has arrived," which was received by a host of welcoming comments. The minister then looked penetratingly at me and proclaimed, "Don's Rabbi, come up and deliver a eulogy for Don," and his words were greeted by many audible statements of agreement from those in attendance.

I looked at Benny in a quizzical manner. "Benny," I murmured as my heart began to race, "what should I do? I didn't prepare a eulogy. No one told me that I should prepare a eulogy. I'm unprepared."

Benny merely smiled at me. "Do it off the top of your head," he advised me. "You can't say no. That would be an insult."

People behind me began orally prodding me in a friendly manner. "Tell us about Don." "Speak to us about Don." "Let's hear about Don." It was a subdued chorus but all the comments seemed to agree that it was the wish of the congregation for me to deliver a eulogy for Don.

I slowly ascended the pulpit, shook the minister's hand, walked over to the lectern, hesitated for a moment, and then, in a very subdued and restrained voice, looked out into the congregation and began. "My friends, I only knew Don for about six months. I was associated with Don at my congregation for only about a half year, but during that time I always found him to be a fine and a reputable human being."

As soon as I completed my sentence, about five men from different parts of the church raised their hands and called out, "Say it again."

I was truly taken by surprise; however, I felt that they probably could not hear me because there was no microphone in the church and I was speaking in a tempered and hushed manner. So I raised my voice and spoke louder. "Don was not only a fine and reputable human being, he was also compassionate and understanding."

But before I could add another word, about twenty-five men and women in the church arose from their seats and also called out, "Say it again. Say it again."

I was truly stupefied. I thought that this time my voice had been loud enough so that all could hear me, but their comments, "Say it again. Say it again," implied to me that many were still having a problem hearing my words.

So, once again I raised my voice. This time I was really loud. "Don was not only fine and reputable, compassionate and understanding, but he was also loved by all the employees at the synagogue and all the congregants of our synagogue."

I waited for a moment after that laudatory comment to see whether all could now hear my comments, but to my amazement about half the church was now raising their hands and calling out, "Say it again. Say it again," and many were now standing at their seats.

For a fleeting moment I felt that they still could not hear me, but it quickly dawned on me that that was impossible. The way I was now speaking I did not need a microphone. The volume of my voice now was comparable to one using a megaphone.

I quickly realized that the format in this church was different from sermons preached at my synagogue. At my congregation the rabbi spoke from the pulpit and the congregants listened courteously. It was a unidirectional conversation. But in this church it was a dialogue. The preacher spoke from the pulpit and the congregants often commented on his statements from the pews. They did this with emotion, with feeling, with gusto, and with zest.

I felt good. I actually felt exhilarated. I don't know what got into me but I kept on speaking about Don for twenty minutes as the congregants encouraged me to go on with comments like, "That was Don," or "Tell it again," or "That was the Don we knew."

And when I concluded the eulogy, the entire congregation gave me a standing ovation. Then one woman began singing "Oh when the Saints, go marching in," and almost everyone made a chain line around Don's casket and began marching and dancing around it. In fact, two men placed me behind the minister as we paraded around his casket. They were celebrating Don's life rather than mourning his death. There was nothing they could do about his demise. He had lived an almost full life and had died of cancer. But they wanted to memorialize him with memories of happiness and joy rather than recollections of sadness and grief. I was truly caught up in the emotions of the moment. In fact, I went around his casket two times in that chain line of singing human beings. A special spirit of community and congeniality encompassed the congregants. And before I went to my seat I kissed Don's wife on the cheek and she emotionally thanked me for "speaking so admirably" about her husband.

When Benny and I left the church, men and women galore approached me to thank me for the way I praised Don. They told me that it meant much to Don's wife and family to see me at his church and to hear me speak in such a praiseworthy manner about him.

As I shook the hands of the congregants as we left the church, I must admit that I saw no color or pigmentation. All I saw were human beings, people who had some customs or ways of life different from mine—but human beings just like my wife and me, my friends and my congregants.

Don's death and funeral service left a deep and indelible impression upon me.

Part II

"Race" was never a very important subject to me when I was growing up in Brooklyn, N.Y. True, I had very few Black friends but prejudice and bigotry were not genetic or hereditary in my parents' family.

In fact, when I was a young boy my father told me the story of Moses marrying "a Black woman" "ha'ishah ha-Kusheet" (Numbers 12:1), and he never referred to her by using a derogatory Yiddish expression when speaking English, "He married a *Shvartze* [a Black woman]."

On the contrary, my father often told me about the Jewish prophet Amos who proclaimed to the Jews of the eighth century BCE, "Halo kivnay Kushiyim atem lee Bnei Yisra'el [You are to Me like the Black Ethiopians, O Children of Israel.]" (Amos 9:7). My father would always tell me that God evaluates a person not by the color of his skin, the wealth of his bankbook, or his country of origin but rather by his personality, his deeds of kindness, and his relationship to others.

My father would always quote to me the Talmudic statement (B.B. 20a):

> There are ten strong things:
> Iron is strong, but fire melts it;
> Fire is strong, but water quenches it;
> Water is strong, but the clouds evaporate it;
> Clouds are strong, but wind drives them away;
> Wind is strong, but man uses it to breathe;
> Man is strong, but fear casts him down;
> Fear is strong, but wine allays it;
> Wine is strong, but sleep overcomes it;
> Sleep is strong, but death is stronger;
> However, loving kindness is stronger than death because it always outlives death.

My father never cared if a person's name was Booker T. Washington or George Washington, if he was Dred Scott of the infamous Supreme Court case of 1857 or General Winfield Scott who won victories for the United States at Vera Cruz and Chapultepec during the Mexican War, if he was Thurgood Marshall, the Supreme Court Justice, or General George Marshall, United States Army Chief of Staff, United States Secretary of State, father of the Marshall Plan, and a winner of the Nobel Peace Prize. My father was interested in a person's character and good deeds, not his outer trappings and ornamental coverings.

But when I moved to Houston in 1965 it quickly became obvious to me that race was a crucial and critical issue in our city—and in the entire "Deep South."

Black people wanted to eat in the same restaurants where Whites ate, but the Whites were angered by this "effrontery."

Blacks wanted to attend Rice University in Houston and not be barred from studying in this prestigious college, but many Whites opposed this "boldness and audacity."

Even White Christian clergymen cried out, "The Bible is opposed to integration. God wanted Blacks and Whites separated, not integrated. That's why the Bible said that Canaan, the son of Black Ham, was cursed by Noah when Ham dishonored and outraged his father, Noah, upon seeing him naked, and he merely joked about it to his brothers, Shem and Japheth [Genesis 9:21-27]."

Houston was truly a racial cauldron when I arrived in 1965 but I never gave it much thought because my congregation's members were 99.9% White. Also, while living in New York, Pennsylvania, and Oregon my path and the paths of local Blacks almost never intersected. My knowledge of the problems of race in the United States came primarily from the television news or newspapers or magazine articles.

As the years went by, I attempted to reach out to African-Americans. I did this for myself, for the Blacks, and for both of us.

I did it for myself because my Bible told me (Genesis 1:27), "And God created man in His own image, in the image of God created He him. . . ." The Bible did not say that God created the White man in His image. It stated that He created all human beings in His image. God did not say that only one group was His family. It said that all his creatures were His "children".

I also did this for the Black people because since 1619 when they were brought to these shores as slaves they were treated with contempt and disdain, ridicule and scorn. Enough was enough! This cycle of hatred and animosity, anathema and enmity had to end—and it was not going to end by itself. Everyone, I felt, had to pitch in to help remove the negative feelings that existed in regard to men and women, adults and children of the Black race.

I reached out to the Black people of my community to help correct some of the ill feelings that had developed over the past three and three-quarters centuries. I always believed that in unity there is strength but in division and fragmentation there is only weakness and impotence. If we wanted a flourishing and prosperous nation it would only come about if all of us—Blacks and Whites together—worked collectively to achieve that goal.

That is why I would invite Black clergymen to address my study groups and speak from my pulpit to tell us about their problems and how we, White people, could help them solve their problems.

Every year, just before Passover, I would conduct a Passover Seder (holiday ritual meal) for one hundred and twenty Black people, members of a specific church, and one hundred and twenty members of my synagogue. The Black church members would be our guests and the Black minister and I would work together to develop a Haggadah (booklet that traditionally told the story of the Israelite exodus from the slavery of Egypt more than three thousand years ago). However, this Haggadah would also tell of the difficulties Jews experienced over the centuries and would also tell of the hurt and pain, misery and agony that the Blacks experienced in the United States. And if Dayaynu (a Hebrew song describing all the miracles God did for us over the years) was a highlight of the Jewish section of the Haggadah, the reading of Dr. Martin Luther King's "I Have A Dream" sermon was surely the apex of the Black presentation of the

Haggadah. The purpose of this joint Seder was to develop friendly relationships between Blacks and Whites.

And during the latter part of the 1960's, when there were marches in Houston to emphasize the importance of integration and equal rights for Blacks I would march with them.

So, too, I always accepted invitations to speak from the pulpits of Black churches and schools whose student bodies were almost entirely Black.

I also accepted an assignment from the Governor of Texas to serve on a committee to develop better relations between Blacks and Whites.

I also helped form at Beth Yeshurun a group consisting of Blacks and Whites where the members of that group could speak freely, in both directions, in regard to racial problems.

And I spoke strongly and emphatically and aggressively from my pulpit about a habit that I found amongst many Jews, even young Jews, that I personally considered derogatory, disparaging, and insulting toward Black people. When speaking of Blacks and African-Americans, I would often hear many Jews referring to them as Shvartzess. Yes, *Shvartess* is a Yiddish word meaning "Black people." But these Jewish people were not speaking Yiddish. They were speaking English. And I personally felt that when speaking English, Jewish people should refer to Black people with the English words meaning Black people—African-Americans or Black people, not *Shvartzess*. And I asked from my pulpit, "If our synagogue would invite Colin Powell to our synagogue to speak from our pulpit would you be happy if I would introduce him by saying, 'I now present to you one of the greatest *Shvartzess* of the century, Colin Powell'? Of course not. It was during the age of our grandparents and great-grandparents, whose use of the English language was limited, that they would refer to the washer-lady as a *Shvartze* [singular for *Shvartzess*, which is plural]. That term was not even good then because it implied a person with little education and from the lowest rung of society, and it is surely improper today when we're speaking English. That word in English has a different connotation from its use in Yiddish. In English, today, it should not be used."

And I went on to belligerently demand, "Would you be happy if you went to a lecture in a church where I was to be the featured speaker and the minister introduced me by stating, 'I now present to you Rabbi Jack Segal, one of the finest KIKES in Houston'? Would you smile or would you take offense, and if you would take offense—why?

"The word 'KIKE'" I continued, "originated on Ellis Island toward the end of the nineteenth century when Jews were migrating en masse to the United States. That word came from the Yiddish word *keikl,* which means 'circle'. At Ellis Island, at that time, immigrants were initially grouped by religion and language in order to make it easier for the immigration officials to communicate with them and for the immigrants to speak to each other. So, too, waiting relatives in the United States who had previously never met them could identify them easier.

"Christians were marked with an 'X', which originally was supposed to be a cross. However, Jews were marked with a circle because they were initially supposed to be marked with a Star of David but that became too difficult for the immigration officers to form and too time consuming. So a fast circle was substituted for the Star of David. The necessity for immigration officers to work quickly converted the cross into an 'X' and the Magen David into a circle.

"The word *'keikl'* was used by the Jews making fun of the poorly drawn stars. The Jews referred to each other as being 'circles', *'keikls'*. But, unfortunately, from this innocent usage the term acquired a derogatory meaning."

Yes, many in the congregation refused to accept my explanation and refused to eliminate the word *Shvartzess* from their vocabularies. "There is a difference between the connotation of the word *Shvartzess* and KIKE," they kept telling me. "The former is a common Yiddish word for Black people while the latter is an insulting and defamatory expression for Jews." However, no matter how many times I repeated my thesis, there was always a small element that always turned deaf ears toward my entreaties and always considered me wrong and misinformed.

But I never gave in because I always believed that it was my duty and obligation to make Jews more sensitive to the feelings of Blacks—and Blacks more sensitive to the feelings of Jews.

Part III

Toward the end of the 1960's I received a call from a Black Baptist minister. "Rabbi Segal," the voice pleasantly and amiably stated, "my name is Rev. Clifton Fleetwood* and I'm the minister of a Baptist church in the Fifth Ward. I am also president of a group of Negro ministers [this was before Blacks received the nomenclature 'African-American'] who are attempting to improve the existence of Negro teenagers in our community."

Rev. Fleetwood's voice rose as he continued. "We would like you to come and speak to a group of about sixty eleventh and twelfth graders who attend our churches and tell them about your Jewish religion. We know Jews, too, have been persecuted throughout the centuries but you have done well in the United States. You live in nice houses, you have nice cars, and you own your own businesses. Maybe we can learn from your successes if you'd speak to our youngsters."

I felt exuberant about this invitation. This was the first non-Jewish group in Houston that had asked me to address its members and I immediately accepted.

Two weeks later, I was greeted by Rev. Fleetwood at his church. But in addition to Rev. Fleetwood there were also five other ministers. They corroborated Rev. Fleetwood's original statement that this new organization was a consortium of local churches with a common goal: help their teenagers better themselves and extricate themselves from the poverty of their neighborhoods.

I smiled and affirmatively shook my head and told them that they were performing a great mitzvah (good deed). I even added an old rabbinic maxim, "The most important thing is not to give a poor, hungry person a fish sandwich to eat because tomorrow he'll need another fish sandwich. It is far more important to teach him how to fish so that he'll always be able to support himself."

The ministers brought me into a large room where I was greeted by the almost total silence of the sixty, or so, seventeen and eighteen year old teenagers. The ministers' welcome was warm, friendly, and with open arms but it seemed to me that the students' greeting was cool and uninviting. Not one student was smiling even though all eyes were focused on me. However, I was undaunted and I was not discouraged.

"Give them a good biblical message," Rev. Fleetwood whispered to me as he ushered me up to the lectern and introduced me.

I smiled and began my talk by telling a story. I wanted to "break the ice." I wanted to "warm up" my audience. So I told them that Jews believed in the old principle, "God helps those who help themselves."

I related to them how a farmer named Mr. Sam Schwartz, eighty years of age, lived in Kansas. Every year he had big crops of wheat, corn, barley, and rye. He would tell everyone that he was a religious man and God was repaying him for his piety.

But one year, the rains came down heavily. It rained, rained, rained—and rained still more. The area around his farm began to flood. Twenty inches of rain had descended on his town and its environs in three days. Finally, Mr. Schwartz noticed that water had penetrated his home. There was about four inches of water in his living room from the flooded river, and about a half hour later the sheriff came by in a jeep and told him that his force was evacuating all the farmers because they were expecting still more rain.

However, Mr. Schwartz replied, "Mr. Sheriff, I am going to remain here because I am a religious man and the Bible says that if you conduct yourself properly, God will take care of you. I'm not going to leave because I know that God is going to take care of me." So the sheriff shrugged his shoulders and left in his jeep.

The next day, the waters were still rising and Mr. Schwartz had to climb the steps to go into his bedroom on the second floor. A few hours later he heard a motor boat dock right outside his bedroom window. Again it was the sheriff. "Mr. Schwartz," the sheriff called out hoarsely. "Everyone is being evacuated. The waters are still rising. Come with me."

"I'm sorry," Mr. Schwartz once again replied. "I told you that God takes care of those who are devoted to Him. I have nothing to worry about. God will protect me." The sheriff merely shrugged his shoulders again and putt-putted away from Mr. Schwartz's home in his motorboat.

But the waters were persistent and aggressive and the next day Mr. Schwartz had to climb to his roof to escape the continuously ascending waters. And once again Mr. Schwartz saw the sheriff. This time he was in a helicopter hovering over his home, and through a bull horn he was shouting, "Mr. Schwartz, the rain is going to continue. This is your last chance to escape this flood. Come with us on the helicopter."

But Mr. Schwartz emphatically and wholeheartedly shouted back, "I told you before, Mr. Sheriff, God takes care of those who are devoted to Him and all my life I've been dedicated to God. I don't need any help. God will save me." So the sheriff, once again, in exasperation, flew away in his helicopter.

However, the waters refused to abate. On the contrary, they kept on rising—and Mr. Schwartz drowned.

Shortly afterwards he came before God and God said, "Good to see you, Mr. Schwartz."

But Mr. Schwartz's face was frozen in confusion. "I didn't expect to be here so soon, God," he replied with sullenness written all over his face. "I believed what you said in your Bible, that You would personally take care of those who were faithful to You, and You must admit that I've been faithful to you all my life."

For a moment, Mr. Schwartz stared at God and then went on. "God, how could You let me drown? God, how could You totally ignore me in my time of difficulty? God, how could You turn Your back on me when I needed You most?"

However, God lovingly and tenderly replied, "Sam, who do you think sent to you the jeep, the motorboat, and the helicopter?"

The six ministers all joined in with a cacophony of laughter. "Mr. Schwartz was blind to God's help," Rev. Fleetwood bleated as he continued to laugh.

"God never ignores those who follow his instructions," another minister attempted to teach his students.

However, not one of the boys even cracked a smile. It was as if I was sitting before cement statues. I smiled at them, waited a moment, but received no response. So I decided to continue.

"God helps those who help themselves. Mr. Schwartz was waiting for someone else to help him while he sat on his backside—SO HE DROWNED. Lesson number one that Jews have learned through history is that we have to help ourselves. The results are sweeter and the results are more positive."

I waited for some recognition but their faces remained frozen, yet still focused on me—so I went on.

"I believe," I continued, "that there are four other major principles that are the columns and posts and foundation stones upon which Judaism and the Jewish people rest today. The first one, I just told you—help yourself and then God will help you.

"But, then, there is the principle of 'family,' the importance of getting married, sharing love with one woman or one man, having children, and sharing love with all the members of your family. That's the second foundation stone of Judaism.

"Remember what God told the first couple on this universe, Adam and Eve [Genesis 2:24], 'Therefore man should leave his father and mother and cleave unto his wife, and they should become one flesh.' "

The ministers responded with "Amen," "Hallelujah," and "That's the word of God." But the students were still stone-faced. There was no response from them. So, again, I went on.

"A third foundation stone of Judaism is education. Jews have been thrown out of almost every country in the world: 1290 from England; six times in the 1300's from France; 1492 from Spain; 1497 from Portugal. We could not take with us our property, silver, gold, or money. Those nations took that away from us. They confiscated them. But they could not take away from us our education, our knowledge, our brains, our intelligence. Maybe that is why the Bible told us [Deuteronomy 6:17] 'You shall teach them diligently unto your children, and shall talk of them when you sit in your house, and when you walk by the way, when you lie down, and when you rise up.' "

Once again the ministers responded with smiles upon their

faces and also with "Amen," "That's what the Bible says," and "Hallelujah." But there was still no reaction on the students' faces. On the contrary, it seemed to me that they were not interested in the subject I was discussing. My subject matter was not a practical issue to them. They had their own problems and they were not interested in how Jews solved their Jewish problems. They were interested in how Blacks should solve their Black problems.

I felt that I had lost my audience. In fact, I felt that I had never gained the interest of my audience.

But then, before I could continue with another "foundation stone of Judaism" a tall and muscular Black student arose and in a defiant voice cried out to me, "Why don't you see to it that your white, Jewish students are taught about Black history, about what the Whites did to us in the United States, about how we were slaves for so many years, and about what they are still doing to us?"

Immediately, the students were resurrected. Many shouted, "Yeah, yeah. Why don't you teach that to your Jewish students?"

I was momentarily taken aback. What had I said? What had I done? Had I insulted someone? Had I spoken arrogantly?

Rev. Fleetwood quickly arose with anger written all over his face but he spoke tranquilly and pacifically to the students. "Rabbi Segal's our guest. We don't shout at guests."

"But why doesn't he answer our questions?" another student brusquely called out. "We're not interested in Jewish history. We're interested in Black history and we're interested in knowing why all the Whiteys don't teach their White students what they did to us and what they're still doing to us."

Cries of agreement and concurrence immediately came forth from almost all the other students. I attempted to speak but the noise was too loud. No one could hear me. The ministers, however, arose and demanded silence and respect, and, to my surprise, their appeal was honored. Silence once again hovered over the assembly even though it was obvious that the students were angry and wanted an answer—"Why aren't the Houston schools teaching Black history? Why are they ignoring the achievements of the Black race? Why are they silently implying that Blacks have done nothing for the advancement of the American nation?"

I told them that they were correct. The schools should teach about the Blacks, the Hispanics, the Jews, the Catholics, the Protestants, the Indians, the Asians, and many other minority groups. One should not emphasize the achievements of one group and ignore the others. Otherwise the groups will shout "Prejudice," "Bigotry," "You're unfair"—and they will be correct. I went on to say that the schools definitely should teach about these groups; however, because there were so many of them it should be obvious that it would only be a peripheral and shallow undertaking, only an aroma of the true history. But, I added, that that would be a good beginning. Better something than nothing.

There was quite a bit of *boortshing* (griping and grumbling) from the students as I spoke, but I have always felt that a strong offense is far better than a weak defense.

I therefore pointed my right index finger at the tall muscular Black student who had raised the initial question, and I forcefully said to him, "Two wrongs don't make one right. Yes, White schools have done very little to teach its students about Black achievements in our country, but have your Black churches attempted to help you?"

I could see frowns on the faces of the six ministers and uncertainty and suspicion written all over the faces of the students. But I did not hesitate. "Have your churches—your Black churches—been teaching you about Black history? Have they been instilling in you pride for your achievements and accomplishments in the United States? Or have they merely taught you how you suffered and were maltreated, how you were beaten and bloodied, and how Whites have merely taken advantage of you? Have they accentuated the negative and eliminated the positive?"

It was obvious that the students were getting restless and edgy. My words were not striking nerves of approval. But I went on. "Yes, we Jews have also suffered much. We were slaves in Egypt. The Church made life miserable for us during the Inquisition and Crusades. Hitler killed six million Jews in

Europe just a handful of years ago. But that's not all I teach my students. I, and my synagogue, teach them the good that we have done and the accomplishments that we have achieved in the United States. I know that the public school is not going to do it, so we do it ourselves."

I did not hesitate to evaluate the students' responses. I merely continued on. "I have to teach my Jewish students Jewish self-pride before I can ask that others learn about my Jewish history," I quickly interjected. Above the din of the students I added, "I didn't wait for the public school to teach the Jewish students of my synagogue about Louis Brandeis, Benjamin Cardozo, Felix Frankfurter, Arthur Goldberg, and Abe Fortas."

But before I could continue, one of the students shouted out, "Who are they?" as if he was not interested in my question or in my reply. Those names were irrelevant to him because he had never previously heard of them.

But I went on. "Those five men were members of the U.S. Supreme Court—and JEWISH members of the Supreme Court. I knew that that fact would not be taught in the public schools, so I taught it to my students. It's my Jewish duty to teach my Jewish students about our Jewish stars and our important Jewish people."

The noise was getting louder and louder. Even Rev. Fleetwood could not stifle or suppress it. So I went on the offensive again. I tugged on my belt, pulled up my pants, and called out in a loud voice, "Who is Thurgood Marshall?"

I thought that at least three-quarters of the students would know the correct answer—but only one student, a slim and short boy, called out, "He's a member of the Supreme Court, a BLACK member of the Supreme Court and he was only recently appointed. He's the first BLACK member of the Supreme Court that's always been WHITE."

"That's right," I half shouted as the noise of the students began to abate.

But then I cried out, even though there was no longer any noise over which I had to vocally leap. "Who is Benjamin Davis?" But this time, no voice was heard with a correct answer.

In fact, only one voice offered an answer, and it was obvious that it was meant to create laughter. "He plays the drums for a Rock Group in Atlanta"—and the result was laughter and snickering, shouting and guffaws. Rev. Fleetwood stood up tall from his chair, grimaced, and twisted his face indicating his anger for the burst of noise. Quickly, the noise once again slackened and weakened.

"General Davis," I loudly pronounced, "is an American hero—and he's BLACK. He's the first Black general in the American Air Force and he was a hero during World War II."

Quickly it became totally quiet. I was surrounded by the silence of a mausoleum, and all eyes were focused on me, even those of the six ministers. I did not hesitate or pause. "General Davis," I went on, "was the leader of the all-Black Tuskegee Airmen."

Again I cried out, "How many of you ever heard of the Tuskegee Airmen?" None of the teenagers raised a hand or called out a reply, even though two of the ministers and Rev. Fleetwood raised their hands and smiled broadly. "The Tuskegee Airmen," I continued, "were a group of Black fighter pilots during World War II, when the United States military was segregated, who fought as a unit—BLACK fighter pilots—who never lost a bomber they escorted during two hundred air-combat missions—a feat unmatched during World War II."

I walked in front of the lectern in order to get closer to the students. Their ears were now all open to my words and their mouths were closed to interruptive horse laughs and meaningless howling. "I teach my Jewish students about Sergeant Isadore Jochman and Lieutenant Raymond Zussman, both JEWS, who won the Congressional Medal of Honor during World War II—and both were killed in battle. I teach my kids about these men because I want them to know how Jews sacrificed their lives so that America could beat the Nazis."

I then pointed my finger at the students and softly stated, so that they had to extend their heads forward to hear me, "I teach those facts to my Jewish students either on Sundays or on Mondays or on Wednesdays in Religious School or on Saturdays and Tuesdays in our Hillel High School. I teach those facts to our Jewish students in my Jewish synagogue."

And before any student could comment, I added, "And I also teach them about General Maurice Rose, a Jew, the son of a rabbi, who became a Major General and led his tanks in combat against the Germans through France, Belgium, and Germany—and was killed in Germany during a fierce battle during World War II."

And before anyone could say a word I went on, "And in Religious School in my synagogue I also teach them about a Jewish rabbi during World War II, Chaplain Alexander Goode, who was on a troop transport carrying nine hundred American soldiers off Greenland when it was torpedoed and sunk."

I stopped for a moment and then strongly asked while poking my index finger into the space between me and the students, "Do you know what he did?"

One student attempted to answer my challenge. "He swam toward the nearest lifeboat," he cried out.

"No he didn't," I replied in full voice. "He took off his life preserver and gave it to a scared soldier who did not have a life preserver. He died that night, and the last time anyone saw him he was holding on to three other Chaplains and reciting the biblical words [Deuteronomy 6:4] 'Hear, O Israel: The Lord Our God, the Lord Is One.'"

I was on a roll and I was not going to stop. "That's what I teach my Jewish students after public school or on the weekends in my synagogue. Yes, it takes time but I want my Jewish students to know their Jewish history. Maybe some time in the future, non-Jews will want to learn our history. But at present, the most important thing is for my Jewish students to learn their own Jewish history to gain self-pride and self-esteem. And at the end of their studies after several years, we have a Bar Mitzvah ceremony to recognize the fact that they have mastered a certain amount of Jewish culture."

I just kept plowing on. "Therefore I'd like to know, why can't you have the same thing in your churches after school during the weekdays or on Sunday mornings? Why can't your churches teach you about your Black history, traditions, and culture? Why can't they teach you what Blacks have done for the United States? Why must you always concentrate on the negative, on being slaves? That's over. That's finished. That's gone. Start concentrating on what you've done in the past for the nation and what you are doing now and what you want to do in the future for this nation."

I waited for just a flashing second, and then something prompted me to add as a postscript, "And after several years you can have a celebration in your church on a Sunday morning called a 'Bar Negro' like we have a Bar Mitzvah, or something else that is more meaningful to you."

Immediately, at least a half dozen students turned toward the ministers and shouted out, "Why are we only studying in our church schools about Adam, Noah, Moses, Jesus, Paul, Peter, and James? Why aren't we being taught about men like General Davis?"

"Yeah, yeah, yeah," were boisterously echoed from at least half the students in the room. "Why don't our Black churches teach us about our Black heroes?"

I turned toward Rev. Fleetwood and the other five ministers and they were all uniformly shaking their heads in agreement and acquiescence.

"Rabbi Segal is quite busy," Rev. Fleetwood called out over the students' comments. "He has to leave now. Maybe he'll be able to come back again. He has other chores to perform at his synagogue." The minister looked at me, put his arm around my shoulder, and instructed the students, "Let's give Rabbi Segal a hand," and all the students arose and gave me a thunderous applause, and some even approached me and patted me on the back. "I never knew there was a Black general in the U.S. military or a Black man on the Supreme Court," one powerful and handsome teenager commented to me. "Thanks for coming here and telling us."

Rev. Fleetwood quickly escorted me to my car and thanked me for the visit.

• • • • •

(In the years afterwards, I was never reinvited to that church to address teenagers, students, or adults.)

• • • • •

"There are two types of birds that fly over the California desert—the hummingbird and the vulture. The vulture ... makes a silent sweep until it spots the carcass of a dead animal and torpedoes down upon it. The tiny hummingbird ... flies over the same terrain never noticing the carcass. Patiently it hovers near a cactus and spots a plant in full bloom. The bird spears the plant, drawing out the honey with its long, thin bill. Each creature, in its own way, puts on mental blinders and finds what it is looking for.

"This is a parable for life: You will find what you look for."

—Dennis Kimbro (Daily Motivations For African-American Success)

Chapter 23

"For Everything There Is A Time"[1]

Every year I would receive calls from mothers in my synagogue who would say to me almost the exact same thing: "Rabbi, you've got to speak to my son. He's twelve and he doesn't want to study for his Bar Mitzvah. He doesn't want to be Bar Mitzvahed. In fact, he doesn't even want to be Jewish any longer."

And I would meet with the children and their comments would almost always be the same. "Judaism doesn't move me. It's not 'cool.' It's the same thing all over again. I'M BORED."

In fact, I even remember reading an article about Franz Kafka, the Austrian novelist, who was considered one of the most significant European writers during the first quarter of the twentieth century.

He wrote a "Letter To His Father" in which he questioned him about remaining Jewish. His father wanted him to remain a Jew but Franz wrote, "With the nothing of Judaism you yourself possessed [how could you] reproach me for not making an effort to cling to a similar nothing?"

---

1 Ecclesiastes 1:1

Franz went on to write, “Four days a year you went to the synagogue. I yawned and dozed through many hours (I don’t think I was ever again so bored, except later at dancing lessons) and did my best to enjoy a few little bits of variety that there were, as for instance when the Ark was opened. This always reminded me of the shooting galleries where a cupboard door would open in the same way whenever one hit a bull’s eye; except that there something interesting always came out and here it was always the same old dolls without heads. That’s how it was in the synagogue. . . .”

So, too, so many youngsters told me that at services they yawned and dozed and stared at their watches, hoping that the time would quickly pass. They were not interested in learning a service that was good and meaningful for their grandparents when they were living in small towns in Eastern Europe but was not good for them. The service had not progressed. It had remained stagnant. It was still in the nineteenth century. It was boring, tiresome, and merely long stretches of Hebrew.

Even though these youngsters were only twelve years of age, and many rabbis might have ignored their criticism and fault finding, my ears were always very attentive to their words. I remembered my father saying, “You can’t sell a product if the customer is not interested in it.” I also remembered an old rabbinic statement: “God gave us two ears but only one mouth so that we should listen more and talk less.”

I always believed in the old aphorism “Nothing ventured, nothing gained.” Therefore I decided to initiate some motion, some spirit, some energy in some of our Jewish traditions. I realized that initiating rituals would not totally solve my problem but I did believe that it might instill a feeling in our youngsters that we were dusting off the ancient traditions and putting a new coat of paint on them.

The young boy Mark* kept telling me how bored he was, how uninterested he was, how monotonous the service was. I had to say something creative, something that would resurrect an interest in him. So I said the first thing that came into my mind without giving any thought as to how I was going to bring it to fruition.

I put my hand on Mark's shoulders and began. "All the children of our Day School are going to be present in the Sanctuary for our Passover Service but after the Service we will serve a delicious lunch and then we will have an 'Exodus March'."

"What's an Exodus March?" Mark quickly growled with doubt written all over his face. "I never heard of it before."

"Well," I began, "we're going to begin something new that all the kids will love and I truly hope you'll be part of it."

Mark did not seem very interested in my hypothetical program and he began to rise as if he was about to leave the room, but I applied pressure to his shoulder keeping him in his seat. "Mark," I emphatically stated, "I need your help to make this project a success."

Mark looked at me with questioning eyes. "Three thousand years ago," I went on, "Moses took tens of thousands of Jews out of Egypt where they had been slaves and led them for forty years through the hot and sweltering Sinai Desert until they arrived at the Jordan River and the Holy Land. Then Joshua finished the task by moving the Israelites across the river and bringing them into the Holy Land. It was dangerous. It was hazardous. It was full of peril and risk, but Moses achieved the impossible and Joshua helped him achieve his goal."

I could see doubt and hesitation, uncertainty and suspicion inscribed all over Mark's face, but before he could say a word I grabbed both of his shoulders and proclaimed like Charlton Heston, "*I* am going to be Moses and you are going to be my Colonel—Joshua. *I* will lead the Israelites through the desert and *you* will bring them into the Holy Land."

Mark merely opened his mouth as if to protest but I had thrown out a challenge to him—to be my Colonel Joshua—and his twelve year old personality did not allow him to turn down a defiant dare.

"OK," Mark hesitantly replied, "but you'll have to help me. I'm not familiar with the Jordan River, the 'Exodus March,' and the forty year trip through the Sinai Desert."

"Don't worry," I enthusiastically assured him, "I'll see you every Tuesday evening after your Bar Mitzvah instruction. We'll discuss details then."

I could see confusion written all over his face. The "Exodus March" sounded interesting to him even though he had not even an inkling of an idea as to what it involved—but it was something new. However, he was not too zealous about the "meetings after the Bar Mitzvah instruction." But the dye had been cast. The Rubicon had been crossed. There was no turning back now.

As the weeks turned into months, Mark marshaled scores of youngsters to participate with him in the "Exodus March." Together we mapped out a "path through the desert," a two-mile trip from our congregation to the Jewish Community Center; however, we would not travel on the streets connecting those two buildings. We decided that we would guide boys and girls along the banks of the bayou that extended from our congregation to the Jewish Community Center.

We began the "Exodus March" with a luncheon for parents and children—for all those who had attended the holiday service. There were well over two hundred who decided to join us at the luncheon and the march. Then we divided those in attendance into twelve groups, each one representing one of the twelve Israelite tribes that marched with Moses, and each tribe had a large pole with a poster on it indicating the name of its tribe: Reuben, Simeon, Levi, Judah. . . . Then I marched out in front of my legions bedecked in a flowing white robe and a large seven foot staff and cried out, "Follow me to the Holy Land," which was answered by a blusterous and clamorous "Let's go" from my followers.

Along the path, we arranged for the Men's Club of the synagogue to hand out "manna" to the children like God showered down upon the Israelites as they traveled through the desert. However, the Men's Club's "manna" was slightly different from God's. They gave the youngsters water, chocolate candy, and apples which the boys and girls enjoyed immensely—especially the water and chocolates. (It was ninety degrees on our march.) However, *we* left behind for the "archaeologists" many half-eaten apples and candy wrappers even though nothing has ever been found by contemporary archaeologists of the debris and refuse jettisoned by the Israelites in the desert more than three thousand years ago.

Unfortunately, the bayou area was not totally dry for us to walk unimpeded to the Jewish Community Center and we had to make several detours out of the bayou. We also experienced an "emergency" when a young girl spotted a garter snake sunning itself on the bayou cement and she began shouting and shrieking. Almost all the boys and girls began dispersing and scattering in all directions and it took about ten minutes to reassemble them once again. Meanwhile the snake slithered away under several rocks. It was my feeling that the snake was more scared of the oncoming horde of children and their bellowing and screeching than they were of it.

It took about two hours to march the youngsters to the Community Center, and at the end of the trail almost all the kids enthusiastically proclaimed, "This was terrific," "I had a terrific time," "Passover was never so much fun." And several youngsters approached me and asked me to introduce a "Cavalry Corps" next year to lead the group on bikes—which we did.

For many years this was one of the highlights of the Passover festival for our youngsters; however, all new things eventually fade and this "tradition" was no different. Its luster began to dull and the numbers attending the "Exodus March" began to wane a bit rather than increase, as it had done in previous years.

I wanted to infuse it with an injection of "insulin", to revive it and resurrect it—and it hit me like a bolt of lightening one night as I was attempting to fall asleep.

The Bible tells us (Psalm 78:23-25), "Then [God] ordained the skies from above, and the doors of heaven He opened: And He let rain down upon them manna to eat, and the corn of heaven He gave unto them. Angels' bread did man eat: he sent them provision to satisfaction."

King David described how the Israelites were fed in the desert for forty years. They could not go to a Kroger's Food Store or a Randall's Food and Pharmacy or a Belden's and order food supplies for a week. The Bible tells us that manna was rained down upon them from the heavens. God acted in the same manner that the American military acted in Europe and the Pacific during World War II, in Korea during the Korean Conflict, and in Vietnam during that war when cut-off troops had to be supplied from the air. The Air Force would drop supplies for them by parachute and in that way they would be able to sustain themselves.

So, too, God "parachuted" to the Israelites manna from the heavens as they traveled forty years through the hot desert.

I therefore decided that I was going to revitalize the "Exodus March" by advertising "ReJEWvenate the 'Exodus March' This Year" and highlight it by convincing a group of synagogue mothers to cook for me several hundred soft matzah balls and place them individually in plastic bags. I was then going to contract with a local helicopter company to have one of its helicopters fly over the group of youngsters and adults participating in the annual "Exodus March" and have its crew drop the matzah balls on the marchers with a sticker on each bag proclaiming, "Manna From The Heavens."

I thought it was a brilliant idea. In fact, *I* thought it was a super-brilliant idea. I felt that I had found my "Religious Insulin Shot" to reestablish interest in the Passover Festival.

However, even before I could get the project rolling, one of the lawyers of the congregation informed me that he had spoken to the City Lawyer and he had been informed that it was illegal to "drop objects from planes or helicopters onto marchers within the City of Houston."

I asked our lawyer if he could get that law rescinded or merely overlooked for only that one day of Passover, but I was told that that was impossible.

I even asked if we could still bypass the law since, in *my* opinion, it was a violation of the principle of "Separation of Church and State." The State was telling me how I could, or could not, perform a religious service; however, I was told that in certain cases the State did have that right. For example, if I would inform the government that I wanted to sacrifice a child to my God as they did in Canaan several thousand years ago, or if I informed the State that I wanted to take another wife *in ad-*

dition to Toby, that would be illegal and not a violation of the principle of Separation of Church and State. Dropping objects from a plane or a helicopter—even soft matzah balls—I was informed, could be dangerous if the matzah balls landed on someone's head.

My brilliant dream had gone up in smoke even before I had a chance to fan the flames.

However, there were other traditions that I reJEWvenated in order to have our youngsters develop an interest in them.

On Rosh Hashanah afternoon, it is customary to go to a body of water (creek, lake, river, Gulf of Mexico, Atlantic or Pacific Oceans, bayou, etc.), recite a number of prayers and cast bread crumbs into the water. This ritual is based on the statement of the Prophet Micah who declared (Micah 7:18-20), "Yea, thou will cast all their sins into the depths of the sea."

True, this statement was not meant to be taken literally but we Jewish people have always believed in the old Chinese proverb that proclaims, "One picture is worth more than ten thousand words," or the aphorism that declares, "Action speaks louder than words." Therefore, during medieval days we developed a tradition called *"Tashlich,"* to go to a body of water on Rosh Hashanah afternoon and *symbolically cast our sins into the depths of that water.* That ritual proclaimed: "God is giving us a second chance. Don't strike out this time."

Unfortunately, it was only our elderly members who were participating in this ritual. Our youngsters merely proclaimed, "We spent enough time already today in the synagogue. Why must we have another service, another ritual?"

I therefore decided to reJEWvenate this tradition, to "dust it off," give it "another coat of paint," and infuse in it new meaning and interest.

During the week prior to Rosh Hashanah I told our Day School and Religious School students to think of two major sins that they had committed during the past year and to inscribe them on a small card that I handed to each student. I asked them to place the "sins" in a wooden box and, before their eyes,

I locked the box with an inexpensive lock that I had purchased at a local hardware store. Then, I informed the students that at the Meyer Park Lake I would personally see to it that their sins were "transported" to God and we would ask that we be forgiven for our trespasses.

Everyone laughed; however, I told them to be present at the Meyer Park Lake on Rosh Hashanah afternoon and they would be able to experience something unique, pleasurable, and religious—and, I informed them, "After the service, ice cream will be served."

That Rosh Hashanah afternoon approximately three hundred and fifty children and parents appeared at the Meyer Park Lake to participate in the "*Tashlich*" ritual, and after the brief ritual six of our synagogue staff brought out two tanks containing helium gas, a box containing the "sins" inscribed on cards, several rolls of scotch tape, and a large box of balloons. The staff members then began blowing up the balloons, tying two-foot strings to them, scotch taping the "sins" to the balloons, and handing the balloons to the youngsters. When all the "sins" had been attached to the balloons I proclaimed, "The Prophet Micah suggested two thousand and seven hundred years ago that we drown our sins in the depths of the seas. But we will send our 'sins' directly into the heavens to God—and we ask for forgiveness. We will not repeat our errors again."

And I turned toward the youngsters and shouted, "Am I correct?"

And they bellowed and clamored back to me, "Yes!"

I then instructed them, "Let the balloons with your 'sins' rise into the heavens toward God. Hopefully, He will accept our plea for forgiveness and we *will* be forgiven."

All of a sudden, three hundred and fifty balloons began slowly ascending into the heavens amidst the tumult and cheers of the roaring youngsters and parents.

Immediately afterwards, everyone was treated to ice cream.

This ritual gained popularity and participants over the next few years but then I heard several youngsters commenting,

"Rabbi Segal is going to send the balloons again into the sky with our 'sins'." However, the comment was not made with enthusiasm or fervor. It seemed to me that it was being stated with ennui and a lack of interest. I therefore felt obliged to think of another way to reJEWvenate this ritual.

That night I could not sleep well so I turned on the TV. The first thing I saw was a replay of the film "JAWS" that I had seen at least a half dozen times; however, I tuned in toward the end of the film when the behemuthian shark opened its carnivorous and cavernous mouth and swallowed whole the middle-aged fisherman who vowed that he would personally destroy the shark.

Right there and then it struck me. "That's the way we are going to commemorate *Tashlich* this year," I proclaimed to myself. This year, I decided, I would hire a scuba diver, outfit him with a shark costume, have him lie submerged in the western part of the Meyer Park Lake while I congregated the children and parents toward the eastern part of the lake, have everyone join me in the recitation of the ritual, take the wooden box with the students' "sins" and float it out on the lake, and then proclaim before everyone, "O God, we ask You for forgiveness for our errors of this past year. We have inscribed them on cards so that they might be vivid in our minds. Show us that they are forgiven by destroying them before our very eyes."

I hoped that at that specific time the scuba diver would have had sufficient time to swim underwater toward the floating wooden box, surface, open his cavernous mouth, swallow the "sins," and then disappear underwater to the other side of the lake. I thought this would "go over big" with the youngsters.

However, to my surprise and chagrin no costume rental businesses in Houston could get for me a shark outfit. I had failed even before I could get it off the ground.

However, during the almost thirty-two years that I served as Beth Yeshurun's rabbi I always felt that one must not remain stagnant in religion. True, the ancient was to be hallowed, but the new was not to be ignored.

• • • • •

1) "The best laid schemes o' mice and men Gang aft a-gley."

—Robert Burns, "To A Mouse"

2) There is always something to upset the most careful of human calculations."

—Ihara Saikaku, "The Japanese Family Storehouse; Or The Millionaires' Gospel"

CHAPTER 14

A Miracle On The High Seas

During the summer of 1996, after serving Beth Yeshurun Congregation for thirty-one-and-one-half years, I retired as its Senior Rabbi. The congregation made me its "Rabbi Emeritus," its retired rabbi.

However, "retired" does not mean "hibernation"—becoming totally inactive, stagnating, languishing, or declining. Therefore, that winter I "signed on" as the Jewish Chaplain aboard a Royal Caribbean Cruise Line ship for a week-long Caribbean cruise. My duties were actually very simple and few. I was to conduct the Chanukah Service every evening and also lead the Shabbat Service on Friday evening.

It was truly a blessed trip. The weather was sunny and balmy, the food was excellent, the entertainment was superb, the exercise room was large and well equipped, the passengers were extremely friendly, the water was waveless, and the accommodations were comfortable and ample.

Every evening we had approximately one hundred men, women, and children at our service for the lighting of the Chanukah candles, the singing, the quiz that I would always give them, the brief talk that I would regularly present, and the refreshments of latkes and apple sauce, cake, and coffee that would always be presented by the ship's chef.

One Friday morning, about 5 A.M., as we were supposedly cruising off the Dominican Republic in the Caribbean Sea I awakened and heard the ship creaking. We had an inside cabin, no portholes, and therefore I could not see how fast we were traveling or whether we were moving at all. The ship was over seventy thousand tons and unless the weather was quite severe and the ship was rolling from side to side it was almost impossible to tell whether the ship was going forward or standing still.

However, the creaking was definite and audible. I therefore turned to Toby, tapped her on the shoulder twice, and when she opened her eyes I commented, "This ship is so new that they haven't even worked out its creaks yet. Listen, you can still hear it moaning and groaning."

Toby opened her eyes widely as if my unexpected comment at that untimely hour had frightened her. "Why is the ship moaning and groaning?" she nervously inquired. "Is everything OK with the ship?"

"There's nothing wrong with the ship," I replied smiling broadly. "A ship is like a new pair of shoes. They creak until you wear them awhile and break them in." I softly touched her hair and convincingly assured her, "Everything is fine—totally fine. Go back to sleep. I'm sorry I awakened you."

Without any further conversation Toby turned over, went back to sleep, and I did the same.

However, about an hour later we were awakened by a voice over the loud-speaker system that broadcast throughout the ship and into each stateroom. "This is your Captain. We've experienced a minor problem. We are a few hundred yards off the Dominican Republic and we are temporarily grounded on a sand bar. It is absolutely nothing. One need not be alarmed or worried because of this temporary delay. We will be reversing the propellers in a few minutes and we should be off the sand bar and back on our cruise in about half an hour."

There was silence for about fifteen seconds and then the Captain began again. "Yes, the ship is listing nine degrees but that is meaningless and should not be any cause for alarm. Just do what you normally do. Breakfast is now being served. In a very short time we will be proceeding as normal."

Toby quickly sat up in bed. "What did the Captain mean when he said that we were listing nine degrees?"

I, too, sat up. We were now both fully awake. "He means that the ship is leaning to one side nine degrees. Ninety degrees would mean that we're totally on our side. Nine degrees means that we're not as it should be. We're tilted somewhat to one side."

Toby's eyes indicated doubt and problems but I told her not to worry. The Captain's voice sounded very confident.

However, an hour later the Captain's voice was heard once again all over the ship. "We have reversed the engines but we have not been successful in dislodging the ship from the sand bar. But," he attempted to reassure us, "do not worry. We have called for three tugboats from the Dominican Republic and we were just informed that they have already left Santo Domingo. They should be here within an hour. That means that we should be off the sand bar in about two hours, before lunch. We hope to be back on our course before many late-sleepers awaken," and he laughed. "They will not even know that we had been stuck on a sand bar," and once again he laughed.

But Toby was not laughing. "Is he sure that the tugboats can pull us off the sand bar?" she prodded me.

I shook my head as if I could not believe her pessimism and her doubts. "Have you ever seen those tugboats? They're gigantic. They're like mechanical Arnold Schwarzeneggers. They'll give one huff and one puff and the ship will be off the sand bar. It'll only take a few minutes and we'll be moving again. In fact, the Captain will probably accelerate the speed of the ship so that he'll make up lost time. We'll probably dock in Curacao on schedule. Stop being a pessimist. Be an optimist."

And as an addendum to get her mind off her dismay and despair I stated, "I'm looking forward to Curacao. I want to see the synagogue there. Its floor is covered with sand to remind us that the Jews traveled in the desert with Moses for forty years when they left Egypt more than three thousand years ago, and Jews began arriving in Curacao way back in 1654 when we had to leave Brazil because the Portuguese invaded that country and made life miserable for us as they had done to the Jews in 1497 in Portugal, about one hundred and fifty years earlier. The Sephardic Synagogue there is the oldest synagogue in use in the Western Hemisphere. It's about two hundred and fifty years old." I smiled at Toby, kissed her quickly on the lips, held onto her shoulders and added, "We're going to have a good time there."

As the Captain stated, about an hour later three tugboats arrived from Santo Domingo—but they were not of the Dinosaur Class as I had mentally depicted them. They were more of the Rowboat Class, similar to the rowboats in which my father would weekly take me in Prospect Park, Brooklyn when he would take my brother and me for an outing during the summer. And when they came abreast of our ship they looked like three mosquitoes on the back of an elephant.

It was truly pathetic. Hundreds of passengers were standing around the railing of the cruise liner hoping to see these pipsqueaks and twerps budge the ocean liner off the sand bar. The three tugboats huffed and puffed, churned up the water, squealed and screeched, coughed and barked—but the ship did not seem to budge or stir even one inch. It seemed as if the ship was asleep and these three little vermin could not awaken it from its lethargy.

This went on for three full hours—and then the "mosquitoes" gave up. Several passengers stated that the tugboats were burning out their engines. It was a task of futility. That chore was defeated even before it began. There was not enough "muscle" in the three puny tugboats to move the ship. Even a dozen of them would have been ineffective and impotent, let alone three of them.

Then the Captain's voice was heard once again over the loudspeaker system. "Ladies and gentlemen, we have good news and bad news. The good news is that we have radioed Miami for help and they are sending four super class tugboats to move us. Those tugboats are ocean-going tugboats and are regularly used to move ocean liners, and I can assure you that within a half-hour after they arrive we will be on our way again."

The Captain hesitated in order to take a breath. His voice sounded a bit nervous, not his usual jovial self. But then he added in a more subdued tone of voice, "However, there is also a little bad news," and it sounded as if his comment was bracketed by nervous giggles. "The super tugboats cannot arrive here until sometime tomorrow morning."

With that comment, a thunderous shout came forth from almost all encircling the railing: "Oh no! Oh no!"

However, the Captain proceeded as if he was oblivious of the response. "That means that we will have to skip Curacao and go on to our next destination. The reason is that we must be at the Panama Canal on the date and time scheduled. Ships make arrangements with the Canal months in advance and if one misses his schedule, he has to cancel his trip through the Canal—and that is a very expensive faux pas."

It was obvious that the passengers were very upset. In fact, they were more than upset. They were agitated, anxious, and disquieted.

"The shipping line should extend our trip one day," one passenger cried out. "R.C.C.L. should reimburse us ten percent of the cost of this trip," another passenger angrily growled at me as if I was one of the owners of the Line. "All drinks should be free," one young man vigorously shouted, and all his friends standing nearby cried out, "Amen," "Yes sir," "Say it again," or "That's the truth and the whole truth."

For the remainder of that afternoon almost all the shipboard conversation was about the ship and being stuck on the sand bar. Some indicated great fright while others merely used this as an excuse to drink more since the Captain did state that until the ship was refloated all drinks would be half-price.

That day was Friday, and at 5:30 P.M. when our Shabbat Service was scheduled to begin we were still languishing on the sand bar like a beached whale. For the previous Chanukah Services we had had about one hundred at our services. But on this Friday evening we had one hundred and seventy-five in attendance—standing room only, even after the porters brought in an additional thirty chairs. It was obvious that many were nervous, tense, and fidgety.

I knew that I had to do something to break the tension at our Service so I began by saying, "Please join me in prayer. O God, there were many in the Bible who experienced difficult moments but they knew where to turn, and their problems were solved and resolved. When Jacob was running away from his brother Esau he turned to You, O God, and asked for help and aid and You said [Genesis 28:15], 'I am with you and will watch over you wherever you go.' When King David found himself in the midst of trouble and difficulty he raised his hands and head toward the heavens and prayed to You and he said [Psalm 86:7], 'In the day of my trouble I will call to You, for You will answer me.' And so, too, when the Prophet Isaiah found himself in the midst of political problems, when the fate of the Jewish people hung in the balance, he turned to You, O God, and prayed, and You responded [Isaiah 41:13], 'I am the Lord your God, who takes hold of your right hand and says to you: Do not fear; I will help you.'

"Today, we aboard this ship have a minor problem, O God. We seem stranded off the Dominican Republic. We are stuck on a sand bar. But we pray that the tugboats from Miami will soon be here, get us off the sand bar, and we will once again be continuing on our voyage. We pray for Your protection, O God. We pray for Your safekeeping, O God. We pray for your security, O God."

The entire congregation responded with a boisterous "Amen!"

However, one elderly woman shouted, "From your mouth, O Rabbi, to God's ears," and again there was an effervescent, "Amen!"

The brief and abbreviated Service proceeded with spirit, enthusiasm, and verve. The congregation joined me in the singing, even though some of us were off key. However, toward the end of the Service I could feel some of that malaise reemerging amongst the congregants. I felt that I had to again say something to break the tension, to ease the stress, so I said the first thing that entered my head.

"Ladies and gentlemen," I stated as I attempted to hide the smile that was endeavoring to spread all over my face. "I didn't know if I should tell you this but right now I can find no reason to hide it from you."

Those who were looking in their prayer books immediately looked up. Everyone was now staring at me.

"My friends," I went on, "early this morning, right after the Captain announced that we were stalled and stopped on a sand bar, I had several strong feelings in my stomach," and I pointed with my index finger to the exact position on my stomach where I claimed I had the stirring. "At first, I thought it was a reaction to the heavy dinner I had last night, but as the seconds passed by I felt that I was receiving a message. The message seemed to say to me, 'Jack, everything will be all right. Everything will be OK. By the end of dinner tonight the Captain will announce good news—we're back on the cruise.' That stirring in my stomach went on and off, as if someone was telling me, 'Listen, I have a message for you. Don't ignore it.'

"Ladies and gentlemen," I went on as my smile expanded and expanded, "I think that message was from God telling me to tell you not to worry, not to be perturbed, not to be distressed. The problem will quickly disappear."

My comment was met with roars of laughter. The tension had obviously been broken. One elderly gentleman even called out, "Now we have a rabbi who gets telephone calls from God," and that comment was also met with strong laughter.

But when the mirth and guffaws receded, another elderly man raised his hand and calmly proclaimed, "Rabbi, I, too, get those stirrings in my stomach. But with me, it's not God who is speaking to me, and do you know how I know that?"

He waited for about five seconds for me to shake my head indicating that I did not know a response to his question and then he emphatically stated, "I take Maalox and those stirrings quickly disappear."

His quip caused an eruption amongst the congregants. Everyone was laughing and talking. Everyone was joking with relatives and strangers, those in front of them and those in back of them, those to the right and those to the left. The tension really had been broken.

That evening at dinner, people continually passed our table and in jest commented, "We're still waiting for a fulfillment of God's comment to you," or "I hope the tugboats from Miami will arrive soon so that God's timetable will be achieved," or "Is your stomach receiving any other messages now?"

Toby shook her head at me. "Jack, you opened a hornet's nest. What made you make that absurd comment about receiving a message from God?"

Exhaling in embarrassment I merely commented, "I was merely attempting to break the tension and bring some smiles to their faces. I thought a joke would help."

The waiters were extra-slow that evening. It was already 9:55 P.M. when they began serving the dessert. As usual, I ordered a double scoop of chocolate ice cream, but as the waiter was putting the dish before me a voice burst forth from the public address system. It was the Captain.

His voice was extra-cheery and extra-ebullient. "Ladies and gentlemen," he seemed to sing, "we do not—I repeat, we do not—need the tugboats from Miami." Immediately, there was total and complete silence in the dining hall. The atmosphere quickly became aphasic. "We are no longer stuck on the sand bar. The high tide has floated us off the sand bar."

All at once, the dining room erupted in pandemonium. People were kissing each other and slapping each other on their backs. Others were embracing each other and some were even dancing in the aisles.

The Captain's voice was once again heard over the public address system. "However, we're going to anchor here overnight until the Coast Guard arrives tomorrow morning. They're sending divers to check our hull just to make sure that everything is proper. So, enjoy the evening; attend the entertainment programs in our theater; and at midnight enjoy our special midnight dinner." And he concluded his good news with a hearty, "God bless all of you."

Immediately, our table was flooded with men and women who had been at our Shabbat Service. One woman said to Toby, "Did you know you married a holy man who speaks to God?" A middle-aged man said to me, "The next time my stomach rumbles I'm not going to go to Walgreen's to get a pack of Tums. I'm going to Radio Shack to buy an electric receiver that will allow me to get God's messages."

That went on for at least fifteen minutes. Smiles were written all over the faces of those who came to visit us at our table and make a comment.

And as Toby and I were about to leave, a woman who was surely ninety years of age and in a wheel chair being pushed by a grandson and surrounded by a dozen or more members of her family, stopped by my table, touched my hand, smiled, and slowly said, "From the moment I saw you at Services tonight I felt you were a prophet. But now that I have heard the Captain's comment I know that you are a prophet."

The elderly woman then indicated to me by motioning with her right index finger that she wanted me to bend down toward her wheel chair so she could whisper something in my ear. I bent down and she mumbled to me, "Rabbi, what horse is going to win the fifth race at Gulfstream?"

She winked her eye at me, turned toward her grandson, and motioned with her hand, "Let's go see the show."

• • • • •

1) Someone once asked James J. Corbett what was the most important thing that a man must do to become a champion. He replied, "Fight one more round."

—Author Unknown

2) If it were not for hope the heart would break.

—Author Unknown.

Chapter 25

"Frank, There's A Guy In The Hall Who's Bothering Me"

In 1954, when I moved to Homestead, Pa., my first pulpit, I found an apartment in a renovated movie house. It was really one room in the former balcony of the Stahl Movie House and it contained only a refrigerator and a divider that could hold a few pots and pans. In fact, the "apartment" did not even contain a stove.

But my mother came down from New York to help me furnish the "apartment," and after perusing the empty room she skeptically commented, "I guess you don't need a stove. You don't bake and you don't cook very much. I guess what you need more than a stove is a wife."

She hesitated for a moment hoping that a positive comment concerning matrimony would be forthcoming but when she was accosted by a wall of silence she merely shrugged her shoulders and continued. "But you will need something to prepare the meals that you will have at home. I'm going to give you as a gift a hot plate with two burners and I'm also going to get for you an electric broiler. You can use the hot plates to heat your vegetables and the broiler to prepare steaks, lamb chops, or chopped meat. But mind you, get yourself a wife."

I sighed heavily and went with my mother to buy the hot plate and broiler.

However, before my mother returned to New York she prepared for me fourteen cylindrical cardboard containers with stuffed cabbage (chopped meat wrapped in cabbage leaves) and placed them in my freezer. "Just defrost them for a few hours and then heat them on your stove," she instructed me. She knew that I loved stuffed cabbage that we called *hulyiptzess* in *Yiddish.*

But she continued, "You can't just eat *hullyiptzess* every day." So she went to the kosher butcher in Pittsburgh and bought for me steaks, lamb chops, and chopped meat and advised me, "Let's place this in your freezer. In this way you'll be able to have variety. One night you can have *hulyiptzess,* the next night you can prepare a steak, the next night you can have lamb chops, and the next night you can broil chopped meat. In this way you won't get bored. It's better than nothing." She hesitated for a moment and then once again added, "But the best advice I can give you is to get a wife. I hope she'll prepare better meals for you."

My mother returned to New York that week and I began to prepare my meals for myself. Generally, I ate at home. I would eat almost the same meals every day for breakfast and lunch. For breakfast, I would have half an apple pie and a glass of milk. In fact, the baker once told me that I bought "more apple pies per capita than anyone else in Pittsburgh." For lunch, I would open a can of peas, dump them into a frying pan, and smother them with two beaten-up eggs to make an omelette. However, for dinner I would always enjoy variety. I followed my mother's suggestion. One night I would prepare *hulyiptzess,* the next night steak, the next night lamb chops, and the following night chopped meat. However, I would always simultaneously open two cans of vegetables to heat on the burner.

It was early February of 1955 and it was truly freezing outside. The Pittsburgh area can be extremely cold in the winter. Snow was on the ground and the outsides of the windows were frosted. Therefore, in order to be more comfortable I had purchased an electric heater to help heat my apartment and minimize the chill that seemed to otherwise permeate my living quarters.

More than six months had already gone by since I had been installed as the rabbi of the Homestead synagogue and I was now also teaching every Tuesday evening at the Pittsburgh College of Jewish Studies from 7:00 to 9:00 P.M. Therefore on Tuesday evenings I would normally prepare dinner at 5:30 P.M. in order to be at class on time.

Unfortunately, on this specific Tuesday in February I arrived home late due to the stalled traffic caused by the snow. I was running late and immediately began preparing my dinner. I opened a can of baked beans and a can of beets and put them in pots on the burners. I also put the electric heater on "maximum" because the room was quite cold and I then went to the freezer to get a steak that I placed in the broiler. Then I realized that I had not shaved that day, so I went to the bathroom to get my electric razor. I also simultaneously put on the radio to hear the news, and as I walked around the apartment and the bathroom I flicked on every light that I had in the apartment. It was truly bright and I prepared to shave while listening to the news and waiting for the food to heat.

It was obvious to me that I was going to be late, so I put the two burners on "high" and I also put the broiler on "high."

However, as soon as I began shaving I noticed something very surprising—the lights in the apartment quickly went out one by one until the room was in total darkness. Luckily, I had a flashlight that guided me to the light switches. I flicked them on and off but there was no response. I went over to the burners and the broiler and noticed that they too were off. It quickly became obvious to me that there had been a failure in the electricity. I said to myself: "I'll bet the whole house is dark. There must be some trouble with the electrical system in the house." And then I looked at the broiler and thought: "That's the end of the steak. It's still red. I can't eat it, and the vegetables are still cold."

I opened my door to see if any other residents of our "apartment house" were in the hall searching for a solution, but to my surprise, I noticed that the hall lights were on and no other people were in the hall. It quickly became apparent to me that only *my* apartment had suffered a blackout. Only *my* room was in an electrical coma.

I looked at my watch and it became quite apparent to me that unless I quickly solved the problem I was going to be very late for class—and without dinner.

Then, as I stared at the cooling broiler, a thought struck me like a prophecy from heaven. It was for me an eye-opener. It was like Moses standing at the Burning Bush when (Exodus 3:4), "God called out . . . 'Moses, Moses'" For me, the words were: "Jack, Jack, go next door and ask the person there to let you plug in your broiler and hot plate. The food will be ready in a few minutes and you won't waste the food and you won't be late for class and you won't be hungry."

A smile quickly erupted over my face and I immediately went next door and knocked on the door. About ten seconds later the door opened and an exceedingly attractive young woman about twenty-one years of age smiled at me and said, "What can I do for you?"

She was tall, had flaming long red hair, was extremely curvaceous and for a moment I hesitated. I thought that all the residents on my floor were elderly, retired men and women. I had never previously seen this young woman in the building or on my floor—especially not next door to me.

Once again she said, "What can I do for you?"

As I looked at her, it seemed to me that my story would not sound too credible or trustworthy to her. So I haltingly said as I grimaced, "I know this may sound a little strange to you, but my broiler has lost its heat and my hot plates have gone dead. I'm without electricity and I live next door." I pointed in the direction of my apartment and continued, "I wonder if you would do a favor for me?"

She was still smiling but it was obvious to me that she did not comprehend my problem.

I therefore went on with my woes and my proposed solution. "My steak is going to get ruined and my beans and beets are also soon going to be worthless. I can't heat them up. The broiler is not working and the hot plate is also kind of dead. There's no electricity.

"Could I ask a favor of you? Could I please bring my broiler and hot plate into your apartment and plug them into your outlets? It will only take a few minutes."

The smile quickly evaporated from the young woman's face and a frown immediately took its place. "Are you a jokester? You must be kidding," she angrily retorted.

I shook my head horizontally from side to side indicating that I was not joking. I was serious. "I only want to save my steak and vegetables."

The young woman quickly took a step back, turned around, and loudly and irritably called out, "Frank*, come quickly. There's a masher at the door."

Within five seconds, Frank was at the door next to the young woman. He smiled briskly at her, held her hands, and said, "What's the matter, Sweetie?"

Frank was big—really big. He was about six foot four inches tall and weighed about 270 pounds. In fact, he looked massive and gigantic to me.

Once again he looked at the pretty, young woman and pleasantly said, "What's the problem Charlene*?"

Charlene spoke quickly as she stepped behind Frank, "This guy says that he lives next door and he wants to bring his broiler and hot plates into my apartment to plug them in. He has some baloney story about the electricity being off in our building and he can't cook his meal.

"I think that he just wants to get into my apartment and he didn't know that you were here."

Frank immediately stepped forward, a big and ominous frown on his face. He grabbed my arm and threateningly growled, "You'd better not be fooling around with my girl friend. Otherwise, you'll quickly find your arm in a cast."

His grip was very tight and I did not doubt the truth of his statement. He was truly menacing and intimidating.

"I'm telling you the truth," I quickly replied. "I live next door and my electricity has gone off. If you don't want to help me, OK. I'll go back to my apartment and throw the steak and vegetables in the garbage. I just thought you'd want to help a neighbor."

Frank quickly turned toward Charlene with an innocent smile on his face. "Maybe he's telling the truth. Let me go to his apartment and check it out. I'll take him with me."

Then he directed his comments toward me. "There are a lot of guys who try to take advantage of Charlene. She's so good looking. In fact, just last night at the bar I had to bop a guy in the nose for acting fresh to her. I don't like when anyone tries to take advantage of her."

"I'm not trying to take advantage of anyone," I attempted to reassure Frank. "I merely want to salvage my steak, baked beans, and beets."

Frank exhaled heavily. "Let's go to your apartment and see if I bust you in the nose or you join us for some wine."

My heart was beating quickly. He was gigantic in my eyes. He reminded me of the twelve spies whom Moses had sent into Canaan to reconnoiter the land. Two returned with a positive report but ten came back with a pessimistic account. They proclaimed (Numbers 13:33): "And there we saw the Nephilim, the sons of Anak . . . and we were in our own sight as grasshoppers. . . ." Frank held firmly onto my arm as we went toward my apartment—and I thought of myself as a grasshopper in the hands of a dinosaur.

I opened the door—but it was pitch black. "Put on the lights," Frank aggressively called out to me.

"I can't. There's no electricity."

Frank himself went to the light switch and impatiently moved it up and down three or four times, but the electric current was not resurrected.

I took him in the direction of the broiler and hot plates and he could still feel some heat coming forth from those appliances.

"Hey," Frank remarked, "you're going to ruin your food unless you heat it up quickly. It's a pity to foul up such a good piece of meat. It smells terrific."

Quickly, Frank realized that I was not bluffing. I was telling the truth. "Grab the wagon under the hot plate and I'll take the broiler. Let's bring it into Charlene's apartment. She's got plenty of electrical outlets where you can plug them in. Come on in. You'll have some wine with us. We were about to sit down for dinner anyway."

I breathed easier and went along to Charlene's apartment. She met us at the door and surprisedly exclaimed: "What's happening here?"

However, Frank smiled at her as he shook his head. "He was telling the truth. There's no electricity in his apartment. He must have burned out a fuse and I don't know where the circuit breakers are. I invited him in to plug in his broiler and hot plates—and to have some wine with us."

Frank smiled again at Charlene and added: "Now you know your next door neighbor. He's not a masher. He's a nice guy."

Once again he turned toward me. "By the way, what's your name and what do you do for a living? I hope you're not unemployed."

I shook my head: "No, I'm not unemployed. I'm a rabbi at the synagogue on the next block and my name is Jack."

Both Charlene and Frank indicated surprise on their faces as they simultaneously exclaimed: "You're a rabbi?"

Frank grabbed my arm again and enthusiastically pumped it. "It's good to have a man of God next to Charlene. By the way, are you Jewish rabbis permitted to get married? Are you permitted to date?"

It was obvious to me that he was probably Catholic and extrapolating his priest's marital restrictions to rabbis. I answered his many questions and Charlene's too and we sat down while they had some wine and I had a Coke. However, it was difficult for them to understand why I insisted on only eating *my* food and turning down the ham that Charlene had prepared.

Frank told me that he played football for the Pittsburgh Steelers and that Charlene was a secretary at Jones & Laughlin Steel Mill. In fact, for the remaining year and a half that I was in Homestead Frank often gave me tickets to the Steelers' home games.

The burned out fuse incident could have ended in a bloody

and broken nose—for me. But thank God it merely culminated in new friendships and free tickets to football games.

• • • • •

> "A friend is not so much one to whom you can go for help when *you* are in trouble. . . . But a friend is one to whom you can go when *he* is in trouble."
>
> —*L.O. Dawson*

ABOUT THE AUTHOR

RABBI JACK SEGAL was the rabbi of Congregation Beth Yeshurun, Houston, Texas from 1965 to 1996 (Associate Rabbi 1965-1973; Senior Rabbi 1973-1996). He retired in 1996 and was designated Rabbi Emeritus. Under his tenure the congregation rose from 1,450 family members to over 2,200 family members.

Rabbi Segal previously served congregations in Homestead and McKeesport, Pennsylvania, and Portland, Oregon.

Rabbi Segal received his secular education at New York University (B.A. in Physics), the University of Pittsburgh (B.S. in Mathematics), Oregon State University (M.Ed. in Counseling and Religion; M.A. in Counseling and Psychology), and the University of Houston (Ed.D. in Counseling and Psychology). He also did additional graduate work at the New School For Social Research (in New York) and Columbia University.

He was ordained at the Mesivita Rabbi Chaim Berlin (Brooklyn, N.Y.) and received a Doctor of Hebrew Letters degree (D.H.L.) from Hebrew Union College in Cincinnati, Ohio.

Rabbi Segal is a member of the Rabbinical Assembly (Conference of Conservative Rabbis) having served five years on its Committee on Law and Standards and is also a member of the American Psychological Association.

Rabbi Segal and his wife Toby are the parents of four children (Jeffrey-married to Shelley, Michael-married to Sharon, Lisa- married to Matt, and Scott-married to Dena) and have six grandchildren (Shawn, Ali, Nicole, Zachary, Josh, and Jordan).

Rabbi Segal's previous book, *Modern Problems—Some Jewish Solutions,* is often used as a text for confirmation classes.

The present book is the second of a trilogy, the first one having been *When Man Closes Doors, God Opens Windows.* Rabbi Segal is currently writing the third book of this trilogy, *Remember What You Still Have Left, Not What You Have Lost.*